D1806908

JANUA LINGUARUM

STUDIA MEMORIAE
NICOLAI VAN WIJK DEDICATA

edenda curat
C. H VAN SCHOONEVELD
Indiana University

Series Practica, 131

THE D-STEM IN WESTERN SEMITIC

by

STUART A. RYDER, II

Judson College

1974

MOUTON

THE HAGUE · PARIS

© Copyright 1974 in The Netherlands
Mouton & Co. N.V., Publishers, The Hague

No part of this book may be translated or reproduced in any form, by print, photoprint, microfilm, or any other means, without written permission from the publishers.

Printed in The Netherlands by Mouton & Co., The Hague

Dedicated to
Stuart A. Ryder

TABLE OF CONTENTS

FOREWORD

Consideration of the origins and functions of the D-stem in the Western (or Eastern) Semitic languages confronts one with a complex and often confusing exercise in historical, comparative and structural linguistics, raising considerable doubt about the validity of the so-called 'traditional' explanation of this form without providing evidence of sufficient weight to enable one to substitute for it some certain alternate solution. Indeed, this study raises more questions than it will answer. Probably no final statement is either possible or desirable. This is the case, because the practice of a spoken language, as it develops through such devious and deceptive means as leveling and analogy into a set of fairly stable rules (or a grammar, as we call it), will necessarily rest upon the shifting sands of the linguistic substratum, which will from time to time work their way to the surface as the 'exceptions' which may plague and confound us in the literature.

This study, though, does not purport to resolve all the problems involved in consideration of the D-stem. Rather its purpose is, first, to state some of these problems and, second, to provide linguistic data from which the reader like the writer may draw his own conclusions. These data will be of two principal types. First, data from historical, structural and comparative linguistics, derived primarily from Semitists but also from specialists in other languages. Second, examples collected from texts in the three languages which we are taking as representative of Western Semitic: classical Arabic, Biblical Hebrew and Aramaic, including Targumic Aramaic, Reicharamäisch and Syriac. Illustrative material obtained second-hand from Ugaritic, Ethiopic, Akkadian and the Hamitic languages will be introduced when it supplements or illuminates the material compiled for this study, but such material will not, since these languages lie outside the writer's area of competence, form the basis for any conclusion, explicit or implicit, which the study may produce.

I

THE D-STEM: A HISTORICAL SURVEY

The traditional approach to the D-stem has been predicated upon three assumptions, the first two of which have usually been implicit, the third explicit.

(1) The verbal stem with 'strengthened' (or 'geminated' or 'lengthened') middle radical found in all the major Semitic languages has a single origin and a basic function to which its usages in those languages may be traced.

(2) This stem is 'derived from' (or 'constructed upon') the so-called B(ase)-stem or G(rund)-stamm, which conveys the 'simplest' meaning of the verbal root. It thus resembles those stems employing a prefix or infix/ʾ/, /n/ or /t/, therefore its meaning must be distinct from that of the B-stem.

(3) The initial connotation of this stem was a 'strengthening' or 'intensification' or 'pluralization' of the verbal concept expressed in the B-stem, symbolized by the doubling or 'strengthening' of the middle radical. Other usages, such as the causative, denominative, factitive and declarative, are subordinate to and derivable from the connotation of intensity in the performance of the activity.

One must remember that these are indeed assumptions, or better, hypotheses, no matter how obvious any or all of them may appear to be. As hypotheses, they are subject to trial, and may accordingly be accepted or rejected. One could conceivably formulate these three alternate hypotheses.

(1) In an individual Semitic language, gemination of the middle radical may have had two or more phonological and/or morphological origins and thus have expressed two or more functions of the verbal root. Furthermore, any one or more of these functions may be unique for that Semitic language, or may be common to one or two rather than to all of its sister languages. In short, the 'Semitic D-stem' may be a conglomerate of forms similar only orthographically.

(2) This stem may have developed independently of the B-stem, either directly from the verbal root or indirectly through the medium of nominal formations. In this case it would properly be described as a form parallel to rather than derivable from the B-stem, and would not need to be related semantically to the latter.

(3) This semantic independence would obviate the need for the pseudopsychological correlation of 'strengthening' between form and meaning (a confusion of linguistic

forms with that which they symbolize), and one of the usages of the stem now considered 'subordinate' or 'secondary' could, as a result of comparative study of texts, emerge as the 'original' usage, if such exists. This would not, of course, rule out the possibility that intensification of action became a function of the stem in one or more individual languages.

Before affirming either of these contradictory sets of hypotheses or some third set combining elements or emphases of each, we shall examine much linguistic evidence. But first we will consider the 'traditional' first set of hypotheses as earlier grammarians and modern scholars have handled them.

The view that the D-stem originally signified intensification has been based upon the work of early Arab grammarians. Though these scholars were mostly indifferent to the morphological or phonological aspects of the development of the D-stem it is useful to consider a few of the brief comments they offer concerning the meaning of the stem, since we can find here an original and spontaneous response to the need for definition. Sibawaihi finds it necessary to consider the D-stem in conjunction with the causative Stem IV. The latter he describes as having been "rejected" in some verbs in favor of the D-stem (II), citing such pairs as *ẓarufa-ẓarraftuhu* 'it is elegant'-'I adorned it', and *nabula-nabbaltuhu* 'He is noble'-'I ennobled him'.[1] In other cases Stem IV 'shares' its causative function with the D-stem, *e.g. nazzala* and *'anzala* 'he sent down' and *kaṯṯarahum* and *'akṯarahum* 'he increased them'. One may note in Sibawaihi's account that *nazzala-'anzala* provides the only case of causative usage of the D-stem for which the corresponding B-stem is not a stative-type verbal. Furthermore, although he cites several examples of D-stems related to stative verbs without any Stem IV counterpart, he offers no example illustrating that the reverse situation can also exist. Finally, although he cites *mallaḥtu* 'I have beautified' as the regular causative corresponding to *maluḥa*, he states that he has 'heard from the Arabs' some who say *'amlaḥtu.*

The inference drawn by the modern reader is that these D-forms, rather than sharing the causative function of Stem IV, represent the normal means for transitivizing the stative verb, a usage upon which Stem IV, normally employed for double transitives, will sometimes impinge by false analogical extension, even as the D-stem sometimes impinges upon the normal semantic province of Stem IV. This inference is strengthened by Sibawaihi's listing of several D-forms which are employed to form a transitive verb from deverbals (what we call a denominative-factitive usage), such as *zannaytuhu* 'I have called him an adulterer', literally 'I have caused (brought) adultery upon him', and *ḥayyaytuhu* 'I have greeted him', literally 'I have made the greeting *ḥayyâ* to be upon him'. The connection between these and the preceding group of D-forms is clear. One is safe in inferring that within this grammarian's scheme the basic function of the D-stem is denominative-factitive (bringing someone into a state of being embodied or described in a noun or adjective or stative verb), as opposed to

[1] Sibawaihi, *La Livre de Sibawaih*, H. Derenbourg, ed., 2 vol. (Paris, 1881-1889), section 444.

the primary causative function of Stem IV (bringing someone into a state of activity embodied in an active verb). However, either will at times infringe upon the domain of the other.

In addition, Sibawaihi discerns a second, more distinctive function of the D-stem "in which Stem IV does not share",[2] namely its use to express "more of an activity" (Ar. *takṯîr*), as in the pair *kasartu-kassartu* 'I broke'-'I continued breaking' or *yajûlu-yuwajjilu* 'he wanders'-'he increases his wandering' (*i.e.* 'he wanders about'). Moreover, he cites such instances as *mawwatat* 'they died' and *qawwamat* 'they stood' as being in the D-stem as a result of a plural subject. Presumably an increase in dying or standing takes place when a group is involved. It is possible to express continuity of action without employing the D-stem, but this stem serves as a 'clarification' of the increase, much as the *maṣdar* acts as a special construction to emphasize the force of the verb. Thus in the sentence *mâ ziltu 'uftaḥu 'bawâban wa'uḡliquhâ* 'I continued opening the gates and shutting them' Sibawaihi declares that the D-form *fattaḥtu* would be a "preferable" construction as compared with *ziltu 'uftaḥu*, as in the sentence *fajjarnâ 'l'arḍa 'uyûnan* 'we continued to pour forth streams on the earth'. One may well wonder why, if the augmentative force of the D-stem was so strong, it was NOT employed in the former sentence. Nevertheless, where such forms as *mawwatat* and *qawwamat* exist, one must give serious attention to Sibawaihi's assertion that in some case gemination possesses augmentative significance, or at least allow for the possibility that in Arabic it came to have such significance in some contexts.

The comments of the grammarian Ibn Jaiš are even briefer. He calls the D-stem the "brother" of Stem IV in transitivizing, and notes additionally that in some cases the stem is employed for a negative connotation.[3] He cites such examples as *fazza'tuhu* 'I have frightened him', *qaḏḏaytu 'aynahu* 'I have irritated his eye', *jalladtu 'lba'îra* 'I flayed the camels' and *qarradtuhu* 'I deloused him'. Ibn Jaiš apparently groups two slightly different uses of the D-stem for semantic reasons. All four are denominatives but the latter two are what we call 'privatives', *i.e.* they involve the removal of something from the object of the action (English *delouse* is a perfectly parallel denominative, as is *skin*). Finally, comparing the D- with the B-stem, Ibn Jaiš like Sibawaihi concludes that "its presence is for augmentation", but goes beyond Sibawaihi to declare that this is true in a majority of the occurrences of the D-stem, as *rabbaḍa 'ššâ'u* 'the sheep lay down'. He notes also that the D-stem can be used in connection with a plural object.

These two classical grammarians essentially prefigure most scholarly comment concerning the D-stem which has since transpired. For instance, the early Hebrew grammarian Saadia-ha-Gaon described the D-stem thus: "When a verb is changed from intransitive to transitive it takes a dagesh, as, *e.g.* *lāmaḏ* changed to *limmēḏ*;

[2] Sibawaih, *Livre de Sibawaih*, section 445.

[3] Ibn Jaiš, *Commentar zu Zamachšaris Mufaṣṣal*, nach den Manschriften zu Leipzig, Oxford, Constantinopel und Cairo, herausgegeben von Dr. G. Jahn (Leipzig, 1882), section 449.

or when it is changed to denote a modification in meaning, as *šālaḥ* 'he sent' and *šillēḥ* 'he sent away' ...; or when the verb denoting a single action is changed to denote a repeated, as *rāṣaḥ* and *riṣṣēḥ*, or an intensive action, as *šābar* and *šibbēr*. In all these and similar instances there is a distinct modification in meaning".[4]

Most significant in the accounts of Sibawaihi and Ibn Jaiš is their failure to mention that which Western scholars have usually called the 'intensive' function of the stem, that which Reckendorff describes as "sich um die von der ersten Konjug. bezeichnete Handlung bemühen, mag die Handlung vom Subj. selbst ausgehen (intensive) oder von einem andern (kausativ)".[5] What Western Semitists have often inferred from Arabic *takṯîr* is a kind of subjective heightening of experience, a greater physical effort or special enthusiasm.[6] Such an 'energic' interpretation is inapposite to the examples proposed by the Arab grammarians we have cited. While they refer to 'increase', their examples clearly show that they mean by this an expansion of the scope of the action of the root, whether expansion in time (continuative/iterative) or expansion over a number of subjects or objects (plurative): what Höfner in his description of the putative Old South Arabic reduplicated form *qatâtala* calls "(eine) Mehrheit, die nicht als geschlossenes Ganzes, sondern in einzelne Gruppen unerteilt erscheint. So ist es verständlich, dass reduplizierte Formen einerseits verstärkende, andererseits aber, eben auf Grund jener Unerteilung und Zerstückelung, abschwächende Bedeutung erhalten können, je nachdem, ob die Mehrheit als solche oder die einzelnen Stücke, aus denen sie aufgebaut ist, ins Auge gefasst werden".[7] Thus, for example *qaṭṭaʿa* might have been conceived by Sibawaihi as having had an original meaning 'continue to cut', which could serve as the basis for either a specialized syntactic use '(many) cut' or 'cut (many things)' or a specialized semantic use 'continue cutting (into ever smaller pieces)'. It is the latter which presumably is reflected in the classic example *šabar-šibbēr* 'break'-'smash'. While such a semantic development could have been projected by Sibawaihi and Ibn Jaiš from the grammatical origins of the form, no such projection is explicitly noted by either grammarian.

Even allowing for a misinterpretation of the term *takṯîr* on the part of later grammarians, however, one finds the same weakness in the two Arab grammarians as in their successors of the West, namely that no clear connection is made between the 'augmented' meaning of the D-stem on the one hand, and the causative and denominative/factitive meaning on the other; nor is the link between the latter two unambiguously demonstrated. One may say, echoing Flügel, that "im Ganzen und Grossen hat die ordnende Überblick und eine rationelle Behandlung gefehlt und durch den Gang, den die grammatischen Studien von ihrem Ursprung an nahmen, war allem folgerichtigen Systematisiren der Weg abschnitten".[8] This weakness has proved fatal

[4] S. L. Skoss, *Saadia ha-Gaon, the Earliest Hebrew Grammarian* (Philadelphia 1955), 17.
[5] H. Reckendorf, *Die syntaktischen Verhältnisse des Arabischen* (Leiden, 1895).
[6] H. Bauer and P. Leander, *Historische Grammatik der hebräischen Sprache*, (Halle 1922), 281.
[7] M. Höfner, *Altsüdarabische Grammatik* (Leipzig, 1943), 86.
[8] G. Flügel, "Die grammatischen Schulen der Araber", in *Abhandlungen für die Kunde des Morgenlandes*, II Band: No. 4 (Leipzig, 1862), 74.

for any consistent definition of the place of the D-stem in Semitic grammar, and accounts for the feeling of one careful scholar surveying the data available, that the stem is 'ill-defined'.[9]

Generally speaking, European Semitists of the early 19th century were less preoccupied with the 'energic' view of the D-stem than some of their successors have been. In 1831, de Sacy noted that "La seconde et la quatrième forme donnent aux verbes neutres et aux verbes actifs absolus, la signification doublement relative".[10] He continues: "Les verbes, à la seconde forme, sont fréquemment synonymes de ceux de la première forme". He finally describes the denominative, including the privative aspect of the D-stem. Two years later Caussin de Perçeval, in his *Grammaire Arabe Vulgaire*, wrote: "L'on ne peut réduire à des règles bien précises les altérations que les formes dérivées apportent au sens de la racine; mais, en géneral, la deuxième forme donne au verbe la signification transitive".[11] He then mentions also the 'doubly transitive' and 'energic' aspects. And finally, Fürst, writing from the standpoint of an Aramaist, carried over the conceptions of the Arabist thus: "Die semitische Intensivform ist ganz imperfectiv, sie drückt sowohl die Stetigkeit der Handlung oder des Seins".[12]

It is only in the later 19th century that we find the beginnings of an effort to make a general statement related and relevant to all the semantic categories previously associated with the D-stem. Porges, noting that vulgar (*i.e.* colloquial) Arabic had in many cases substituted the D-stem for Stem IV where the written language would require the latter, speculates that "doch unterscheidet sich wenigstens ursprünglich der Intensitätstamm mit annähernd kausativischer Bedeutung von eigentlichen Kausativum erstens dadurch, dass ersterem die Kraft eines ächtens Kausativum, aus einfachen Transitivis doppelt transitive Verba zu machen, völlig abgeht".[13] He appears to have inferred this from such examples as Heb. *yillēd-hōlīḏ* 'act as midwife'-'beget', and *giddēl-higdīl* 'bring up'-'make large', in which the true causative function is vested in Stem IV, while the D-stem "immer den Nebenbegriff der eifrigen beabsichtigen, mit Mühe und Sorgfalt verbundenen Thätigkeit hat, welcher dem eigentlichen Kausativum stets fehlt".[14]

The acceptance of this hypothesis as a universal principle of the Semitic languages would demand, of course, that in such a case as Ar. *kaṯṯara-'akṯara* such a distinction was originally present but was later lost. A more likely alternative explanation would be that, if Hebrew can be shown consistently to reflect this distinction between Stems II and IV, this represents a specialized development in that one language. Yet, thirty years after Porges wrote, and throughout subsequent editions of his *Grundriss*

[9] A. Götze, "The So-Called Intensive of the Semitic Languages", in *Journal of the American Oriental Society* 62 (1942), 12ff.
[10] S. de Sacy, *Grammaire Arabe*, 2 vol. (Paris, 1831), 130-132.
[11] A. P. Caussin de Perçeval, *Grammaire Arabe Vulgaire* (Paris, 1833), 39
[12] J. Fürst, *Lehrgebäude der aramäischen Idiome* (Leipzig, 1835), 126.
[13] N. Porges, *Über die Verbalstammbildung in den semitischen Sprachen* (Vienna, 1875), 45.
[14] Porges, *Über die Verbalstammbildung*, 45.

der vergleichenden Grammatik der semitischen Sprachen, Brockelmann maintained that: "Diese Bemühung um das Zustandekommen einer Handlung führt ... oft zur kausativen Bedeutung, der aber meist noch der Nebensinn der Sorge und des Eifers anhaftet".[15] The example he cites is, once more, *giddēl-higdīl*. König posits a similar link between the causative and 'intensive' meanings of the D-stem, but defines this link more appropriately as "Steigerung einer Handlung ... welche soweit gehen kann, dass Andere unter die Einwirkung der vom Qaṭal bezeichneten Handlung gerathen oder zur Versetzung in dem vom Qaṭal bezeichneten Zustand veranlasst oder als mit demselben behaftet erscheinen".[16] He then goes on to distinguish between Stem II ('directly causative') and Stem IV ('indirectly causative'). In the latter a middleman would be brought to the state or action indicated by Stem I, while in the former the state or action is itself brought to realization. Presumably he would have regarded an example such as *yillēḏ-hōlīḏ* as appropriate to his contention.

Nevertheless, any such link between 'intensivity' (arising from the iterative) and causation fails to satisfy in two respects. First, it demands that a long list of apparent exceptions be regarded as resulting from some weakening in the force of the form. Second, it does not account for the existence of other categories of D-stems, notably denominatives and factitives (which sometimes have a transitive meaning but sometimes do not) and cursives. Yet the basic weakness of the argument, the reason that we must regard it as an artificial, ex post facto line of reasoning, is that it begins with the origins of meanings rather than with the origins of the form. Aware that difference in form implies a difference of function, yet aware also that a diversity of functions seem to be associated with the D-stem, as reflected in the 'meanings' of some D-stems in various Semitic languages, solutions such as those just cited attempt to find a link between these functions, not by analysis of the original form of the D-stem in an attempt to determine how it might have served as the basis or vehicle for the development of these later functions, but by a kind of verbal rationalization based on the effort to find a lowest common denominator of 'meaning', a common denominator which has in fact been too often drawn from the meanings as translated into the Indo-European languages. This method seeks to impose upon the D-stem a type of semantic uniformity which it in fact lacks, and the lack of which is inevitably reflected in the qualifications expressed or exceptions noted in such accounts. Form-analysis, however, may turn out to reveal a common structural element within this diversity of functions which will reveal these functions as being mutually consistent, though not necessarily mutually dependent or engendered by the same process of development. We may indeed find that, as Nyberg remarked in a different context, "in der Reduplikation des Stammes nur das Bildungsprinzip ursemitisch ist".[17]

[15] C. Brockelmann, *Grundriss der vergleichenden Grammatik der semitischen Sprachen* (Berlin, 1908), 508.

[16] E. König, *Historisches-Kritisches Lehrgebäude der hebräischen Sprache*, vol. I (Leipzig, 1895), 186.

[17] H. S. Nyberg, "Zur Entwicklung der mehr als dreikonsonantischen Stämme in den semitischen Sprachen", in *Westöstlische Abhandlungen R. Tschudi*, ed. Meier (Wiesbaden, 1954), 129.

In Chapter II we shall attempt to analyze this principle of construction and to relate it to the meanings which have developed around it. Presently, however, we are concerned with those Semitists who have sought to approach the D-stem from a fresh viewpoint, who have indeed sought, not a synthesis of apparently inconsistent 'meanings' but a linguistically viable explanation which as Christian demands, "muss an die Entstehung der Form anknüpfen".[18] It is significant that all three of the scholars whom we shall cite here, Poebel, Götze and von Soden, are specialists in Akkadian. Not only are Akkadian studies a comparatively recent phenomenon, less bound by traditional scholarship; in addition Akkadian texts from the start have received only objective analysis, since unlike the Hebrew and Arabic texts which provided the material for early Semitic grammar, they possess no sacred status for their interpreters, nor has the 'meaning' of the texts necessarily been the over-riding consideration in linguistic study of them.

Poebel seems to have been the first to deny in any systematic way the intensive meaning of the D-stem, yet he came to a conclusion already suggested by Sibawaihi but later rejected by Götze and von Soden when he wrote, "... there cannot obtain the slightest doubt that the function of the pi'el is to express not the idea of intensity but that of plurality".[19] He then goes on to posit, as did Bauer and Leander,[20] a proto-Semitic doubling of the entire root, the plurality of which indicates to him a plurality of action as well. He goes on to buttress this hypothesis by an appeal to the nomina professionis, which he sees as representing men who repeatedly perform the action denoted by the stem. This part of his statement applies, however, only to verbs which are originally transitive in the Qal and remain transitive in the D-stem. He continues, in an effort to explain those D-stems which do not fulfill both conditions, by describing as a second function of the stem that of giving a 'transitive-causative' meaning to intransitive B-stems. He believes that there was in proto-Semitic a transitive and intransitive *Qal* theme of each verb, each having a corresponding (but distinctively vocalized) *Pi'el*, but that the intransitive *Pi'el* then dropped out, so that the transitive *Pi'el* (which already was serving the 'pluralic' function for transitive B-stems) was forced to serve also as the causative for the intransitive B-stems. Thus, in his scheme ...

	Qal	*Pi'el*		*Qal*	*Pi'el*
Trans.	*qatal*	*qattal*	became	*qatal*	*qattal*
Intr.	*qatil*	*qattil*		*qatil*	

Such a formulation, of course, does nothing to explain the origin of the gemination in 'causative' D-stems. In effect, it solves the problem of establishing a link between intensive and causative by denying that such a link existed in the early stages of the

[18] V. Christian, "Zur inneren Passivbildung im Semitischen", in *Wiener Zeitschrift für die Kunde des Morgenlandes* 42 (1935), 267.

[19] A. Poebel, *Studies in Akkadian Grammar* (Chicago, 1939).

[20] Bauer and Leander, *Historische Grammatik*.

Semitic languages, and attributes the apparent link to orthographic similarity and combination of forms. Insofar as it raises the possibility that there is no need to reconcile the variant functions of the D-stem semantically, that *qattala* is in fact a 'portmanteau' form, Poebel's hypothesis represents a useful departure from the work of earlier Semitists, even though his execution of it may well seem arbitrary and confusing to the reader.

Götze's article, "The So-Called Intensive of the Semitic Languages",[21] was the first serious effort to reconstruct the original significance of the D-stem on the basis of forms actually occurring in a Semitic language, in this case Akkadian, and on the basis of morphology rather than semantics. He reaches conclusions which he feels may well be applicable to the West Semitic languages as well as to Akkadian, on the tacit assumption that the grammar of proto-Semitic is likely to have been better preserved in Akkadian than in its western counterparts. The notion of 'intensity' he rejects outright, at least as regards Akkadian. In his view the primary force of the D-stem is that of a denominative-factitive formation. In Akkadian, he holds, this stem was derived from and parallel to the stative verbs, which were themselves basically nominal forms; and it stands in a more or less causative relationship to these forms.

There are three types of stative verbs.[22]

(1) The Durative Stative, which "denotes an inherent quality of a person or things", *e.g. ṭāb* 'is good'. This is "identical with the predicative form of the adjective".

(2) The Perfect Stative, which "denotes a condition which results from the subject's own action with reference to a person or thing", *e.g. aḫiz* 'holds' or *lamid* 'has learnt'. The object which the subject 'has' or 'holds' is invariably indicated. This category may also incorporate some intransitive verbs, in which case it "denotes the rest after movement", *e.g. wašib* 'is seated'.

(3) The Passive Stative, which "denotes a state of affairs which results from another person's action, but the agent remains unspecified. This type always goes with transitive verbs; one may call it a passive participle in predicative use", *e.g. aḫiz* 'is held' and *walid* 'is born'.

For each of these there is a corresponding D-stem formation.

(1) Durative, *i.e.* "put a person or thing in the condition which the stative indicates" *e.g. ṭubbum* 'make good'.

(2) Perfect, *i.e.* "make somebody have something", *e.g. lummudum* 'make somebody instructed, teach' or *zuzzum* 'make somebody divide'.

(3) Passive, *i.e.* "put a person or thing in the state which the stative describes", *e.g. uḫḫuzum* 'make something fitted (held)' or *zuzzum* 'make divided'.

[21] Götze, "The So-Called Intensive".
[22] Götze, "The So-Called Intensive".

Since the stative verb is a nominal form, the basic function of the D-stem is then seen to be denominative. Wherever derived from adjectives the D-stem denotes 'make a person or thing that which the adjective indicates', *i.e.* it is factitive. Other denominative verbs occurring in the D-stem, *i.e.* those derived directly from nouns, are not introduced into this scheme, since Götze regards them, quite arbitrarily, as remaining "outside the verbal system in the stricter sense of the word". Moreover, in addition to the denominative-factitive D-stems he finds a "small" number of forms not derivable from the same original, which he calls "cursives" of a type Bn (B-stem with cursive infix *-n-*), which physically resembles the D-stem through ubiquitous assimilation of the *n*-infix to the second radical of the root, and which therefore has mistakenly been attached to the D-stem in grammatical surveys, thereby adding to one's confusion in analyzing the actual D-forms. Both the denominative-factitive and cursive forms, he writes, are found in West Semitic as well. The former, however, was "cut off from its original ground" by West Semitic loss of the fully-developed stative; while the cursives, presumably seen under some sort of an "intensive-frequentative" aspect, obscured the original meaning of the D-form and led to a "faulty classification of the ordinary D-forms". In effect, a minority of the D-forms, perhaps because they seemed to reflect a more striking contrast of meaning with the B-stem, came to be regarded as normative for the entire stem.

Götze thus agrees with Poebel upon the dual nature of the D-stem (in fact the threefold nature, if one does not choose to read noun-derived D-forms out of the verbal system), but goes far beyond Poebel in credibility, insofar as his formulation does not rely upon the re-creation of hypothetical proto-Semitic forms. Therefore his argument must be given most serious consideration as we later come to survey some of the forms actually occurring in West Semitic, in order to determine whether they have, in fact, no common origin, or whether the relationship of this type of D-stem to the factitive D-forms still requires explanation, as von Soden claims.

At several points von Soden departs from Götze's account of the D-stem, and raises several questions which Götze did not answer. While von Soden agrees that the principal function of the D-stem is the factitive, *i.e.* "er drückt vor allem die Herbeiführung des Zustandes aus, der durch den Stativ des G-Stamms bezeichnet wird",[23] nevertheless he does not regard this as the exclusive function of the D-stem, as Götze seems to do (with the exception of the cursives and pure denominatives). For instance, the D-forms which Götze regarded as based upon a Passive Stative von Soden characterizes as "resultative" (*e.g.* *ṣabātum* 'packen' – *ṣubbutum* 'gepackt halten') or "pluralic" (*e.g.* *nakāsum* 'abschneiden' – *nukkusum* 'vieles abschneiden,)' admitting however that the difference in meaning between the B- and D-stems is hardly discernible for the latter forms. While he regards such an example of Götze's Perfect-Stative class as *lamādum-lummudum* as factitive, some other examples, such as *aḫāzum-uḫḫuzum* he takes as being denominalized from verbally-derived sub-

[23] W. von Soden, "Grundriss der akkadischen Grammatik", in *Analecta Orientalia* 33 (1952), section 88, par. c.

stantives, *e.g.* *aḫāzum* 'seize' – *iḫzum* 'a seizing upon' – *uḫḫuzum* 'fasten upon', and classifies them with denominative verbs of action formed within the D-stem. Furthermore, von Soden points out that although the D-stem is most clearly factitive with (Durative) Stative verbs, "Allerdings findet sich als Faktitiv dieser Verben nicht in all Fällen der D-Stamm; die Gründe dafür bleibt noch zu untersuchen".[24] Finally he makes a provocative suggestion that "Bisweilen scheint nur der vollere Klang zum Gebrauch des D-Stammes verleitet zu haben".[25] As opposed to Götze, then, von Soden reaffirms the place of denominatives and cursives (or duratives) in the mainstream of the D-stem, although he does not explain the connection between them and the factitive; in general he stresses the diversity of the D-stem rather than the unity proposed by Götze. In this sense, he takes a step backward, yet his analysis is accurate insofar as it takes cognizance of all the loose ends present in any comprehensive statement concerning the D-forms which has so far been attempted.

[24] Soden, *Grundriss*, section 88, par. c.
[25] Soden, *Grundriss*, section 88, par. f.

II

THE MORPHOLOGY OF THE D-STEM

"Morphemic analysis is the operation by which the analyst isolates minimum meaningful elements in the utterances of a language, and decides which occurrences of such elements shall be regarded as the 'same' element".[1] If we now wish to subject the D-stem to morphemic analysis we must isolate the element which distinguishes it from the other stems of the verb, *i.e.* the gemination (or lengthening) of the middle radical of the root (R_2). We may then determine whether this gemination is the 'same' as that found elsewhere in the Semitic languages, *e.g.* in the Akkadian present-future *iparras* (associated not with the D-stem but with the B-stem) and its cognate forms in West Semitic, and in the so-called nomen professionis *qattâl.* Finally, since "we can include as members of one morpheme units which are not identical in form"[2] we may consider whether other forms, *e.g.* the Stem III *qâtala* or the present participle *qâtil*, include elements which are part of the same morpheme as geminated R_2.

In considering these questions we will use as our touchstone Nida's statement that:

> An overt formal difference among related forms (forms containing recurrent partials or occurring in complementary distribution) constitutes a morpheme if in any of these forms this difference, together with a zero tactical difference, is the only significant feature for establishing a minimal unit of phonetic-semantic distinctiveness.[3]

Thus, for instance, in the case of *qatala*, *qattala* and *qâtala*, which contain recurrent partials (*q..ala*) and show a zero tactical difference (the items of the forms are similarly arranged), if there is any phonetic-semantic distinctiveness among the three forms the overt formal difference(s) among them will indicate the existence of one or more distinctive morphemes contained in them. If they are not semantically distinct, any two or all three of these forms (and thus their seemingly different morphemes) may be said to be in free alternation (or variation) with one another, *i.e.* "one cannot predict ... which form will occur in a given instance" and "the occurrence of one, rather than of the other, does not produce an utterance different in meaning"[4]

[1] C. Hockett, "Problems of Morphemic Analysis", in *Language*, 23 (1947).
[2] E. Nida, "The Identification of Morphemes", in *Language*, 24 (1948).
[3] Nida, "The Identification of Morphemes".
[4] Hockett, "Problems of Morphemic Analysis".

therefore the three stems may be used interchangeably. In the same way, we may compare forms of the *iparras* and *uparras* types, West and East, and also forms of the *qâtil* and *qattâl* types.

In this chapter we shall be concerned primarily with laying out some of the possibilities concerning the morphology of the D-stem; any conclusions regarding these possibilities must wait until we have the opportunity to survey the textual evidence bearing on the issue and to determine which answer to our problem is most credible.

Certainly the relationship between Stems I, II and III seemed clear to Semitists of the 19th century. Philippi wrote, "Dass diese Stämme *kattab* und *kâtab* ... aus einem *katab* hervorgegangen (sind), bedarf keines weiteren Nachweises".[5] Fürst explained further, "Diese doppelgestaltige Fortbildung des ursprünglich gegeben Begriffs, wozu andere Sprachen häufig eigene, von Hauptstamm entferntere Stämme haben, bildet sich hier regelmässig und consequent aus der ersten Stammform, und zwar harmonisch mit der Begriffserweiterung, die Intensive nur durch innere Steigerung und Iteration des Mittelconsonanten, die Extensive durch äussere Acquisition eines Zusatzes vorn am Stamm".[6] That such unqualified statements are potentially misleading, however, is implicit in Philippi's own comment: "Gegen unsere Beweisführung verschlägt selbstverständlich die Tatsache nicht, dass jetzt öfter neben den abgeleiteten Stämmen kein einfacher mehr existiert, oder dass die abgeleiteten Stämme jetzt öfter eine ursprünglichere Bedeutung bewahrt haben als der einfache, ja dieser selbst denominativ oder deverbal, d.h. aus einem abgeleiteten Stamm erst wieder rückgebildet sein kann".[7] Far more precise was Porges' comment of that year, that "Der Intensitäts- und Extensitäts-Grundstamm werden nämlich nach dem Muster des einfachen aus der Verbalwurzel abgeleitet, und zwar charakteristisch durch das Mittel innerer Wurzelerweiterung gebildet".[8] It is more precise because while recognizing the probable priority of Stem I, it cites this stem only as a model for others and allows for the possibility that the other stems were likewise sometimes the linguistic forms in which the root concept was initially embodied, without the intermediation of Stem I.

Nevertheless, the consensus of Semitists has seemed to be that other stems are 'derived' from the B-stem. As Götze remarks: "The assumption that PS *qatala* (*yaqtulu*) is the basic form of which the other forms are modifications was left unchallenged".[9] All this would perhaps amount to no more than a problem of terminology if this assumption as to the origin of the D-stem did not have as its corollary the further assumption that the D-stem must also represent a semantic modification of the B-stem. Thus, if in Hebrew the two forms *qābar* and *qibbēr* exist, on the assump-

[5] F. W. M. Philippi, "Der Grundstamm des starken Verbums im Semitischen", in *Morgenländische Forschungen, Festschrift Fleischer* (Leipzig, 1875).

[6] J. Fürst, *Lehrgebäude der aramäischen Idiome* (Leipzig, 1835).

[7] Philippi, "Der grundstamm des starken Verbums".

[8] Porges, *Über die Verbalstammbildung*.

[9] Götze, "The So-Called Intensive".

tion that a difference of form implies a difference of meaning, the "derivation" of *qibbēr* from *qābar* must be shown to have some semantic purpose. Thus Köhler defines the two forms as 'bury' (B) and 'bury in masses' (D),[10] *i.e.* he gives the D-stem a plurative connotation. The latter is an acceptable translation in such a phrase as *l^eqabber eth-haḇ^elâlîm* 'to bury the dead (after battle)' (I Kings 11.15) but in Ezekiel 39.11 one finds in a similar context, *w^eqāb^erû šām eth-gôg w^eeth-kol h^emônoh* 'and they will bury there Gog and all his crowd'. Moreover in Genesis 25.10 the passive of Stem II is employed in *qubbar 'aḇrāhām* 'Abraham was buried'. Even assuming that the last example can be explained as a passive of the B-stem (see Chapter III) any distinction of the meanings 'bury' and 'bury many' for Stems I and II respectively is difficult to maintain. Many similar examples could be adduced, which would illustrate the difficulties inherent in trying to demonstrate a consistent semantic relationship between the two stems other than that provided by the root meaning underlying each.

Any attempt to establish such a relationship must inevitably rely sometimes upon artificial and/or pseudopsychological criteria rather than upon an analysis of the form and the contexts in which it may occur. As Götze notes: "Any attempt at interpreting D as a modification of B action type remains unsatisfactory. The question is justified: what, if any, is the relationship between D and B stative?"[11] We have seen his own answer to this question in Chapter I. Insofar as he provides a reasonable explanation for the existence of a pair such as *qāḇar-qibbēr*, where there is no apparent difference of meaning between the two: that the B-form means 'bury' and the D-form 'make buried', his explanation of the D-stem as the causative of a stative verbal adjective is helpful. However it does not account for all D-stem forms which occur, as he recognizes; such forms as Hebrew *dibber*, *hillek*, *y^ezammer* are left outside, to be explained by other means. Such forms suggest to us the possibility of a totally independent origin of the D-stem. Bergsträsser states the problem well when he writes: "Ziemlich häufig ist das Piʿel isoliert, hat also kein Kal (Nif.) neben sich, von dem es sich ableiten liesse ... z.T. werden diese Piʿel in Wirklichkeit Intensiva (oder Kausativa) zu verlorenen oder im Alten Testament nicht vorliegenden Grundformen z.T. aber Denominativa sein".[12] The difficulty which he attempts to resolve here arises out of the fact that the D-stem is always assumed to have been derived from some prior form, therefore the isolated form must have a parent form somewhere. Most scholarly effort in reference to the D-stem, including Götze's, has been aimed at demonstrating the connection between Stems I and II, or between Stem II and deverbal stems (verbal and non-verbal nouns and adjectives), an approach which inevitably ends up by ignoring or rejecting as an irrelevant accretion to or secondary development from the D-stem those forms which are not in the mainstream of the stem's development, whatever the individual scholar may consider that mainstream

[10] L. Köhler and W. Baumgartner, *Lexicon in Veteris Testamenti Libros* (Leiden, 1948-1953).
[11] Götze, "The So-Called Intensive".
[12] G. Bergsträsser, *Hebräische Grammatik*, II Teil (Leipzig, 1918).

to be. To date, no one has started with the D-stem whole and begun by seeking the connection, if any, among its apparently unrelated aspects. Yet such a connection must be sought, in the interest of an accurate description of the scope of the D-stem in grammars of the Semitic languages; and if it does not exist, the preponderant significance of the stem must be determined and extraneous forms reclassified. Morphemic analysis, or analysis of the distinctive phonemic features of the stem in terms of the meaning they add to the root, may aid us here.

The nub of any discussion of the D-stem is a determination of the origin and significance of the gemination of the middle radical, its most distinctive phonetic feature (vocalization distinguishes it in some languages but not in all). The range of possibilities is suggested by A. F. Pott's statement that the linguistic phenomenon of repetition may serve: (1) "to indicate repetition (reiteration of an activity), thus for construction of an Iterative or Frequentative to which the concept of longer persistence of an activity (Continuative) ... is easily joined"; (2) "to indicate greater force in an activity, therefore as Intensive or Desiderative"; (3) "more in the interest of inflection for the recognition of tenses".[13] Although the D-stem probably does not arise from an actual repetition (reduplication) of the entire stem (unless one accepts Poebel's analysis of the form as an original *y-qtl-qtl* by analogy with the pilpel formation *kilkel*, originally *kul-kul*),[14] the gemination of the D-stem would seem to be a related phenomenon and, as Pott suggests, might be (1) temporally relevant (expressing duration), (2) quantitatively relevant (expressing a specific type of action) or (3) grammatically relevant (not expressive in itself, rather serving as an arbitrary tense or aspect indicator). In all three cases the gemination might be said to be morphologically determined, *i.e.* it carries with it a meaning which is added to the meaning of the root with which it is associated; in the third case it might equally well be referred to as tactically determined, *i.e.* it is a function of the larger sequence of morphemes of which it is a part (the structure of the sentence in which it occurs).

We can at least partially illustrate this range of possibilities from the Western Semitic languages. As Ullendorff points out, "in Arabic, the alternation of simple and doubled radical may take place in most verbs and import morphological value. In Ethiopic ... very few verbs have both the simple and the doubled stem, and verbs with a geminated radical present no morphological or semantic distinction".[15] In other words, while Arabic *yuqattilu* would seem to contrast in meaning with *qatala*, Ethiopic *y^{e}qatt^{e}l* would not, but would instead complement *qatala* in certain grammatical environments. Can the implication of the gemination present in both forms be the same in each? Rundgren would distinguish them semantically, describing the Ethiopic form as a "réemploi de l'intensif", the 'intensive' D-stem pushing into the semantic domain of the B-stem as a simple indicative, losing in the process its intensive

[13] A. F. Pott, *Doppelung (Reduplikation, Gemination) als eines der wichtigsten Bildungsmittel der Sprache*, 1862.

[14] Poebel, *Studies in Akkadian Grammar.*

[15] E. Ullendorff, *The Semitic Languages of Ethiopia* (London, 1955).

significance, retaining only its phonological identity.[16] However, this statement rests upon the assumption that *qattala* represents an original modification of the meaning of *qatala*, and does not deal with the origins of the gemination in the case of either the Arabic or the Ethiopic form. In this regard there are two possibilities. The first is, that gemination in each case may have had an independent origin; the second, that the original significance of the gemination may be accurately reflected in one of the forms but have acquired a secondary meaning in the other. That is, either *yuqattil*, which is distinctive in Arabic, lost its qualitative or quantitative significance in Ethiopic, or it was originally only aspectually relevant as in Ethiopic and acquired a meaning different from *qatala/yaqtul* in Arabic as a secondary development. This whole question, of course, assumes that Ethiopic $y^{e}qatt^{e}l$ goes back to a form like Akkadian *uparras*. If, as seems more likely, it is to be associated with *iparras*, the problem becomes even more complex, as we shall see when we discuss 'continuative' forms.

In order to decide whether gemination has a single semantic value wherever it occurs we must speculate concerning its origin. Again there are two possibilities. To put the problem in its simplest form: it may represent either the lengthening of a consonant or the assimilation of an infix. The actual situation is not quite so simple, and involves the question, whether gemination of the middle consonant presents us with a segmental or with a suprasegmental phoneme.

Nida defines these last two terms as follows:

> Segmental phonemes are the consonants and vowels of a language. They are the significant phonemic segments into which the continuum of speech may be broken. There are in addition the suprasegmental phonemes, which do not occur as separate units in the continuum, but extend over more than one segmental phoneme. They are superimposed entities. In English, stress is a suprasegmental phoneme, for it is associated with the entire syllabic unit. ... In general segmental phonemes are written on the line and suprasegmental phonemes written over segmental ones.[17]

He later continues: "Length in some languages patterns as a segmental phoneme and in other languages as a suprasegmental phoneme". If the impetus for lengthening (gemination) of the middle radical comes from an actual repetition of that radical or from the assimilation of an infix so as to create an apparent repetition, we may say that length here is a segmental phoneme, and in such a case the morphological significance of gemination will be original, beyond doubt; it will have an inherent and consistent meaning. If, however, the impetus comes from some quantitative shift either within the entire word or within one of its syllables, gemination may be said to be suprasegmental in origin, and may result from either phonetic or grammatical impulses, *i.e.* from such causes as shift in accentuation or the need to distinguish tenses or aspects of the verbal concept.

In the latter case, it would be inaccurate to speak exclusively of the lengthening of

[16] F. Rundgren, *Intensiv- und Aspektkorrelation* (Upsala, 1959).

[17] E. Nida, *Morphology* (Ann Arbor, 1946).

the middle radical; rather one would speak also of the lengthening of the syllable which precedes it. The lengthening of R_2 would then be the result of what Gray called "secondary gemination" (as opposed to gemination which is etymologically justified) which "occurs when a short vowel plus a doubled consonant corresponds to a long vowel plus a single consonant".[18] Thus in his example Hebrew *hâ-malk* (original) becomes *ham-meleḵ*. In other words, the gemination would be phonologically determined, as an alternative means of lengthening a syllable in the Semitic languages, and would not necessarily have any semantic significance in itself. It would be only a phonetic alternant of a suprasegmental phoneme 'long first syllable'. This is the phenomenon to which Kurylowicz refers when he writes of the "équivalence fonctionelle *qattala/qawtala, qaytala/qâtala*".[19]

This explanation of gemination has the virtue of appropriateness to the connection between Stems II and III which has long been recognized by Semitists. These have generally assumed the priority of *qattala* over *qâtala*, as when Fürst declared that "die Verdoppelung des Mittellaute musste sich wieder einem andern Gesetze unterwerfen, nämlich die Auflösung einer Verdoppelung durch Vokalverlängerung, wenn die Verdoppelung nicht statt haben kann".[20] The last would be the case often with 'weak' middle consonants in Hebrew and Aramaic; however it does not explain the far more common use of *qâtala*-forms in Arabic and in some Ethiopic dialects, seemingly unconnected with the 'sound' of R_2.

Alternatively, Semitists have derived both *qâtala* and *qattala* from some third form, as when Botterweck posited a reduplication of the final radical in the form PS *qatlala*, to become PS *qatʾala* and finally *qattala* and *qâtala*, the latter arising from "qualitätsmetathese"[21], a phrase picked up by Christian and altered to "quantitätsmetathese".[22] Priority of one form over the other, or of a third form over both is not, however, a matter of key significance. What is important is their joint consideration, and their possible relationship to such other forms as the present participle (nomen agentis of the B-stem) which, according to Rosenthal, who sees a possible denominative origin for Stem III, "could conceivably have formed the starting-point for qâtala".[23] If so, this gives support to Kurylowicz's belief that "le gémination est un procédé d'origine deverbale"[24], *i.e.* is denominative in origin.

If *qattala* and *qātala* are indeed linked, their distinctive characteristic is the weighting or lengthening of the first syllable: a suprasegmental phonemic feature. The morphological significance this feature may have is by no means clear; one may only say

[18] L. Gray, *Introduction to Semitic Comparative Linguistics* (New York, 1934).
[19] J. Kurylowicz, *L'Apophonie en Sémitique* (Warsaw, 1962).
[20] Fürst, *Lehrgebäude der aramäischen Idiome.*
[21] G. Botterweck, *Der Triliterismus im Semitischen*, (Bonn, 1952).
[22] V. Christian, "Untersuchungen zur Laut- und Formlehre des Hebräischen", in *Österreichische Akademie der Wissenschaften*, Phil.-Hist. Klasse, Sitzberichte 228, Band 2 (Vienna, 1953).
[23] F. Rosenthal, "Review of H. Fleisch, *Les Verbes à l'Allongement vocalique en Sémitique*", in *Orientalia* 16 (1947).
[24] Kurylowicz, *L'Apophonie en Sémitique.*

that when it becomes desirable to define the meaning of verbal gemination its phonemic link with these other forms will help to delimit the area within which such a definition could be formed. For instance, Rundgren's suggestion that "fâʿil weist dem langen â zufolge sog. grammatikalisierte Durativität auf"[25] might serve to strengthen the concept of the D-stem as expressing durative or continuative action. On the other hand, it is possible that the lengthening of the first syllable would have had at first no morphological significance, that it arose instead from some shift in accent or pitch patterns within Proto-Semitic, perhaps not in all dialects, and acquired a special meaning or meanings as it was assimilated into the individual languages side-by-side with the simple stem. This is the process described by Nida when he writes that "what may have been originally quantitative differences become qualitative differences as well"[26], *i.e.* changes in the length of a consonant or vowel become a part of the structure of a language and acquire some grammatical or morphological significance. In such a case we need not expect to find a semantic link between *qātala*/*qattala* and *qātil*, or even between the first two.

Another explanation of gemination which initially excludes semantic considerations as such would see it as the outcome of a suprasegmental alternation R_2: R_2R_2, or short consonant: long consonant, similar to the short vowel: long vowel alternations found elsewhere in the Semitic languages, as in some types of the Arabic broken plural and in the Hebrew and Aramaic segholate nouns. Also similar would be the alternation of vocalic and consonantal morphs, as in the inflectional endings of 'feminine' nouns. Such alternations are automatic, in that they are determined phonemically by the environment in which they occur, *e.g.* *-â(h)* becomes *-at* before a vowel, /a/ becomes /â/ in an open syllable; these alternations are theoretically applicable to all roots which appear in the form under consideration. For instance the *ā:at* alternation will occur in all nominal forms of 'feminine' determination (not necessarily gender) regardless of the meaning of the underlying root. Thus *-â* and *-at* would be described as morpheme alternants, or "the smallest sequence of phonemes which have what we consider the same meaning".[27] Together they constitute a morpheme unit: they have the same meaning but different phonemes, and do not occur in the same environment.

Can the same terminology be applied to the gemination of the second radical in the D-stem? The fact that gemination occurs only in a particular phonetic environment (between two vowels, since before a consonant or at the end of a word only a short consonant is possible) would lead one to seek some kind of automatic alternation. Some writers, indeed, have suggested that the alternation R_2:R_2R_2 can best be described not as non-gemination: gemination but in purely phonetic terms as simple consonant: strengthened consonant, contingent upon the phonetic environment Thus König wrote of Hebrew: "Man sollte in diesen Formen gar nicht mehr von

[25] Rundgren, *Intensiv- und Aspektkorrelation.*
[26] Nida, *Morphology.*
[27] Z. Harris, "Morpheme Alternants in Linguistic Analysis", in *Language* 18 (1942).

einer Verdoppelung, sondern durchaus von einer Verstärkung der betreffenden Laute reden; denn der mittelste Laut von *qiṭṭel* wird nur mit einem stärkeren Luftstrom als der von *qāṭal* gesprochen. ... Die Verdoppelung des Buchstabens ist bloss eine Mittel, jene Verstärkung zu versimlichen".[28] This view is generally applicable to Semitic languages, and defines gemination as an aspect of what Spüler calls the "Reichhaltigkeit der Nuancierung" in Semitic[29], *i.e.* the employment of weakened, simple and strengthened vowels and consonants (at first phonetically determined, then assuming morphological status) to express variants of root meanings, where the Indo-European languages employ compound verbs, *e.g. exeō, mitmachen, compare.* An obvious item of evidence for König's opinion is the Hebrew language's employment of the same orthographic device, the dagesh, for expressing gemination as well as strengthened (or 'hard') consonants, and the fact that the West Semitic languages in general are less likely to indicate gemination through writing the consonant twice. Saadia ha-Gaon, in fact, does not employ the term 'gemination' when describing the D-stem, rather describes its "distinct modification in meaning" and its capacity for changing the verb from intransitive to transitive as "reasons for having a dagesh".[30] We may note here also MacLean's account of the D-stem in Modern Syriac, that "If a verb is conjugated according to both conjugations (I and II) ... we may often distinguish them by the second radical being soft in the first, hard in the second conjugation: as *zaḇēn* 'to buy' (I): *mzabēn* 'to sell' (II), but there are exceptions".[31] All these suggestions that the so-called R_2R_2 is actually a 'hard' single radical do not rule out the possibility that this hard consonant acquired morphological significance. Yet König's description of the phenomenon as a stronger breath of air, an already existent phonetic distinction seized upon, presumably, for the purpose of distinguishing two types of verbal form, does not comport well with any pseudo-psychological explanation of gemination as a conscious doubling of the sound in order to symbolize a doubling or repetition of the action. Rather, it strengthens the aptness of suggestions that the gemination is often used merely for variety of timbre.

Nevertheless R_2 and R_2R_2 are not in free alternation with one another, thus do not constitute a single morpheme unit. Nor does there seem to be any phonetic context which demands automatic alternation of the two, as both occur in intervocalic position. In the verbal context, one sees quickly that Stems I and II are not in free alternation, since some roots are found only in the *qatala-*, others only in the *qattala*-form, unless Sibawaihi is correct in believing that a D-stem with plurative meaning (e.g. *qawwamat*) can occur for any root. Despite the probability that the alternation of 'hard' and 'soft' consonants had no morphological significance in early Semitic, some selection does seem to have taken place, resulting in the associa-

[28] E. König, *Gedanke, Laut und Accent* (Weimar, 1874).
[29] B. Spüler, "Der semitische Sprachtypus", in *Handbuch der Orientalistik* B. Spüler, ed. (Leiden, 1954).
[30] Skoss, *Saadia ha-Gaon.*
[31] A. J. MacLean, *Grammar of the Dialects of Vernacular Syriac* (Cambridge, 1895).

tion of specific root concepts with one stem or the other. The alternation of R_2 and R_2R_2 is thus meaningful.

One is then required to find the reason for this alternation in semantic considerations. While an alternation determined by the phonetic environment could have developed from a quantitative to a qualitative differentiation, it appears that in this case the differentiation was qualitative from the outset, an example of what Kurylowicz calls "grammatic gemination", *i.e.* gemination arising out of the need to express or denote some specific grammatical concept such as case, number, tense, mood *etc.* The implication of this is that the 'long' or 'hard' second radical of the D-stem is a segmental phoneme, with a morphological value either in its own right or as a result of its use in this connection, and that it therefore represents an addition to the root meaning. Moreover, since this stem does not occur for all known roots, while for others it is the only existent stem, we may well expect to find some element in common among those for which it does occur. In short, what Kurylowicz noted concerning apophony, or vowel alternation, that "l'apophonie sémitique a souvent un caractère morphologique pertinent"[32] may here be equally true of consonant alternation, though its application may be less general than that of vowel alternation, which is associated in a regular manner with all roots.

We will take up some of these points again later, when we discuss the semantic domain of the D-stem (Chapter III). But now we shall look at the possibility that gemination represents not strengthening of the first syllable or of the middle radical, but rather the combination of the second radical with an infixed phonemic element. This might be either a literal repetition of the middle radical or some other phoneme with morphological significance introduced directly before or directly after R_2. Both of these possibilities have found widespread acceptance among Semitists. There are three principal opinions as to the origin and identity of the infixed element which is posited.

(1) The infix is an original nasal (*n*/*m*) or liquid (*l*/*r*) consonant. Joly has cited, as possible evidence for the insertion of a liquid, the following Arabic examples: *karsafa* 'hamstring' and *kassafa* 'cut into several pieces'; *zaḫrafa* 'adorn' and *tazaḫḫafa* 'adorn oneself'.[33] The fact that the 'inserted' /r/ occurs in a different position within each of the two verbs, however, makes it unlikely that we are here dealing with a regularly determined infix, which would normally occur either before OR after the middle radical, not in both positions. A more likely explanation of these cases is that we have in each dissimilation from an already present gemination which had some other origin.

Speculation concerning a nasal infix has been far more widespread, and more evidence of an *n*-infix exists in the physical traces it may have left behind. Thus

[32] Kurylowicz, *L'Apophonie en Sémitique*.

[33] A. Joly, "Sur les Dérivations du Trilitère et les Origines du Quadrilitère", in *Actes de XIVe Congrès International des Orientalistes, Alger* 1905 (Paris, 1907).

Spitaler wrote: "In reichsaramäischen Texten ist die Schreibung von etymologisch berechtigen n-konsonant in Fällen, wo an sich totale Assimilation des n an diesen Konsonanten zu erwarten wäre, als etymologische Schreibung anzusehen und berechtigt weder zu der Annahme, dass sekundäre Dissimilation verliege".[34] Some examples of such 'etymological writing' occur for the D-stem. Elsewhere, examples not etymologically justified occur. These are described by Spitaler as "graphische Analogie zu betrachten, die in gewissem Umfang ein Mittel zum schriftlichen Ausdruck von Konsonantverdoppelung abgegeben hat". In a sense, the existence of these latter forms makes the case for an *n*-infix stronger, since they imply a regular association of such an infix with gemination. However, Rosenthal regards these forms as nasalization of geminate clusters and states that "wherever original n appears unassimilated, secondary nasalization, instead of retention of the original sound, may be involved".[35] Similarly in Mandaic, Nöldeke points out that "die Verdoppelung des mittleren Radicals im Pael wird zuweilen durch ein n(m) vor dem einfachen Radical ersetzt, z.B. *hambēl* 'he destroyed', *hambēb* 'he burned', u.s.w.".[36] While Nöldeke seems to regard this phenomenon as dissimilation, it could equally well be seen as etymological orthography.

As to the meaning of an *n*-infix, there is disagreement among scholars. Götze, who regards the presence of this infix as being restricted to a few isolated D-stems, mostly verbs of motion, ascribed to it a "continuative" force, as in the infix *-tan-*, although Speiser responded that "the iterative-durative force of an infixed -n- by itself is nowhere unambiguously demonstrated".[37] Kurylowicz, on the other hand, refers to the Semitists' reconstruction of infixed *-tan-* as "une interprétation morphologique particulière des consonnes géminées"[38], *i.e.* not etymologically founded, and questions the existence of the *n*-infix as well. (One may wonder whether he is aware of such Akkadian forms as *ittanallak* and *iptanarras*, in which the *tan*-infix is quite evident). He concludes by reminding the reader that a geminate cluster can represent $R_2 + R_2$ as well as $n + R_2$. Before discussing this possibility we may note a further variation on the 'infix' hypothesis.

(2) The infix is an original /ʾ/, identifiable with that found in the causative Stem IV but differently placed among the root consonants. This suggestion has its origin in Dillmann's comments concerning Stem III, that "the influencing stem was once used more extensively. ... Two kinds of formative principles seem to have cooperated in its production. In part the doubling of the second radical was replaced by a semivowel, which coalesced with a foregoing /a/ into ô or ê; in part an originally causative form consisting of the prefix (alif) was brought within the word, and this (alif) became

[34] A. Spitaler, "Zur Frage der Geminatendissimilation im Semitischen", in *Indogermanische Forschungen* 61 (1952-54).
[35] F. Rosenthal, *A Grammar of Biblical Aramaic* (Wiesbaden, 1961).
[36] T. Nöldeke, *Mandäische Grammatik* (Halle, 1875).
[37] E. Speiser, "The Durative Hithpa'el", in *Journal of the American Oriental Society* 75 (1955).
[38] Kurylowicz, *L'Apophonie en Sémitique*.

established as â after the first radical".[39] While Dillmann's description of the process is somewhat naive, when he speaks of a prefix being "brought within the word" to form a new stem, there is nothing improbable about the idea that the *â* of *qâtala* has its origin in the sequence /a/ + /ʾ/, and that the latter element is the same morpheme as the /ʾ/ in *ʾaqtala*. It would be preferable, however, to describe *qâtala* and *ʾaqtala* as variants, the latter of which survived in all the West Semitic languages, the former primarily in the South Western languages. A parallel case exists in the instance of the element /t/, which we find both as prefix and as infix in the South Western languages but primarily as a prefix in the Western group of languages as a whole. Semantic differences between *qâtala* and *ʾaqtala* would have emerged from usage.

How does *qattala* fit into this picture? Surely not as Dillmann suggests, as part of a developmental sequence *qattala/qawtala*, *qaytala/qôtala*, *qêtala*, for he can cite no parallel for a dissimilation of R_2R_2 to wR_2 or yR_2. On the other hand, a sequence *qaʾtala/qattala* presents a by no means improbable assimilation. Such a reconstruction would reveal *qattala* and *qâtala* semantically equivalent in their origin and would present both as variants of *ʾaqtala*, again in origin and not in later usage. In their origins at least, they would then differ from the root meaning of the verb by the same morphological factor /ʾ/, although this single original morpheme could have developed into two or three if the meanings of the stems had become sufficiently specialized. However, no such specialization in fact exists, and in individual languages we find all three stems used in similar ways, in particular as vehicles for denominative and causative concepts. In fact this is the most compelling argument for attributing gemination to the assimilation of an *alif*-infix, whether directly, through the assimilation of $ʾR_2$ to R_2R_2, or indirectly, via a dissimilation (or metathesis of quality) from original $aʾR_2$ to $âR_2$ to aR_2R_2. The latter is perhaps the likelier of the two possibilities, since there is no evidence elsewhere that an /ʾ/ will automatically assimilate to a following or a preceding consonant. For instance, in the Arabic Stem VIII the /ʾ/ of *ʾaẖaḏa* assimilates to the infix *-t-*, whereas in such verbs as *ʾamata* and *ʾamana* it does not (the fact that *ʾaẖaḏa* may be an original *waẖaḏa* only weakens any case for the assimilation of /ʾ/ even more). On the other hand, the disappearance of an aspirate with corresponding lengthening of the preceding vowel is a well-known Semitic phenomenon. Yet, while this variation on the infix-hypothesis offers an attractive explanation of the D-stem (as well as the other two basic derived stems) it does not in itself offer any explanation for those D-stems which do not, seemingly, bear a causative or denominative relationship to the root.

(3) The infix is an actual repetition of the middle radical. This is immediately recognizable as the hypothesis which underlies the intensive-frequentative definition of the D-stem. In morphological terms, according to this view, the relation R_2(*qatala*):

[39] A. Dillmann, *Ethiopic Grammar* (London, 1907).

R_2R_2(*qattala*) would be described semantically as 'one: more than one (literally or metaphorically)'. We have already discussed the opinion of Götze, Christian and others, that such an explanation is "romantic" or "pseudopsychological". Is there any parallel or precedent in the Semitic or other languages, however, for such an interpretation of gemination? We may assume that this hypothesis arose either by analogy with the well-known phenomenon of word-gemination or from the assumption that root-gemination underlies gemination of the middle radical. Word-gemination is, of course, a familiar construction in English, *e.g.* 'many, many' and 'naughty-naughty', and is employed in the Semitic languages also for expressing the comparative or superlative degrees of the adjective. Wundt speculates concerning the origin of such constructions: "Das nächste ... Motiv zur Lautwiederholung ist offenbar da gegeben, wo das Wort Schalleindrücke wiedergibt, die sich selbst wiederholen. ... Den nächsten Übergang bietet hier die Bezeichnung einer Mehrheit von Gegenständen. ... In der Anwendung auf den Eigenschaftsbegriff ... die Verdoppelung gibt den verstärkten Eindruck wieder, den die Empfindung der Eigenschaft auf den Redenden macht, und damit wird sie zum Ausdruck einer auch objektive grösseren Intensität der Eigenschaft selbst. ... Ähnliche Anwendungen der Verdoppelung ... finden sich beim Verbum. ... Am nächsten liegt hier der stärkeren Betonung der Eigenschaft der Ausdruck der gesteigerten Tätigkeit durch vollständige oder verkürzte Verdoppelung des Verbalstamms".[40] This last is what Poebel was getting at with his reconstruction of the form underlying the D-stem as PS *y-qtl-qtl* or PS *y-prs-prs* becoming *yprrs*[41], which, according to Heidel in his comment on Poebel's hypothesis, "originally was pronounced *yuparáras* or *yuparárras*, the latter with doubling of the second /r/, owing to the accent"[42], and which presumably implies as original vocalization PS *yu-paras-paras*. The 'original' meaning of the D-stem then would be 'he kill-kills' or 'he cut-cuts', parallel to such adjectival formations as 'the holy-holy (one)'.

There is linguistic evidence of two kinds which bears upon the validity of this hypothesis. The first is the actual existence of forms corresponding to Heidel's reconstruction, described by Kienast as the R(eduplication)-stem of Akkadian which, although it is inflected after the model of the D-stem and is "seiner Bildung und Bedeutung nach eng zum D-Stamm"[43], he regards as independent of the latter, as in this chart:

R. PS ya-pararras	PS ya-pararris	PS ma-pararris-um
D. PS ya-parras	PS ya-parris	PS ma-parris-um

Despite this, one might well imagine, in light of the fact that Kienast comments: "Nur in wenigen meist literarischen Beispielen finden sich noch Spuren dieses R-Stammes"[44], that this R-stem could have been only a transition stage from PS *yu-*

[40] W. Wundt, *Völkerpsychologie*, I Band: *Die Sprache*, Erster Teil (Leipzig, 1900).
[41] Poebel, *Studies in Akkadian Grammar*.
[42] A. Heidel, *The System of the Quadriliteral Verb in Akkadian* (Chicago, 1940).
[43] B. Kienast, "Verbalformen mit Reduplikation im Akkadischen", in *Orientalia* 26 (1957).
[44] Kienast, "Verbalformen mit Reduplikation".

paras-paras to *uparras*, a stage of which a few examples survived in Akkadian literature. Such an impression would perhaps be strengthened by the distribution of similar forms in other Semitic languages, particularly those of the west. Kienast refers to the so-called Frequentative form PS *parârasa* found in Old South Arabic and in Ethiopic. In unvocalized Old South Arabic texts the form in question would resemble the D-stem. However Höfner refers to Pa'â'al forms as frequentatives of the B-stem[45], on the assumption that since the geminated R_2 of the D-stem is not ordinarily written twice in other Semitic languages, Old South Arabic *qttl* must have stood for an original *qatâtala*. In the case of the Ethiopic languages the matter is clearer. Leslau, for instance, refers to a frequentative stem *nädaddala-y^{e}nädadd^{e}l* as existent in "all the Ethiopic languages, with the exception of Ge'ez".[46]

The second point in favor of the 'reduplication' hypothesis is that parallel or analogous formations can be easily found in Semitic. Thus, Toy wrote of "triliterals of the form qal.al made by reduplication of the second root letter, in which we can perceive a notion of intensity (e.g. Ar. *darra* 'go rapidly', Syr. *ḫ^{e}mam* 'burn with anger'). ... The idea of intensity seems to be attained by the addition of a substantive element of the root...".[47] While the analogy with the D-stem or R-stem is not clear in the case of these verbs, such is not the case with the quadriliterals cited by Poebel as being analogous to his PS *y-qtl-qtl*, such as Hebrew *kilkel* 'comprehend' and *galgal* 'wheel' (*i.e.* that which goes round and round). "Ces quadrilittères", Eitan remarks, "peuvent facilement tirer leur origine de toutes sortes de racines faibles aptes, par conséquent, à se débarrasser d'une de leurs trois radicales. ... La réduplication donne à ces verbes de formation secondaire une nuance nettement itérative ... à peu près comme les fréquentatifs latins à l'infinitif en *itare* (crepitare, cantitare, volitare etc.)". Finally, he continues, "Quant aux racines trilittères saines, ne pouvant pas facilement se répeter en entier, ce qui produirait un radical secondaire de six lettres inapte à la conjugaison – elles se sont contentées de redoubler les deux dernières radicales pour former ainsi des soi-disant quinquilittères. Comme verbes, ils ont surtout un sens superlatif".[48] However, *saḫarḫara* 'turn about' and *ḫ^{e}marmar* 'become heated' which, according to Brockelmann are the two examples of quinqueliterals occurring in the Old Testament, hardly lend themselves to interpretation as superlatives. Rather, they are examples of partial reduplication, a device little employed in Hebrew but, according to Dillmann, of frequent occurrence in Ethiopic, expressing "in a very picturesque way the notion of ... 'unremittingly', 'again and again'", *e.g.* *'ansafsafa* 'pour out drop by drop'.[49] Arabic Stem XII likewise employs this means of reduplication, though with dissimilation of the third radical, *e.g.* original *iḫḍarḍara* becoming

[45] M. Höfner, *Altsüdarabische Grammatik* (Leipzig, 1943).
[46] W. Leslau, *Étude Descriptive et Comparative du Gafat* (Paris, 1956).
[47] C. H. Toy, "On Hebrew Verb-Etymology", in *Transactions of the American Philological Association* 7 (1876).
[48] I. Eitan, "La Répétition de la Racine en Hébreu", in *Journal of the Palestinian Oriental Society* 1 (1920-1921).
[49] Dillmann, *Ethiopic Grammar*.

iḫḍawḍara 'be green' which, if we wish to preserve the iterative nuance of the construction, would have to be an original 'become green'.

Complete or partial reduplication of the root is, then, a well-established if secondary element in the evolution of the Semitic stem system, nominal and verbal. Moreover, one of the types of reduplication found corresponds to the hypothetical stem *ya-pararras* posited by Heidel. The question remains, (1) Is the D-stem with its gemination actually a remnant (or apocopation) of this stem and (2) If so, does this imply an intensive and/or plurative meaning for the D-stem? Neither proposition can be unambiguously demonstrated, though neither can be clearly disproven.

Taking the second question first, we note that one of the few consistent elements in our survey of reduplicated stems is that the iterative nuance is characteristic of each of them, including the Ethiopic *nädaddala* form; iterative, however, not in the sense of repeating an action a number of times but of continuing an activity over a period of time, or of developing a characteristic trait. This is also typical of the adjectival use of reduplication in Semitic. Thus, if *uparras* should represent PS *yu-paras-paras*, pluralic meaning (a number of individuals performing an act, or one individual performing an act upon many subjects) would not be typical of the normal Semitic use of reduplication. If the first proposition is valid, however, one might still draw the conclusion that the D-stem is therefore iterative/continuative in meaning. But there is no reason to assume that even *ya-pararras* resulted from apocopation of an original *ya-paras-paras* (nor does Kienast so indicate), when partial reduplication of the root is attested in the case of the other radicals (in particular R_3 as in Arabic Stem IX) and combinations of radicals. Moreover, an evolution from the simple stem to word-gemination to gemination of a single radical seems an unnecesarily involved process, a process for which no parallels can be adduced and which was perhaps put forward primarily with the goal of promoting a particular interpretation of the meaning and function of the D-stem, yet which neither Poebel nor others can relate clearly to other uses of the stem. Finally, Poebel's explanation assumes that the D-stem was derived from an already formed and defined B-stem, an assumption which we have already questioned.

For these various reasons, we feel that the gemination of R_2 is not a byproduct of word-gemination. If the 'extra' R_2 exists as a morpheme with the meaning 'intensity/frequency' it is for some other reason. We would agree with Götze that these reasons, as they have generally been presented, are "romantic". They arise from a confusion between the word as symbol, *i.e.* a sign with no natural qualification to denote an object or concept, and the word as index, *i.e.* a sign which has a natural association with that which it denotes, such as a facial gesture has. Only a few onomatopoetic words bridge the gap between the word as symbol and that which is symbolized. Having written of the D-stem that "Verdoppelung eines oder mehrerer Wurzelkonsonanten kennzeichnet die Intension oder Extension der Handlung; eine vocalische aber verwandte Verstärkung", König noted half-disappointedly that "bei den übrigen, durch Zusätze gebildeten 'Formen' der Verba springt die übereinstimmung zwischen Bedeutung und Laut nicht so unmittelbar in die Augen".[50] It would be surprising if such an agreement did exist. Words arise autochthonously and become associated with meanings arbitrarily, even in mature languages. The word exists phonetically before it acquires its peculiar significance. Only after it has acquired this meaning in some particular linguistic environment is the more visible process of analogical extension and leveling able to get under way. The D-stem may be the result of such an extension, or its form may have existed with some other meaning before it acquired its particular connotation.

[50] König, *Gedanke, Laut und Accent.*

III

THE SEMANTIC DOMAIN OF THE D-STEM

"Als ein Bedeutungssystem ist die Sprache auch ein Zeichensystem. Das linguistische Zeichen hat zwei Seiten, die phonische Form und die Bedeutung oder den Bezeichner und das Bezeichnete. Alles, was zum Zeichensystem, der kollektiven Sprache gehört, ist Form, nicht Substanz". ...[1]

In the last chapter we were concerned with investigating the occurrences of a particular linguistic phenomenon, gemination, and speculating about the connection between these occurrences and the possible origin of the phenomenon in the Semitic languages. Substance (meaning) was a secondary consideration; but hereafter it will assume primary importance, since the ultimate significance of any linguistic form lies in the substance which is given to it by those who employ it in their speech. As Nida describes the situation: "All morphological items have some semantic value. ... This meaning may be quite difficult to define, but nevertheless it is present. The linguistic meaning of a form may be stated in terms of the situation in which the form may occur. The positions of occurrence of a form are, however, of two types: structural and semantic. The positions of occurrence in terms of grammatical structure may be called the 'structural domain' of an item. The positions of occurrence in terms of the meaning may be called the 'semantic domain'. ... The semantic domain of any item must be described in terms of the natural and cultural phenomena of the language area in question".[2]

The meaning of gemination, and the semantic domain of the items in which it figures as a morpheme, are then separate, the former being associated with the origin of the D-stem in Proto-Semitic, the latter resulting from the linguistic practices of various Semitic peoples, who individually may employ "une seule des possibilités renfermées en germe dans la signification générale ou valeur des morphèmes".[3] An example demonstrating the difference between the semantic value of a morpheme and its semantic domain is the Semitic verbal theme *yqtl*. In Akkadian, and probably

[1] F. Rundgren, *Das althebräische Verbum: Abriss der Aspektlehre* (Uppsala, 1961) 27.

[2] Nida, "The Identification of Morphemes", 166.

[3] L. Hjelmslev, "Essai d'un Théorie de Morphèmes", in *Actes du 4. Congrès International de Linguistes* (Copenhagen, 1936), 148.

Ugaritic, it is used as a preterite; in Arabic, Aramaic and Ethiopic as an 'imperfect'; in Hebrew primarily as an imperfect, but in a special narrative construction as a preterite also. This is the semantic domain of the theme which, in its unpronounceable consonantal skeleton, may be considered a single morpheme (actually a portmanteau morph with two or more separate elements). Obviously, it will be the semantic domain of any form which first comes to the attention of the linguist, and from it he will usually try to deduce the semantic value of the form. For instance, in the case of *yqtl* there have been two principal lines of development, which have application to our D-stem problem also.

The first holds that since *yqtl* was employable for such diverse temporal concepts it must have been in Proto-Semitic a 'universal' tense dependent upon the grammatical context for its specific meaning (the Hebrew constructions with and without the '*waw* consecutive' are held to corroborate this). This line of thought typifies what Nida describes as the linguist's attempt to "recognize some common denominator that will permit us to group the various occurrences as one morpheme",[4] and meets Hjelmslev's criterion, that "définitions sémantiques doivent être d'un tel degré d'abstraction qu'elles permettent d'expliquer, par un simple déduction, toutes les variants (significations particulières) manifestées et toutes les variants possible".[5] It is what one might call a 'statistical' approach, rejected by those who are inclined to follow the second line of thought possible, which seeks to establish one meaning of *yqtl* as 'primary', then to demonstrate how other meaning may be derived therefrom. Rather than regarding *yqtl* as an original universal tense, this method would begin with the assumption that *yqtl* was an original preterite theme which during the evolution of the Western languages came by some means to usurp or acquire the function of the older present-future theme *uqttl*, probably because of the development of the *qtl* theme (used primarily for stative forms in the East) into a preterite in the West. In short, the preterite *yqtl* is accepted as primary because the other later uses of the theme can be explained with reference to an original preterite, while no equally plausible scheme can be advanced to support the idea that the imperfect *yqtl* was the original and the preterite somehow secondary. The application of this diversity of approach to the D-stem is clear. Shall we seek a lowest common denominator of meaning for the stem (such as enthusiasm or plurality) and show how this varies in different contexts, or shall we seek a single primary meaning with reference to which all other uses of the stem may be explained? In the last chapter, insofar as we were seeking the meaning of the stem's characteristic gemination, we concentrated upon the latter approach, with no conclusive results. We shall now concentrate more upon the former, more upon the semantic domain than on morphological analysis.

This can, perhaps, best be done by reference first to the semantic domain of the verb itself, then to that of the D-stem in particular. One device we shall employ for this purpose is the opposition of 'marked' and 'unmarked' terms, in a formula *A*/*Ax*

[4] Nida, "The Identification of Morphemes", 79.
[5] Hjelmslev, "Essai d'un Théorie des Morphèmes", 148.

in which "der merkmallose Term A besagt prinzipiell nur, dass es dem A an der x-Signalisierung fehlt, nicht eigentlich positiv, dass A die Negation von Ax ankündigt. Wäre dies der Fall, würde A in unserem Beispiel einen einheitlichen Wert im System der Sprache besitzen. A hat jedoch ... sowohl einen neutralen Wert als auch einen negativen Wert, der sich aus der Negation von Ax ergibt".[6] As an example we may take the masculine-feminine opposition, in which the feminine (*cf.* Eng. *actress*, Arab. *ḫimāra*, Heb. *naḇî'ah*) is marked, *i.e.* has an *x*-signification (the ending) not found in the masculine nominal counterparts, while the latter are unmarked, *i.e.* have both a negative (non-feminine) and neutral (generic) value, the latter reflected in the plural form for mixed groups, and in the singular when sex is not specified or indicated by the context.

How may we apply this to the verb? We assume first concerning the verb that, in the words of Wundt, "man kann sich unmöglich denken, der Mensch habe irgend einmal bloss in Verbalbegriffen gedacht. Das Umgekehrte, dass er bloss in gegenständlichen Vorstellungen gedacht habe, könnte man nach den psychologischen Eigenschaften viel eher verstehen".[7] The verbal concept then is probably secondary to the nominal. Whether this or its reverse is true, or whether some verbal or nominal concepts developed simultaneously, is relatively unimportant; the important fact is, that verbal and nominal forms can clearly be seen to have some elements in common. These elements are what we usually call 'roots': "diejenigen Lautbestandteile welche den in der Reihe begriffsverwandter Wörter vonkommenden Begriffselementen entsprechen".[8] The root itself is neither verbal nor nominal. In itself it has no independent existence, for "we have to do merely with the stem and can determine its meaning equally well from an ideal as from an objectively actual root".[9] Thus if we speak of a verbal stem as 'derived' from a root we do not mean (as do those who describe the D-stem as the result of a 'mentally-formed' doubling of R_2 corresponding to intensity or plurality) that the root existed prior to that stem (glossaries of the Semitic languages include many words for which no root is known). Rather, while recognizing that at least a minimal form, such as a nominal *qatl* (*cf.* Heb. *melek* from a hypothetical original *malk*) or a verbal *qtal* (*cf.* Semitic imperative forms) must have been the starting-point for the root concept, we employ the terminology of 'derivation' from the root solely as a useful descriptive device.

If we try, then, to set up a series of marked and unmarked terms within the verbal system, the most fundamental opposition would exist between the root and its derived forms, both collectively and individually, the root reflecting both the absence of time, person, mode *etc.* found in the verbal stems, as well as the 'neutral' generic prototype of the verb (a similar statement could be made for the root in relation to nominal stems). Does this imply then that each of these stems is derivable directly from the

6 Rundgren, *Das althebräische Verbum*, 38.
7 Wundt, *Völkerpsychologie*, 556.
8 Wundt, *Völkerpsychologie*, 559.
9 Toy, "On Hebrew Verb-Etymology", 65.

root, and that they are therefore independent from one another, save for their common source? In order to clarify this, let us see whether other oppositions can be set up among those forms which actually exist.

Such an opposition may be said to exist between the imperative and narrative forms of the B-stem (and the other stems). In the two formulae, *qṭôl/qāṭal* and *qṭôl/yiqṭôl*, the shift of accent and the addition of a prefix, which are the *x*-significations for *qāṭal* and *yiqṭôl* respectively, have added a temporal aspect to the root, whatever their morphological or phonological origins. *Qṭôl* is here the unmarked term, since there is inherent in it the negation or subtraction of the temporal aspect, and since in itself it is the generic prototype of the verb (or word of action): *qṭôl* is both negative and neutral. Does a similar opposition exist between the B-stem and its alternate stems? In the formula of Heb. *qāṭal/hiqṭīl* and Arab. *qatala/ʾaqtala* the answer would seem to be "Yes". The relationship of the second term of the pair to the first is virtually invariable; the *x*-factor (embodied in the prefix *h/ʾ*), whatever its origin, adds the signification 'causation' or 'indirect action'. The B-stem then is negative as 'non-causation' or 'direct involvement'; it is neutral or prototypical in that it presents transitive action or intransitive state in its simplest and purest form. A similar statement could be made concerning the pair *qatala/iqtatala* in Arabic (perhaps also Heb. *qāṭal/hithqaṭṭēl*), substituting 'reflexivity' for 'causation'.

The question is, of course, "Can such an opposition be set up between the B- and D-stems?" The answer is "Probably not". Whatever the origin of the 'extra' R_2 of the D-stem, it is impossible to assign an invariable or even regular signification to this *x* which would be negativized by the B-stem. Does *x* equal plurality of object or subject? Then the B-stem would indicate non-plurality of both, which is prima facie not the case. Does *x* indicate intensity of feeling? Neither Hebrew nor Arabic takes advantage of such an opposition, for example, to provide a D-stem for *ʾāhab* and *ḥabba* respectively, in order to distinguish between 'like' and 'love'. Indeed, the Arabic D-stem associated with this root means not 'like intensely' but 'cause to like'. Does *x* denote continuity or iteration of action? If so, the B-stem should reflect non-continuity of action in addition to its fixed 'neutral' value. Such an opposition might be set up for, *e.g.* *hālaḵ/hillēḵ* 'go/go about', but how does it pertain to *dāḇar/dibbēr* or those cases where the D-stem clearly adds what is translated as a causative meaning to the B-stem?

Is 'causation', then, as in Stem IV, the *x*-signification of the D-stem? If so, we would expect the B-stem once more to imply contrasting direct involvement and to embody the simplest temporal aspect of the root. This is often the case; the direct overlap of Stems II and IV at points, particularly their confusion in colloquial speech, might lead us to search for our answer in this direction. Yet such an explanation does not account for such pairs as those cited above from the roots *dbr* and *hlk*, nor for the many other pairs in which the B- and D-stems would seem, in light of textual evidence, to have the same meaning. Even less does this, or any of the possible oppositions so far suggested, account for the many cases in which the B-stem exists without a corresponding D-stem, even though "... aus dem blossen Fehlen eines entsprechenden Qiṭṭel in der übriggebliebenen Literatur lässt sich nicht das Fehlen desselben in der lebenden Sprache eschliessen".[10] Nor does it account for the less frequent though more significant and more troublesome cases in which the D-stem exists in isolation or alongside other 'derived' stems, despite the suggestion of Bergsträsser that for Hebrew "... z.T. werden diese Piˁˁel in Wirklichkeit Intensiva (oder Kausativa) zu verlorenen oder im Alten Testament vorliegenden Grundformen.....".[11] Such resort to 'lost' or 'non-occurring' forms loses much of its appeal when one consults Arabic texts and lexicons, only to find a situation similar to that of classical Hebrew, with a parallel distribution of stems for many roots which occur in both languages.

The unpredictability of the relationship between the B- and D-stems becomes most striking when it is contrasted with that existing between the B- and Š-stems. In the latter case the opposition of meaning is a consistent one virtually wherever the two forms exist for a given root; moreover, in the few instances of an Š-form found in isolation, most will have a clearly causative meaning. The rest of the cases may be described as *réemploi de matériaux*, *i.e.* employment of the causative stem as a vehicle for denominatives, much as the feminine signification, final *â*, is employed as a signification for abstractions. The comparative disarray of the B- and D-stem 'opposition', in which the *x*-signification has been claimed by various commentators to have plurative, intensive, iterative and causative connotations (to name only the most prominent), each one of which has been regarded by some commentator as 'fundamental', and in which there is an obvious overlap with the usage of other stems, suggests strongly that either (1) there is an extremely widespread and diverse *réemploi de matériaux* in play here or (2) no such opposition of B- and D-stems is in fact demonstrable.

The first of these two possibilities has been most seriously and fully advanced for the Ethiopic languages, in which the relation of *qatala* and *qattala* is apparently even more ambiguous than in the other western languages. For instance, although Dillmann states at the beginning of his discussion of the D-stem, that its essence lies in "indicating more or less frequent repetition, or to signify force, eagerness or completeness in the action"[12], he notes almost immediately thereafter, without advancing any explanation, that "Ethiopic ... has mostly given up the first stem, in the case of those verbal notions which it has developed in the second. ... Besides, in most cases, when both stems are fully formed, there is no longer any essential difference in the meaning." Such apparent contradiction between theory and practice led Cohen some years later to conclude that "en amharique, l'opposition sémitique ancienne du thème trilitère simple et du thème intensif à gémination de la seconde radicale a cessé de fonctionner."[13]

[10] E. König, *Historisches-Kritisches Lehrgebäude der hebräischen Sprache*, vol. I (Leipzig, 1895), 193.
[11] Bergsträsser, *Hebräische Grammatik*, 94.
[12] Dillmann, *Ethiopic Grammar*, 143.
[13] M. Cohen, *Nouvelles Études d'Ethiopien Méridional* (Paris, 1939), 217.

Rundgren, having referred to the 'relevant' opposition *t:tt* in Arabic, concludes that:

So besteht die eben erwähnte Opposition z.B. im Amharischen nicht mehr, indem hier qatala und qattala in der einzigen Form qättälä zusammengefallen sind. ... So stellt z.B. *faṣṣama* 'vollenden' nur noch eine lexicalische Grösse dar. Es ist nicht etwa von einem *faṣama* funktionell deriviert, sondern zur Normalform eben für diese Handlung geworden. ... Wenn nun aber qattala nur noch eine nicht funktionell deriviert lexicalische Grösse wie etwa 'töten' neben 'vernichten' darstellte, konnte es als eine 'verbrauchte' Form des Grundstammes ein neues System bilden, wie sich im Amharischen umgekehrt *näggärä* mit *y^{e}ngar* verband. Hier erbor sich ein geeignetes Mittel zu einem réemploi de matériaux.[14]

In the same way, Rundgren states, the Ethiopic indicative *y^{e}qatt^{e}l* is associated phonetically with the Proto-Semitic intensive *yu-qáttil*, but semantically with the B-stem preterite *qatala* – again a *réemploi de matériaux*. Later in this chapter we shall be discussing further the relationship of the Akkadian *iparras* (B-stem) and *uparras* (D-stem) forms, and will consider the Ethiopic indicative. This whole question is important to us because, as we shall show in later chapters, Cohen's statement concerning Amharic quoted above is substantially correct for Qur'anic Arabic as well. If there was an original opposition between *qatala* and *qattala*, the idea that it has been diluted by *réemploi de matériaux* may turn out to be most useful.

However, there is still the second possibility, that no such opposition is demonstrable. The difficulty we have experienced in setting up the opposition indicates that this possibility is a strong one. Therefore, since such oppositions as *naḇî/naḇî'ah* or *qatala/'aqtala* imply that the second term is in each case 'derivable' from the first (in the ordinary sense of the word, that their relationship is predictable) the non-existence of a consistent opposition between B and D may imply that their relationship, unpredictable in terms of the meaning of each form, involves no possibility of 'derivation'. At the same time, although "hingegen kann zwischen zwei Zeichen (Morphemen) eine Differenz vorkommen, ohne dass dieser Differenz auch eine Bedeutungsopposition zu entsprechen brauchte ..."[15] we cannot say, on the basis of those B- and D-forms which have the 'same' meaning, that the phonetic differences between the stems are non-significant. We mean only to note that there is no significant opposition between them insofar as their meanings are not explicable in terms of one another.

If this is the case, then can there be any other opposition which might be set up, with the D-stem as one of its terms, which could help us to clarify the stem's semantic domain? Of course, as with all verbal stems, an opposition with the root itself can be envisioned; such an opposition is useful only insofar as it symbolizes the fact that the D-stem is not derived from the root through the mediation of the B-stem, but has a more direct relationship to it. However it is NOT useful, in that no other stem either was formed consciously from an abstracted or abstract root. Far more useful will be a description of other forms to which the D-stem may be related and/or opposed, a description which would leave open the possibility that "die Verdoppelungsform in

[14] F. Rundgren, *Intensiv- und Aspektkorrelation* (Uppsala, 1959), 50-55.
[15] Rundgren, *Das althebräische Verbum*, 36.

solchen Fällen möglicherweise nicht das abgeleitete, sondern das ursprüngliche Wort ist,"[16] at least insofar as its presence within the verbal system is concerned. We must even leave open the possibility that the D-stem represents a development external rather than internal to the verbal system, or that at least it did not develop as a part of the stem-system, but became a later accretion to that phase of the verbal system, the term "stem-system" presupposing a series of inter-related forms with stable and definable oppositions in meaning, *e.g.* simple, causative, reflexive, causative-reflexive etc. This at first glance far-out possibility is given some initial credibility by the failure of grammarians during a period of a thousand years to fix or define the particular role of the D-stem or its coordinate Stem III.

For whatever it is worth, we may here refer to Skoss's comment that Saadia ha-Gaon "states in accordance with his computation and including the forms of the *'stmʿ* type (hithpaʿel) there are approximately 20,000 verbs, but to be more exact there are 19,169 forms, and he adds that he could not find one more form to make their number 19,170, but it is impossible to enumerate them all. Dunash ... quotes this statement with amazement and mentions the piʿʿel forms, omitted by Saadia, which would add a great many more verbal forms to the number given by him."[17] Does this mean that Saadia regarded the D-stem as somehow not being a verbal form? This would not necessarily displace it from the verbal system, which may legitimately include all those forms which function as verbs and take verbal endings. 'Nominal verb' is after all a no more anomalous concept than 'verbal noun'. Nevertheless, such a novel approach might alleviate many of the problems associated with fixing the place of D verbal forms.

This line of thought, of course, leads us to the so-called 'denominative verb' which, if it does not stand outside the normal verbal system, remains at best an external rather than internal development in relation to it. As Hirschfeld puts it, "... Zeitwörter, welche abstrakte und komplizierte Handlungen ausdrücken, nicht ursprünglicher Natur sind. Zu dieser Klasse gehören auch die meisten den Zeitwörtern ... da bei dessen Ausführung gewöhnlich mehr als eine Handlung erforderlich ist."[18]

In short, the seemingly obvious comment of Rundgren, that "im Arabischen die Formen *qattala, qâtala, 'aqtala* einerseits morphologisch vom Grundstamm *qatala*, andererseits aber auch im System funktionell abgeleitet"[19] may, since it leads to many contradictions, at least when applied to *qatala* in opposition to *qattala* and *qâtala*, not be the simplest means of determining the functional and semantic domain of the D-stem. Instead, on the possibility that Ullendorff's comment concerning the Ethiopic B- and D-stems, that "we have here two separate types of verbal stems and not

[16] Wundt, *Völkerpsychologie*, 581.
[17] Skoss, *Saadia ha-Gaon*, 17.
[18] H. Hirschfeld, "Bemerkungen zum Verbum denominativum im Hebräischen" in *Monatschrift* 69 (1925), 223-230.
[19] Rundgren, *Intensiv- und Aspektkorrelation*, 50.

morphological variations of a given root" since "in most cases the geminated form cannot be considered the intensive stem of the non-geminated one without doing violence to semantic development,"[20] has wider application to comparative Semitics, we shall now consider some of the suggestions which have been advanced concerning the possibility of a D-stem developed outside of the verbal system and drawing upon some source other than the verb stems for its significant opposition. Most of these involve opposition to nominal forms.

H. S. Nyberg has stated clearly what one may describe as a considered orthodox interpretation of the relationship of denominative verbs to the verbal system:

Die Bildung von denominativen Verben ist von je her der schwache Punkt der semitischen Wortbildung gewesen. Sie konnte nur im engen Rahmen des schon früh erstarrten Verbalsystems stattfinden: die Kernkonsonanten des Nomens wurden unter Weglassung aller äusseren und innern Bildungselemente in das gewöhnliche verbals Schema eingereiht. Teils ging dadurch der äussern Zusammenhang mit dem Nomen verloren, teils konnte ein und dieselbe Verbalform neben ihrer ursprünglichen verbalen Bedeutung auch die eines Denominativums tragen.[21]

This statement is particularly relevant to our consideration of the D-stem, since there is a clear affinity between this stem and denominative formation as such, both in the classical, written languages and in the contemporary, colloquial dialects. This affinity is so pronounced that Hartmann, having in mind an intensive-privative interpretation of the D-stem, stated concerning Semitic pluriliteral formations in general, that their significance was "Intension in der Quantität und Frequenz, Abschwächung in der Qualität und Stärke der Handlung."[22] Despite the difference in approach and intent, it is not difficult to see in the two statements cited the presupposition that the formation of the verbal system preceded the creation of denominative verbs. Placed in the context of our discussion, the assumption here would be that the quadriliteral denominative verbs familiar in all the Semitic languages during all periods were assimilated to an already-existent D-stem (whether intensive, iterative or causative) because "this stem is the simplest of the enlarged formations, its four consonants being due merely to a doubling of the middle radical, not to the addition of a different consonant."[23] Yet, is not the reverse also possible, that the D-stem came into being by analogy with quadriliteral denominatives (or 'nominal verbs') and came later to be incorporated into a 'verbal system' still in process of evolution, by assuming verbal endings and prefixes?

Any attempt to interpret quadriliteral verbs as 'intensive-privative' in meaning, even such forms as Arab. *karsafa* with its parallel D-form *kassafa* which according to Hurwitz "clearly shows that to the Semitic mind these infixed forms have an inten-

20 Ullendorff, *The Semitic Languages of Ethiopia*, 219.
21 Nyberg, "Zur Entwicklung der mehr als dreikonsonantische Stämme in den semitischen Sprachen", 132.
22 M. Hartmann, *Die Pluriliteralbildungen in den semitischen Sprachen* (Halle, 1875), 6.
23 Heidel, *The System of the Quadriliteral Verb in Akkadian*, 133.

sive connotation,"[24] must fail to convince us when textual evidence is considered. Far more consonant with the evidence is Heidel's statement concerning the Akkadian quadriliteral *paršum*, that "in spite of its pi‘‘el features, it is a quadriliteral *qal* form, corresponding to the (Stem I) form of the triliteral verb. ... The genuine pi‘‘el formation of this root could be only *puraššum*."[25] As the author points out, his statement applies just as well to Western forms such as Hebrew *kirsēm* and Arabic *qamṭara*. And it applies equally well to contemporary colloquial and written Arabic, in which "die vierkonsonantischen Bildungen sind auf kräftigen Vormarsch und haben schon viel Boden erobert. Fast alle lautmalenden oder in irgendeiner Weise konkret veranschaulichenden Verba, fast alle irgendwie expressiven Benennungen werden vierkonsonantisch gebildet, während die dreikonsonantischen Bildungen nur dem abstrakten Wortschatz angehören. Auch hier ist die Aufnahme von nichtarabischen Fremdwörtern ...."[26] In the latter category are such words as *tarjama* 'translate', *saflata* 'pave with asphalt' and *ta'amraka* 'become Americanized'; in the former such terms as *darbasa* 'bolt (a door)' from *dirbās* 'bolt' or *taktaka* 'ticked'. Similar examples could be cited from any Semitic language. Moreover, the Arab Murad Kamil points out that "in der Umgangssprache überall eine besondere Häufigkeit der vierradikaligen Verben zu beobachten ist. Dieselbe Person braucht zum Ausdruck eines Gedankens, den sie in der Umgangssprache mit einem vierradikaligen Verb ausdrückt, in der Schriftsprache in der Regel lieber ein dreiradikaliges Verb und vermeidet das vierradikalige."[27]

One may suppose that the phenomenon noted here is not exclusively of recent origin, that the ready transformation of nouns into denominative verbs (quadriliteral or triliteral) has always been an important factor in the spoken Semitic languages, even though such forms may appear relatively infrequently above the surface in the classical literature. In fact, to judge from Kamil's statement, such usages may have been suppressed in literary language because of a lack of 'elegance', appropriateness to what is often a sacred text conservative in language use. Such demonstratives are, nevertheless, "das treueste Merkmal der Fruchtbarkeit lebender Sprachen."[28] Can forms which arise so readily and spontaneously really be regarded as 'employing' an already-fixed verbal stem so that, as Brockelmann wrote, the D-stem and its offshoots "liefern namentlich in den jüngeren Dialekten das Hauptkontingent der Verbalbindung?"[29] Can the formation of quadriliteral denominatives be contingent upon the prior establishment of a stem with a geminated middle radical? Is it not equally, rather more likely that gemination of the middle consonant was a means of

[24] S. T. H. Hurwitz, *Root-Determinatives in Semitic Speech* (New York, 1913), 49.
[25] Heidel, *The System of the Quadriliteral Verb in Akkadian*, 71.
[26] Nyberg, "Zur Entwicklung der mehr als dreikonsonantischen Stämme in den Semitischen Sprachen", 136.
[27] M. Kamil, "Zur Bildung der vierradikaligen Verben in den lebenden semitischen Sprachen", in *Studi Orientalistici in Onore di Giorgio della Vida*, vol. I (Rome, 1956), 459.
[28] Hirschfeld, "Bemerkungen zum Verbum denominativum im Hebräischen", 224.
[29] Brockelmann, *Lexicon Syriacum*, 510.

stretching out triliteral nominal stems to conform to a pattern already established by the denominatives based upon quadriliteral nouns, when for some reason the B-stem, which surely must also have been denominative in origin, was inappropriate or insufficient for the purpose, perhaps because it was already acquiring the more abstract verbal connotation?

We must not allow ourselves to think of the Semitic 'verbal system' as a Tablet of the Law fallen from heaven in its final and fixed form; we must think of it rather as a collection of general principles, arrived at by trial and error, with many dead ends surviving as anachronisms and many living ends too dynamic to be contained within the guidelines which the system provides. Any grammatical system is no more than the grammarian's attempt to explain what usually does occur in a language; it can never bring that language under control. The content of any language is that "qui est en elle-même amorphe, mais qui se fait décrire à travers les démarcations fixés posées par la forme linguistique."[30] Thus "... il est bien entendu qu'aucun système verbal ne possède des formes distinctes pour toutes les idées que le verbe peut théoretiquement représenter; c'est précisement le choix entre les idées exprimables qui définit le système verbale d'une langue donnée."[31] A 'system' which does not fit all the facts of a language or aspects thereof (*i.e.* the forms which actually occur) is inadequate and must be revised. Denominative D-stems are neither outside the verbal system nor could they be regarded so except by a grammarian whose principal concern is orderliness within the system. Therefore we must find out what these denominatives really do, and how the D-stem is connected with this. Most particularly, we will be interested to evaluate Nyberg's idea, that the D-stem must carry its denominative meaning "in addition to" its "original verbal meaning."

It is probably true that "Qal diejenige Konjugation sei, mit der zunächst Verba denominativa gebildet worden sind,"[32] and that the causative and reflexive alternate stems, as well as the D-stem and its variants, are often associated with denominative verbs (particularly Stem IV). Yet Gerber discovered that, of the one hundred forty-six Hebrew denominatives, only four appeared not at all in the *Pi‘‘el* or its associated stems (*pu‘‘al, pôlel, hithpa‘‘el, hithpôlel, hothpa‘‘el*), while fifty-eight appeared in those stems alone. At the same time, the most common denominatives, the *verba dicendi*, from the roots *dbr, mll, qll, brk, etc.* were found either exclusively in the *pi‘‘el* or, if in other conjugations, the *pi‘‘el* was demonstrably the oldest in usage. Furthermore, Gerber points out that even in the relatively numerous cases where the *Qal* was the conjugation longest employed many of these roots had later become associated with the D-stem. These observations seem to point to a relationship between the 'nominal verb' concept and the form which we call the D-stem, but which we may better call the simple quadriliteral stem as opposed to the simple triliteral Stem I. This relationship goes beyond the mere employment of the D-stem for denominatives, to a pos-

[30] Hjelmslev, "Essai d'un Théorie des Morphèmes", 147.
[31] M. Cohen, *Le Système Verbal Sémitique et l'Expression du Temps* (Paris, 1924), 2.
[32] W. J. Gerber, *Die Hebräischen Verba denominativa* (Leipzig, 1896), 3.

sible origin of the stem in denominative usage. Such usage would have given this stem predominance in the area of denominative verbs, tending to usurp this function when it arose in the simple triliteral stem and only later yielding some ground to the *hiphʿil* forms, which "belong almost exclusively to the younger language" according to Gerber.

Ewald's suggestion, that "Steht aber ein vermehrter Verbalstamm vereinzelt und in ganz besonderer Bedeutung, so verliert sich allmählich die ursprüngliche Kraft der Form ... und zurückfällt in den einfachen ohne die Bedeutung zu ändern,"[33] could even be applied in this instance to indicate the reason for existence of a Qal-form where a *Piʿʿel* denominative might be expected. In any event, the predominant D-stem form of the denominative verb in Hebrew which we have just been describing has its counterpart in Arabic, in spite of the frequency of Stem IV denominatives in that language and the large number of Stem I denominatives which stand side-by-side with those of Stem II; those developments correspond to what Gerber and Ewald described as later stages of Hebrew, and as such could be one more illustration of what Heidel has aptly called "the tendency of the Semitic languages to develop common patterns for their verbal systems."[34] Even so, we have already taken note of the continuing Arabic use of the quadriconsonantal stem for verbs which fulfill some concrete illustrative purpose. This last phrase aptly describes denominatives in general; it should not surprise us if the gemination of the D-stem arose through analogical extension of the quadriliteral principle of construction to triconsonantal roots, as denominative verbal concepts proliferated.

One need not, of course, accept the extension of triliteral into quadriliteral roots in order to accept the general premise of some special connection between the D-stem and the quadriliteral denominative stem. Rather, one may approach the situation as several commentators have already done, beginning with an already-existent geminated nominal stem as the basis for nominal verbs patterned on the quadriliteral verbal stem. We are now to be concerned with several variants of the nominal stem, PS *qattal/qâtal*, forms which have sometimes been put forward as possible bases for the verbal forms *qattala/qâtala*. The basic assumption of such hypotheses is that an opposition of the type *qattal/qattala* or *qâtal/qâtala* might be set up, with the *x*-signification of the D-stem embodied not in the geminated R_2, as we have previously assumed, but in the verbal endings *-a*, *-at etc.* The signification would be the addition of the concept 'act, perform, make' or the like to a nominal stem, noun or adjective.

For instance, we have already mentioned Rosenthal's suggestion that we might seek the origin of the *qâtala*-form in the B-stem participle *qâtil*, for "it would not seem impossible or far-fetched to construe a basic similarity between the two forms and to arrive at the meaning of the 'third conjugation' from the original meaning of 'to act as affecting someone else in the manner of a...' ",[35] taking *qâtil* as nomen agentis

[33] H. Ewald, *Grammatik der hebräischen Sprache* (Leipzig, 1838³), 131.
[34] Heidel, *The System of the Quadriliteral Verb in Akkadian*, 115.
[35] F. Rosenthal, "Review", 548.

of the first conjugation. If Garbini is correct in saying of the D-stem that "il tema intensive presenta la riduzione della forma con la prima vocale allungata (qâtil) attestata in 'cananaico' e in ugaritico,"[36] then we would have in the opposition *qâtal*/ *qātala* (qattala) the origin of the D-stem, *x* having the signification noted by Rosenthal in addition to the aspects of tense, number and person which it manifests in the contexts of other opposed pairs. Garbini's evidence for his conclusion is, however, uncertain.

Specifically, as concerns the 'Canaanite' material he cites, Dhorme states only that one may "rétrouver dans *puḫer* et *mušer* des infinitifs *pôḫer* et *môšer*, appartenant non plus à la forme *qaṭṭil* mais bien à *qâṭil* (infinitif de *qâṭala*). Nous avons donc un double infinitif cananéen pour la forme intensive: *qaṭṭil* (d'où *qaṭṭēl*) et *qôṭēl*."[37] No conclusion can be drawn from this, save that the infinitives of the two stems (and thus the stems themselves) supplement one another. The supplementary nature of the two stems has long been recognized. For instance, Cohen commented: "Comme l'ancien intensif, l'ancien conatif ou 'extensif' à â est en amharique une forme qui ne fonctionne pas regulièrement; les verbes à â apparaissent au thème simple du trilitère comme un 'type C' de conjugaison, sans valeur définie."[38] Already in 1886, Praetorius knew that "der 3. Stamm ist meist nur im Imperfektum gebräuchlich. Dieses Imperfektum des 3. Stammes tritt ergänzend als Indikativ Imperf. zu dem Imperf. des 2. Stammes (y^{e}qatt^{e}l) ...."[39] Moreover, in Qur'anic Arabic Stems II and III are likewise virtually complementary in their distribution, which tends to confirm that they proceed in form and in meaning from the same impulse and are, so to speak, identical in embryo. To say this, however is not to say that we need derive one from the other, as Garbini would do. Furthermore, the fact that "qâtala dans sa forme matérielle ne paraît pas être une formation du sémitique commun, mais une innovation du sémitique de l'Ouest,"[40] coupled with the general linguistic principle (confirmed elsewhere in the Semitic languages) that when a phoneme is lost there is frequently a compensatory lengthening of the contiguous phoneme, would suggest that *qâtala* is more likely to be the secondary form, as Fleisch concluded in his full-length study of Stem III. Thus, omitting the question, whether *qâtala* is thus derived, or whether it is a denominative from original *qâtil*, we think it unlikely that the D-stem can be traced to this last form; it may rather reflect the *nomen agentis* type *qattal.*

Another nominal stem with an obvious link to this last form is the familiar *nomen professionis* type *qattâl*. Many attempts have been made to link this with the D-stem, *e.g.* Götze's suggestion that *qattâl*, along with such pseudo-D-stems as Akk. *ruppudum* 'roam' and Heb. *hillēḵ* 'walk', is an outgrowth of an old Bn form, the -n assimilating to the middle radical to give an impression of gemination, giving the verb

[36] G. Garbini, *Il Semitico di Nord-Ovest* (Naples, 1960), 134.
[37] E. Dhorme, "La Langue de Canaan", in *Receuil Edouard Dhorme* (Paris, 1951), 433.
[38] M. Cohen, *Nouvelles Études*, 225.
[39] F. Praetorius, *Äthiopische Grammatik* (Leipzig, 1886), 37.
[40] Fleisch, *Les Verbes à Allongement vocalique en Sémitique*, 421.

a continuative force. In another vein, Wright regards *qattâl* as an intensive formation, *viz.* "From verbal adjectives of the form *fâ'il* ... is derived an adjective *fa''âl*, which adds to the signification of its primitive the idea of intensiveness or of habit ... *e.g.* *'âkil* 'eating', *'akkâl* 'glutton' ... *šârib* 'drinking', *šarrâb* 'a drunkard'."[41] Loretz, however, objects that "die Idee des Berufes hat an sich nichts mit dem Intensivum zu tun."[42] He arrives at a conclusion similar to Götze's, writing that "diese Nominalbildung zum Durativ-Präsens-Stamm (gehört). Die parras-Bildung ist also von Haus aus sehr geeignet, gewohnheitsgebundenes Tun und Berufstätigkeit zum Ausdruck zu bringen."[42] Speiser holds that "the nominal form *qattâl* cannot illuminate phenomena of the verbal D-stem."[43] This is so, insofar as the D-stem is not clearly derived from *qattâl*. However, it is equally clear that *qattâl* and *qattala* both have some connection with the *qttl* theme, and insofar as this is true any form derived from this theme might be helpful in defining the rather vague limits of the meaning which the theme connotes.

This is particularly so, if we follow the argument of Fleisch, who derives *fa''âl* from a primitive form of the *nomen agentis fa'al*, by reference to "les renforcements habituels en sémitique dans la formation des noms: allongement de voyelle, gémination de consonne."[44] Thus he derives both *fa''al* and *fa'âl*, either one of which, in his view, could have provided the impetus and basis for *fa''âl*. According to Fleisch, "Dans la langue de l'ancienne poésie et du Coran, *fa''âl* n'a que cet emploi de nom d'agent intensif et peut exercer la rection d'un verbe, (*cf.*) Coran V. 46. XII. 53, LXVIII. 12."[45] The later use of the form as nomen professionis, he claims, arises from Aramaic influence.

While we may disregard temporarily the description of the D-stem as 'intensive', the connection with *fa''âl* is significant. Seemingly, both *fa''âl* and *fâ'il* can be linked to an original stem *fa''al*, and both manifest the verbal aspect of continuing action. Another nominal stem worth noting here is that embodied in Heb. *qiṭṭûl* and *qaṭṭûl* forms. Böhmer refers to these as "Reste des Passivums, genauer seines Partizipiums, im Steigerungsstamm" in forms without the characteristic *m*-prefix,[46] analogous to the passive participle of the B-stem *qatûl*. Elsewhere such geminated forms, along with *qaṭṭûl*, have been regarded as comparable with but not incorporated within the D-stem, as noun formations "either emphasizing the energy of the action or relation, or else indicating a longer continuance of the action or relation or state."[47] For instance, we have Rundgren's conclusion that "Die Elativität, die gesteigerte Zu-

41 W. Wright, *A Grammar of the Arabic Language* (Cambridge, 1859), 137.
42 O. Loretz, "Die hebräische Nominalform qattâl", in *Biblica* 41 (1960), 415.
43 Speiser, "The Durative Hithpa'el", 120, n. 28.
44 H. Fleisch, "Le Nom d'Agent Fa'al", in *Mélanges de l'Université St. Joseph* 32 (1955), 167.
45 Fleisch, "Le Nom d'Agent Fa'al", 171.
46 J. Böhmer, "Spuren von Passiv-Participien des Steigerungsstamms im Hebräischen", in *Zeitschrift für Semitistik* 10 (1935), 317.
47 W. Gesenius, *Hebrew Grammar*, E. Kautzsch, ed.; 2nd English edition by A. E. Cowley (Oxford, 1910), sec. 84b.

ständlichkeit wird im Semitischen durch Formen wie qattil, qittil, qattal, quttul ausgedrückt. ... Demzufolge können wir annehmen, dass zwischen Elativen wie qattil, qattul und den Stativen *qatīl, qatūl* ein genetischer Zusammenhang besteht. Weil ferner der Elativ nicht nur essivisch-durativisch ist, sondern auch einen Grad von Intensität aufweist ... ergibt sich von selbst, dass die Base qattil in (PS) yu-qattil mit der Elativ-Base qattil genetisch identisch ist."[48]

One may wonder whether the 'intensive' connotation sensed by these commentators in such Hebrew nominal forms as *ḥannûn* 'gracious', *šiqqûṣ* 'contemptible thing', *limmûd* 'disciple' results from reading back into them the assumed intensive meaning of the D-stem, despite the effort of Rundgren to employ them in turn as evidence of that stem's intensive value. It seems more reasonable to believe that these *qaṭṭûl*-forms are extensions of the *qaṭûl* type, the gemination not having any morphological significance initially, rather resulting from the strengthening of the first syllable characteristic of Biblical Hebrew. In other words, *qaṭṭûl* would be an alternative form of *qaṭûl*, as the pu"al form provides an alternative for a potential but non-existent passive of the B-stem (*qūṭal*), *e.g. luqqaḥ* 'he was taken' (for which no D-stem exists) or *yullᵉdah* 'she was born' (for which a passive of the D-stem would have the very different meaning 'she was helped to bear'). Where *quṭṭal* "in seiner Bedeutung mit dem Qaṭal übereinstimmt, vertritt es das Passivum auch zu diesem."[49] In a later chapter will shall be discussing these ambiguous *quṭṭal*-forms as they occur in our texts. For now, they serve mainly to indicate that gemination in itself does not necessarily assure the connection of a nominal or verbal form with the D-stem, nor even assure us they can be profitably compared with it.

Insofar as we may, however, assume such a mutual relationship between the 'elative' nominal forms cited and the D-stem, the consensus of critical opinion would have it, that since they signify a continuing state of affairs as opposed to a momentary state or action, *e.g.* Aram. *ṭabbâḥ* is one who continually slaughters, Arab. *kurrâm* signifies a man who is very noble because this is his continuing state of being, Heb. *limmûd* is a disciple because he continues learning; therefore the D-stem must have similar connotations, *i.e.* it should point us toward 'extension' rather than 'intension'. This would lead us to the conclusion that some sort of assimilated infix is involved, probably the much-mentioned *-n-*. On the analogy of Rosenthal's statement concerning *qâtala* the semantic domain of *qattala* might then be generalized as "act in the manner of one who is continuing to. ..."

Christian sees here two different themes, parallel yet seeming to intersect only coincidentally as a result of the degree of homonymy between them: the one the intensive stem, "ursprünglich durch (defektive) Verdoppelung des letzten Radikals gebildet", developing from PS *qatlal* to *qat'al* to *qattal*; the other a durative stem in which appears "ein Modificationselement n, das ... in den Stamm eindrang und dem

[48] F. Rundgren. *Intensiv- und Aspektkorrelation*, 261.
[49] König, *Historisches-Kritisches Lehrgebäude*, 192.

zweiten Radikal assimiliert wurde", *e.g.* PS *panras* became *parras.*[50] Elsewhere Christian states that a verbal concept may be modified by one of two means in the Hamito-Semitic languages: "entweder es wird der allgemeine Begriff auf eine bestimmte Teilbedeutung eingeengt oder es wird eine bestimmte Phase im Ablauf des verbalen Sachverhaltes gekennzeichnet. Wir sprechen im ersten Falle von einer Bedeutungsmodifikation, im letzteren Falle von einer Verlaufsmodifikation."[51] Christian, and others, would doubtless regard the majority of D-forms as being in the former category, but the 'pseudo-D-forms' with *n*-infix in the latter.

Christian's understanding of denominative verbs is the key to his understanding of the diversity within the D-stem, and his reconciliation of that diversity. He maintains: "Dass er auf den iterativen zurückgeht, unterliegt wohl kaum kein Zweifel. Es kann nur der der ständigen Beschäftigung Ausübenden beziehen"[52], *i.e.* the nominal concept is identified with the person performing the action, as in Heb. *kihhēn* 'serve as priest' ... Arab. *ṣabbaḥa* 'be morning, come in the morning' ... Syr. *maggēš* 'be a Magian'. But the underlying noun can also be the object of the activity, thus not identical with the subject, as Arab. *sallama* 'speak the salâm' ... Eth. *ʿammada* 'set up a pillar'. These denominatives, initially intransitive, can become transitive if an external object is named, *i.e.* if the nominal concept in question is related to someone or something other than the subject; it then becomes a causative, *e.g.* one brings the dawn into conjunction with something (does something early) or brings the *salâm* into conjunction with somebody (greets him). This progression from iterative to transitive usage would then make these denominatives comparable with the causative-factitive D-stems from stative verbs, by which a state or quality is brought into conjunction with the object. The naming of an object then becomes crucial for the causative meaning of the D-stem. This process may be implicit in what Christian writes, following his discussion of Akkadian *iparras* and *uparras*: "Die ungeheure formale Ähnlichkeit des Durativstamms mit dem Intensivstamm hat es im Verein mit der nahen Bedeutungsverwandschaft der beiden Stämme dahin gebracht, dass es in den übrigen semitischen Sprachen der Intensivstamm den Durativstamm völlig absorbiert. Dass aber beide Themen ursprünglich nichts mit einander zu tun haben, lehrt ihre Entwicklungsgeschichte."[53]

Most Semitists would agree that Akk. *iparras* and *uparras* had different origins and development, which became obscured in the West Semitic languages by the similarity of the forms after Western phonology had altered the (presumed) Proto-Semitic forms reflected in Akkadian. Thus, although the Old West Semitic present-future corresponding to Akk. *iparras* lived on for a time in Canaanite-Hebrew as

[50] V. Christian, "Bemerkungen zu Bergsträssers 'Einführung in die semitischen Sprachen'", in *Wiener Zeitschrift für die Kunde des Morgenlandes* 42 (1935), 209.

[51] V. Christian, "Untersuchungen zur Laut- und Formlehre des Hebräischen, in *Österreichische Akademie der Wissenschaften*, Phil.-Hist. Klasse, Sitzberichte 228, Band 2 (Vienna, 1953), 76.

[52] V. Christian, "Die Kausative Bedeutung des semitischen Steigerungsstammes," in *Analecta Orientalis* 12 (1958), 43.

[53] Christian, "Bemerkungen", 209.

yaqaṭṭal and *yaqâṭal*, according to Meyer[54], it eventually disappeared. As West Semitic formed an active perfect stem around the *qtl*-theme (Akkadian stative) the old preterite *yaqtul* (attested in the West by Ugaritic, the Hebrew *waw*-consecutive clause and Arabic negative clauses) was displaced as the vehicle for expressing past action and in turn began to usurp the function of the present-future theme *y-qttl*, which gradually disappeared, while those remnants of it which persisted were seemingly assimilated to the D-stem, which likewise utilized the *qttl*-theme.

This generally familiar reconstruction is helpful in explaining (or explaining away) the existence of Hebrew D-forms which seemingly have no relation to the commonly accepted meanings of the stem, such as *yᵉhallēḵ*; and eliminates the necessity of positing an n-infix, unless one assumes with Christian that Akk. *iparras* contains such a durative morpheme. This view, of course, might provide a point of intersection in the morphological features of *iparras* and *uparras*, if one interprets the latter not as original *yuparsas* but as containing the same morpheme found in *iparras*, thus giving the D-stem a primary iterative character. The most obvious limitation of this entire reconstruction is, that it is truly helpful only for Hebrew, and to a lesser extent Aramaic; it is of doubtful assistance in clarifying the verbal systems of the other Western languages. In Arabic, for example, it is not necessary to posit the pre-literary existence of a present-future tense. The imperfect B- and D-stems, *yaqtulu* and *yuqattilu*, when compared with the corresponding Akkadian preterites *iprus* and *uparris*, would suggest that, although the final loss of original *yaqtul* may have come about in Arabic through the evolution of an active qtl-form (except in negations), the development of a modal system *yaqtulu*, *yaqtula*, *yaqtul* for all stems may have been the factor which limited and thus weakened the hitherto universal force of the preterite, to the extent that the emergence of *qatala*-forms could have been a response to a need for clarifying the usages of the verbal forms. In any event, the Arabic evidence does not compel one to consider the existence of an earlier present-future in the West, and thus does not allow us to seek the explanation for aberrant D-forms in that direction.

On the other hand, in Ethiopic we have the situation presented in Brockelmann's statement that "Die Verdoppelung des zweiten Radikals als Zeichen des kursiven Aspekts haben nur die Südaraber und ihre Kolonisten in Abessinien beibehalten"[55], this feature having been given up elsewhere because of its strong resemblance to the D-stem. Rundgren, seeking an explanation for this, and for the fact that when a separate D-stem DOES exist in an Ethiopic verb it shows no morphological or semantic distinctiveness from the B-stem, concluded that what had taken place was "das Eindringen der alten Intensivform *yuqattil* als Indikativ im Grundstamm"[56], a *réemploi de l'intensif* for strengthening of the 'stative-durative' aspect of the Ethiopic present-

[54] E. Meyer, "Spuren eines westsemitischen Präsens-Futur", in *Von Ugarit nach Qumran* (Berlin, 1958), 126.

[55] C. Brockelmann, "Die 'Tempora' des Semitischen", in *Zeitschrift für Phonetik* 5 (1951), 144.

[56] Rundgren, *Intensiv- und Aspektkorrelation*, 18.

future *y^{e}qatt^{e}l*. Thus he also posits two originally separate strands coming together into one form. He likewise follows Brockelmann with regard to the latter's conclusion that both *iparras* and *y^{e}nagg^{e}r* embody a durative action type lost elsewhere in the West. Rundgren then extends this hypothesis to *iparras* itself, *viz*. "Die Gemination ist hier kein Ausdruck der 'objektiven' Durativität, sondern der formale Ausdruck für die Erneuerung des kursiven Aspekts ... Das sog. Präsens stellt in der Tat den merkmalhaften Term der aspektuellen Opposition kursiv/konstativ dar, und hat somit im System der Sprache einen einheitlichen Wert."[57] *Iparras* is then a 'marked term' with the *x*-factor signifying cursivity. Thus, while commentators on Hebrew forms explain why the D-stem sometimes will seem to have a durative aspect, Rundgren here seeks to explain why some Ethiopic remnants of the present-future have 'energic' overtones. Meantime, Arabists have no particular problem at all.

The accuracy or inaccuracy of any of these hypotheses is not our real point of contention in this chapter; we introduce them to demonstrate that it is unwise to generalize concerning the semantic domain of the D-stem from a hypothetical course of events within any one Semitic language which has been formulated to explain or account for specific cases in that language. Rather, we wish to seek out the elements common to the forms of this stem as they occur in the literatures of these languages, then to determine whether these common elements provide a basis for the explanation of different usages in the various languages. If this common element is denominative usage then we must show how this use is consistent with what others have seen as intensive, causative or iterative meanings in the languages of their specialization, and show whether there is a common thread running through these seemingly diverse and incompatible usages, or whether the D-stem is truly a 'portmanteau' form exercising *réemploi de matériaux* for diverse purposes. Presentation of the evidence upon which such conclusions can rest will be our matter for concern in succeeding chapters.

The only other matter to be handled now is a preliminary definition of what we would conceive to be a 'denominative' usage, and how we might expect it to appear, if it turns out that this is the basic orientation of the D-stem. The origin of our definition lies as far back as Philippi's comment of 1875, that "die Sprache wenigstens in der Periode, wo sie ihre jetzige Formation erhielt und das Verbum sich entwickelte, unserem Grundstamm zunächst als eine participiale Form betrachtet und behandelt hat, und demnach im Semitischen das Verbum aus einer Nominalform hervorgegangen ist."[58] Any conception of the D-stem as a denominative which is to go beyond the superficial conception that a 'denominative' verb is one which 'employs' an already-existent stem, must take into account the denominative aspect of the verb in general. Close to Philippi in spirit is Harris's statement that "Proto-Canaanite and East Semitic both had a stative perfect aspect developed out of a pronominally-inflected nominal sentence ... but because of the West Semitic internal passive formations this 'nominal' form functioned as a complete stative perfect, whereas in East

[57] Rundgren, *Das althebräische Verbum*, 67.
[58] Philippi, "Der Grundstamm des starken Verbums im Semitischen", 82.

Semitic it functioned just as a passive adjective (permansive) ... (then) on the analogy of stative qatila and qatula there was formed qatala, for roots referring to active situations."[59]

The permansives are, of course, the basis for Götze's interpretation of the D-stem as factitive in Akkadian. The question is, how could a similar relationship exist for the 'active' form of the *qtl*-theme as it developed in West Semitic. It is at this point that Rundgren makes a helpful suggestion, beginning with his assumption that the Akkadian permansive is "nicht als ein Partizipium perfecti, sondern als ein possessivisches Denominativum aufzufassen"[60], *e.g.* *salim* 'he has health', *yalid* 'it has a birth, is borne'. From this developed a perfective meaning, as *kašid* 'to have something conquered' *i.e.* 'to conquer something'. But the stative itself does not indicate the condition resulting from an action, only the condition of the subject. When one comes to the 'active' *qtl*-theme in West Semitic, Rundgren construes its fundamental meaning as 'have *qtl*', which is parallel with the purely possessive conditional type *zaqēn* 'has a beard, is old', *kabēd* 'has *kbd*, is heavy'. If the original pair *kabid/kabbad* means 'have weight, be heavy'/'make heavy, cause weight to exist (for someone)', then the pair *qatal/qattal* may well mean 'possess a killing, kill'/'cause a killing to exist for someone' *i.e.* possibly 'kill' *or* 'cause someone to kill'. This last example hints at how the D-form might have both transitive and causative aspects, express both direct and indirect action.

This is, generally, what we would regard as a denominative origin of the D-stem: to effect the bringing of a person or thing into conjunction with the object or state which provided the initial impetus for the creation of the particular D-stem action. This, if the textual evidence will bear it out, may also prove to be the fundamental semantic domain of the stem.

[59] Z. Harris, *The Development of the Canaanite Dialects* (New Haven, 1939), 83.

[60] Rundgren, *Das althebräische Verbum*, 58.

IV

THE USE OF THE D-STEM IN THE PENTATEUCH AND ITS TRANSLATIONS

The purpose of this chapter is to illustrate the uses of the D-stem as they were understood by Hebrew scholars responsible for translating the scriptures into Arabic or Aramaic dialects. Specifically, we are to examine the material contained in Table I, which constitutes primarily a listing of those roots of Biblical Hebrew which in the Pentateuch are employed in the D-stem, along with a listing of corresponding roots and forms utilized for their translation into (1) the Aramaic of Targum Onkelos, (2) the Syriac of the Peshiṭṭa and (3) the Arabic version of Saadia ha-Gaon. Secondarily, Table I includes a listing of those Biblical Hebrew roots which are employed in some other stem in the Pentateuch (usually Stems I or IV), but which are translated by a D-form in Targum Onkelos, again with the corresponding forms in Syriac and Arabic. Finally, the table includes a few Hebrew forms translated by a D-form in Syriac alone. These three categories have been incorporated into a single list, alphabetic according to the Hebrew alphabet and according to the Hebrew root involved, since there is considerable overlap between the three groups.

Following the example(s) given for each root, there will be a brief comment upon what, if any, insight that example may provide into the nature of the D-stem, and in most cases a translation of the forms. At the end of the chapter we shall comment selectively upon the material presented in the table, in order to draw from it some tentative propositions which, if they are not decisive for our understanding of the D-stem, will at least illuminate the practical usage of the stem, particularly in its relationship to other stems, insofar as any sampling is able to do this. Through our analysis we hope to discover both the functions imputed to the D-stem by translators who were far closer to the language of the Pentateuch both in time and in spirit than we, and the use which these scholars made of the D-stem in their own languages.

Each page of the table contains five columns. The first gives the Hebrew root and the stem in which it was employed; the second does the same for Targum Onkelos; the third for the Peshiṭṭa; the fourth for Saadia's Arabic translation. These four are headed by the abbreviations BH, TO, SP, AS respectively. The fifth column gives the scriptural reference, employing the chapter and verse division of Kittel's ***Biblia Hebraica*** (Stuttgart, 1949).

TABLE I

BH		TO		SP		AS		
’bd	2	*’bd*	2	*’bd*	4	*byd*	4	Dt. 12.2
’bd	2	*’bd*	4	*’bd*	4	*byd*	4	Dt. 12.3

All forms mean ‘destroy’. BH-2 is translated twice in verse 2 by TO-2, then by TO-4 in the succeeding verse, indicating full interchangeability of TO-2 and -4 in the mind of the translator. In SP and AS, BH-2 is everywhere translated by Stem IV, and no D-stem is found in the lexicon.

’dm	2	*smq*	2	—	—	—	—	Ex. 25.5

BH and TO both employ the D-stem passive participle ‘made red’ as an adjective, paraphrased in SP by *’espaynig* ‘red’ and in AS by *’adīm* ‘a tanned skin’.

’wy	2	*r‘y*	8	*rgy*	1	*šhy*	8	Dt. 14.26

BH-2 ‘have a desire for’ is translated by the B-stem or its reflexive (8) for various roots meaning ‘desire’ or ‘delight in’.

’ḥr	2	*’ḥr*	2	*nṭr*	1	*’ḥr*	2	Dt. 7.10
’ḥr	2	*’ḥr*	2	*’ḥr*	4	*’ḥr*	2	Dt. 23.21

The D-stem ‘make late’ is standard for BH, TO and AS, only SP employing Stem IV of the same root. SP-1 ‘keep’ is a paraphrase.

’kl	2-P	*’kl*	8	*yqd*	1	*ḥrq*	8	Ex. 3.2
’kl	1	*gmr*	2	*’kl*	1	*fny*	4	Lv. 26.38
’kl	1	*qṭl*	2	*’kl*	1	*hlk*	4	Nu. 13.38

BH-2 found only in *pu‘‘al*, translated by the B-stem and seemingly used here as passive of that stem, particularly since BH-1 is elsewhere regular, and is so translated in SP. In the verses cited TO translates BH-1 twice by the B-stem of *qṭl*, twice by its D-stem (not all cited), indicating that the translator uses the two interchangeably; and twice by the D-stem of *gmr*, probably meaning ‘put an end to’ (denominative of *g^{e}mar*). AS translates BH-1 by Stem IV (causative) of stative meaning ‘perish’.

’lm	2	*’sr*	2	*’sr*	1	*jrz*	1	Gn. 37.7

All mean ‘bind’, except AS ‘cut’. In what we shall see to be a common pattern, the same root (here *’sr*) is employed in TO-2 and SP-1, the former being more prone to follow the BH original.

’mṣ	2	*tqp*	2	*‘šn*	2	*qss*	1	Dt. 15.7
’mṣ	2	*tqp*	4	*‘šn*	4	*’yd*	2	Dt. 2.30

All mean ‘strengthen’ except AS-1 ‘seek’. BH-2 is regular, translated by TO- and SP-2 and -4. Note that TO and SP choice of stem coincides each time, despite their employment of different roots. In both verses cited reference is to ‘strengthening the heart of s.o.’, indicating interchangeability of the two stems in Aramaic, where they are associated with stative B-stems.

’ny	2	*msr*	8	*šlm*	4	*sbb*	2	Ex. 21.13

BH-2 paralleled by AS-2, both in sense of ‘give occasion to (a murderer’s hand)’, while SP-4 ‘deliver (into the hand of)’ changes the meaning somewhat. TO-8, ‘be transmitted, handed over into’ changes subject. The use of the B-stem in place of the D-stem of BH in such cases suggests that the translator’s stem usage is dependent more upon the syntax of the original than upon the desire to reproduce an ‘intensive’ or ‘plurative’ connotation.

(Table I, continued)

BH		TO		SP		AS		
ʼsp	2	*knš*	2	*knš*	2	—		Nu. 10.25

All mean 'gather'. The use of the D-stem in both Aramaic texts may reflect a conscious desire to retain the stem, since the B-stem of this root occurs in both dialects.

ʼsr	1	*ṭqs*	2	*pgd*	1	*srj*	4	Gn. 46.29

BH use of B-stem is correctly paralleled in SP, while TO employs the more vivid denominative of the D-stem 'provide equipment for (a chariot)'. AS employs a Stem IV denominative 'place a saddle', apparently misunderstanding the BH object 'chariot' as 'team of horses'.

ʼṣl	1	*rby*	2	*bṣr*	1	*fyd*	4	Nu. 11.17

SP is a direct translation of BH 'take away (the spirit from one, for another)', while TO interprets as 'make great' and AS-4 as 'cause to be useful'. TO thus uses the regular means of expressing the idea of 'increase', the D-stem, without regard to the stem-usage of BH.

ʼrś	2	*ʼrś*	2	*mkr*	1	*mlk*	4	Dt. 20.7

BH- and TO-2 'have a desire for' is used in the specialized meaning 'become engaged'. SP paraphrases as 'buy', while AS employs a denominative of Stem IV, 'take possession of, rule over'.

ʼšr	2	*šbḥ*	2	*šbḥ*	2	*wṣf*	1	Gn. 30.13

The form of the D-stem in TO and SP only superficially parallels the BH form, the meaning being altered from 'think (or call) blessed' to 'give praise to'. The Aramaic root commonly occurs in the D-stem, and this, rather than BH usage, is likely to account for its use here (*cf.* AS 'praise' in the B-stem).

bʼr	2	*prš*	2	*pšq*	2	—		Dt. 1.5

BH-2 'explain, give proof' is paralleled in TO and SP by factitive D-stems ('make distinctive', 'make easy'). AS paraphrases as *ʼamʿana fī bayānin* 'engage in explanation', suggesting that BH *biʼʼer* may be a denominative, though no cognate form exists in BH (but *cf.* Akk. *baʼūru* 'proof').

bwʼ	2	*qrb*	2	*ʼty*	4	*ʼty*	4	Ex. 19.4

All mean 'bring'. The variation of TO from the general usage, despite the existence of a comparable form in TO Aramaic, may indicate the declining distinctiveness of the verbal stems.

bṭʼ	2	*prš*	2	*prš*	1	*lfẓ*	1	Lv. 5.4

BH-2 'speak rashly' is not accurately translated by TO/SP 'explain' or AS 'express'. Thus TO-2 may well reflect BH influence, since the translator could as well have expressed the idea in the B-stem, as SP.

byn	3	*ʼlp*	2	*ḥbb*	2	*fhm*	2	Dt. 32.10
byn	4	*sbr*	2	*byn*	5	*ʿql*	1	Dt. 32.29

BH *pôlel* 'take care of' is interpreted by TO and AS as 'make to know', but by SP as 'make loved', all three translators apparently regarding BH *pôlel* as best translated by a factitive. In the second example, however, BH-4 and TO-2 seem, on the basis of SP and AS 'understand', to be regarded as denominatives 'have understanding', the choice of stem being idiomatic.

(Table I, continued)

BH		TO		SP		AS		
bkr	2	*bkr*	2	*qšš*	2	*fḍl*	2	Dt. 21.16
bkr	2-P	*bkr*	5	*bkr*	5	*bkr*	2-P	Lv. 27.26

Generally, the forms show a denominative use of the D-stem 'regard as the elder son', though in the first example SP and AS paraphrase with factitives.

blʿ	2	*ksn*	2	*ksy*	5	*ǧṭy*	2	Nu. 4.20

The meaning changes from BH 'engulf' to TO 'chastise' and SP/AS 'cover'; but the D-stem is employed throughout, even when the option of using a B-stem exists in an individual language.

bʿr	2	*bʿr*	2	*ʾḥd*	4	*šʿl*	1	Ex. 35.3
bʿr	2	*bʿr*	1	*knš*	1	*šʿl*	1	Lv. 6.5

The general meaning is 'kindle, burn'. Note that TO employs both B- and D-stems as translations for BH-2, while SP paraphrases both as 'gather'.

bqʿ	2	*ṣlḥ*	2	*ṣlḥ*	2	*šqq*	2	Gn. 22.3

BH-2 'split' is preserved throughout, as is often the case with verbs expressing some aspect of the idea 'divide'.

bqr	2	*bqr*	2	*šʾl*	1	*fḥṣ*	1	Lv. 13.36

BH/TO 'make split, attend to' employ the D-stem factitive figuratively, while SP and AS give literal translations 'ask, examine'.

bqš	2	*bʿy*	1	*tbʿ*	1	*ṭlb*	1	Gn. 31.39

Root found only in D-stem in BH, as 'seek to find', translated throughout by B-stems of different roots, reflecting idiomatic usages.

brk	2	*brk*	2	*brk*	2	*brk*	3	Gn. 1.22

The root is constant throughout in the D-stem or its counterpart Stem III, as 'bless'. The importance of the passage may be a factor here.

bšl	2	*bšl*	2	*bšl*	2	*ṭbḥ*	1	Ex. 16.23

TO- and SP-2 seem to be a conscious parallel of the BH original 'boil', but the AS paraphrase 'cook' would seem to be unaware of any special significance in the D-stem of the original.

btr	2	*plg*	2	*plg*	1	*šṭr*	2	Gn. 15.10

BH-2 'cut in pieces' (which exists also in B) is translated by the B- and D-forms of the same root in TO and SP. In verbs of this category a D-form would be expected, and is found again in AS.

gdl	2	*rby*	2	*rby*	2	*rby*	2	Nu. 6.5

All mean 'enlarge, increase', as factitive D-stems associated with a stative B-stem in each case.

gdʿ	2	*qṣṣ*	2	*gdm*	1	*jdʿ*	2	Dt. 7.5

Once again a verb of 'dividing', here 'break, cut', occurs primarily in the D-stem, again with the exception of SP, as in *btr* (above).

(Table I, continued)

BH		TO		SP		AS		
gdp	2	*rgz*	4	*gdp*	2	*ḡdf*	1	Nu. 15.30

BH- and SP-2 show a figurative use of a denominative 'throw stones, revile' (*cf.* Eth. *gdf* 'throw stones'), translated in AS by what may be a cognate root in the B-stem 'revile', and paraphrased by TO-4 from a stative verb as 'cause to be agitated'.

gly	2	*gly*	2	*gly*	4	*kšf*	1	Lv. 18.6

All mean 'reveal', the BH- and TO-2 of the root being translated by SP-4 of the same root, apparently regarded as equivalent, while AS root has its transitive in the B-stem rather than in D.

glḥ	2	*glḥ*	2	*gr‘*	1	*ḥlq*	1	Lv. 14.8

BH- and TO-2 seem to be factitive in origin, 'make bald', though regarded by SP and AS translators as equivalent to 'shave' in the B-stem. Though the vocabulary resources of SP and AS would preclude retention of the precise flavor of the original, there seems to be no effort to preserve a factitive nuance.

gll	1	*gndr*	1	*‘gl*	2	*dḥrj*	1	Gn. 29.3

The contextual meaning is 'roll away'. Only SP has the D-stem, but it is a paraphrase of the original meaning 'make swift'.

gml	1	*kpt*	2	*kpt*	1	*‘qd*	2	Nu. 17.23

BH-1 'finish' is translated by TO-2 'make a knot, conclude'. The SP translator's use of a B-form results from a change of subject; thus the TO seems to have a denominative/factitive and the SP a stative, related to a common nominal form. AS-2 is a usage parallel to TO, both roots being related to 'knot', yet while AS is a clear denominative, this is not necessarily the case with TO, which has factitive connotations.

gnb	2-P	*gnb*	5	*gnb*	8	*srq*	1	Ex. 22.6

The BH influence extends only to TO which, as is customary, substitutes the reflexive of D (5) for the passive 'was stolen'. AS 'steal' changes both subject and object.

g‘l	1	*rḥq*	2	*g‘ṣ*	1	*qly*	1	Lv. 26.11

TO-2 is used in an originally figurative sense 'make distant' to express the idea contained elsewhere in B-forms such as 'loathe, condemn'.

grm	2	—	—	*tbr*	2	*‘rq*	1	Nu. 24.8

BH is a clear denominative 'gnaw (bones)' which in this case has no counterpart in SP 'break' or AS 'strip (a bone) of flesh'.

gr‘	1	*mn‘*	1	*bṣr*	2	*nqṣ*	1	Ex. 5.8

Only SP employs the D-stem as 'diminish', for no discernable reason, as the B-stems used elsewhere have the same meaning.

grš	2	*trk*	2	*npq*	4	*ṭrd*	1	Gn. 3.24

The general meaning is 'drive out'. BH-2 and TO-2 are associated, respectively, with a transitive B-stem 'drive', and an intransitive B-stem 'run about'. The same concept is expressed in SP in Stem IV, again based on an intransitive B-stem, the D-stem of *npq* being used in another, specialized

(Table I, continued)

BH		TO		SP		AS		

meaning. Such an example points up, first, the loss of any truly distinctive aura about the D-stem for later translators, and second, the important role which the normal unpremeditated linguistic process of specialization of forms plays in the asisgnment of function to any verbal stem of any root. This specialization in one language may not be generalized for Semitics as a whole.

dbr	2	*mll*	2	*mll*	2	*ḥṭb*	1	Gn. 8.15
dbr	1	*mll*	2	*’mr*	1	*qwl*	1	Nu. 27.7

The merely occasional use of BH B-stems for the normal D-form 'speak, say' suggests it is a back-formation from an original D-stem, presumably a denominative from the noun 'word'. Such a case calls into question the idea that the D-stem was derived from the B, and suggests that, if such a pattern does exist for some roots, it is a secondary development in Semitics by false analogical extension. The TO translator did not see any difference in meaning between the BH B- and D-stems, while the similarity of stem occurrence between BH and SP seems purely fortuitous.

dmy	2	*ḥšb*	2	*ḥšb*	5	*qṣd*	1	Nu. 33.56

The use of the D-stem in BH and in TO/SP does not seem to be motivated by any need to preserve the stem usage, since BH-2 is originally a factitive 'regard as alike', the others perhaps denominative 'give thought to/give oneself thought for'. Again, AS takes advantage of a richer vocabulary and expresses the idea in the simple stem.

drš	1	*b‘y*	8	*‘qb*	2	*lms*	8	Dt. 12.5

The general meaning is 'seek'. Although SP elsewhere has the TO-8 form seen here, or could even use a B-form of the same root, as in BH, the translator apparently regards the D-stem as equivalent.

dšn	2	—	—	—	—	—	—	Ex. 27.3

The BH denominative, 'clear away the ashes from the fat' has no parallel.

hdr	1	*rḥm*	2	*‘dr*	2	*ḥbw*	3	Ex. 23.3

BH 'prefer' is translated by TO 'love', SP 'help', AS 'award favor'. Since the precise meanings of the four forms vary so considerably, the use of the various stems is not significant.

hlk	1	*hlk*	2	*’zl*	1	*syr*	1	Gn. 2.14
hlk	4	*dbr*	2	*dbr*	1	*syr*	2	Ex. 14.21

The use of TO-2 for BH-1 illustrates the well-known confusion surrounding *hlk* 'walk' in BH, though not in TO, where D is the regular form. If it were not for this last fact one would suspect the BH D-form of being a back formation from the *hithpa‘‘el* form (original reflexive of B). As it is, however, if one is not to posit two disparate forms with the same meaning, either the D-stem must be regarded as an original denominative 'take a walk' or the BH B-form must be taken as a back-formation from an original D. Another point to be noted here is the exact parallelism of BH-4 and AS-2, a sign that the two stems had come to be regarded as similar by those knowing the grammar of both languages.

hrg	1	*qṭl*	2	*qṭl*	2	*qtl*	1	Gn. 4.8

The use of the D-stem in the Aramaic forms, and of B in BH, reflects the predominant association of root and stem in each case, and has no relation to the translators' understanding of the BH meaning. Such an example as this undermines the idea that D is plurative in function.

(Table I, continued)

BH		TO		SP		AS		
hrs	1	*pgr*	2	*rḥq*	4	*hjm*	1	Ex. 19.21

The varied meanings: BH 'ruin', TO 'break up', SP 'cause to be far', AS 'terrorize', preclude profitable comparison.

zbḥ	1	*dbḥ*	2	*dbḥ*	1	*ḏbḥ*	1	Gn. 46.1

The isolation of TO-2 in this example illustrates the interchangeability of the B- and D-forms for practical purposes of translation. Otherwise one would have to assume that the TO translator was reading something into the original 'sacrifice', whereas he clearly intends to be accurate.

zkr	4	*dkr*	2	*dkr*	8	*ḏkr*	1	Ex. 23.13

The use of TO-2 for BH-4 'cause to remember' indicates that the translator regarded the stems as equivalent for this root, at least in some circumstances. In SP and AS the meaning is somewhat different: 'remember' as opposed to 'mention'.

zny	1	*zny*	2	*zny*	2	—	—	Dt. 22.21
zny	1	*zny*	2	*zny*	2	*zny*	1	Gn. 38.24

All mean 'fornicate'. The predominant use of the B-stem in Hebrew and Arabic, and of the D-stem in Aramaic, suggests that an original Semitic noun was verbalized separately in each language.

znb	2	*qṭl*	2	*qṭl*	2	*ṭrf*	5	Dt. 25.18

BH 'smite the tail', a denominative, is translated by TO/SP 'kill' in its normal stem-usage. AS 'attack the extremity' is a more successful translation, preserving the denominative overtone of the original. The Aramaic paraphrase is unrelated to any understanding of BH-2. This suggests that Saadia may in other passages have understood the factitive-denominative origin of D, but sometimes sacrificed it in translation for the sake of writing clear Arabic.

znq	2	*ngd*	1	*ynq*	1	*ʿrḍ*	1	Dt. 33.22

The BH denominative 'be as an arrow, leap forth' not only is not paralleled in the translations, but is completely mistranslated by SP 'suckle', unless a printing error exists. (In this case SP-1 would differ significantly from BH-2).

zʿm	1	*trk*	2	*ʾbd*	4	*ḏmm*	1	Nu. 23.7

BH 'curse' is paraphrased in all translations, TO-2 being a factitive 'make agitated'.

zry	2	*bdr*	2	*bdr*	2	*ḏry*	1	Lv. 26.33

All mean 'scatter'. TO and SP may consciously preserve the D-stem.

zrq	2-P	*zrq*	5	*rss*	1	*ršš*	1	Nu. 19.13

All mean 'sprinkle'. As often happens, only TO preserves BH D-stem.

ḥbb	1	*ḥbb*	2	*rḥm*	4	*ḥbb*	4	Dt. 33.3

Since BH-1 is an isolated case, a comparison with its translations here is not too significant. We may note, however, that while TO-2 has the usual D-stem denominative 'feel love', AS expressed the same

(Table I, continued)

BH		TO		SP		AS		

idea in Stem IV, illustrating a marked tendency of Arabic (as opposed to the other languages) to denominalize in IV as much as in II. This tendency is also prominent (as above) in Syriac as opposed to Targumic Aramaic. Arabic, on the other hand, employs the D-stem of this root in a causative sense (which one would normally expect in Stem IV of Hebrew and Aramaic) – unless Arabic denominalizes twice for specialization, the D-form meaning 'effect love in another', the Š-form 'effect love in oneself'.

ḥbq	2	*gpp*	2	*ʿpq*	1	*ʿnq*	3	Gn. 29.13

All mean 'embrace'. BH-2 is associated with a transitive, TO-2 with an intransitive B-stem. Each form reflects idiomatic usage.

ḥbr	2	*lpp*	2	*dbq*	2	*lff*	1	Ex. 26.6
ḥbr	1	*lpp*	2	*dbq*	2-P	*ḫbṭ*	2	Ex. 26.3

These two examples, occurring within a few verses of one another, demonstrate clearly that the Aramaic translators did not differentiate between the meanings of the B- and D-stems of the root in BH, but used the stem which has become associated with the various roots in their respective dialects. Thus, for example, SP uses the passive of the D-stem to translate the B-stem stative 'be united', even though a B-stem of *dbq* exists in Syriac with the same meaning. Note also that AS exactly reverses the stem-choices of BH.

ḥbš	1	*zrz*	2	*rmy*	4	*srj*	4	Gn. 22.3

The general meaning is 'saddle', BH-1 being translated by denominatives in TO and AS. SP translates with an apparently idiomatic expression.

ḥgr	1	*zrz*	2	*ʾsr*	1	*šdd*	1	Ex. 29.9

All mean 'girdle, bind'. Here again, while SP and AS provide forms parallel to BH, TO translates with a D-stem denominative.

ḥzq	2	*tqp*	2	*ʿšn*	2	*šdd*	2	Ex. 4.21
ḥzq	2	*tqp*	4	*qšy*	2	*šdd*	2	Ex. 9.12

All mean 'strengthen'. The BH, SP and AS D-stems, spread over a number of roots, reflect the most persistent type of D-stem, the factitive linked with (not derived from, since both probably go back to an original adjective or noun) a stative B-stem. Nevertheless, the example of the Š-stem, used in TO in close proximity to a D-stem translation (making it likely the same person was at work) indicates that the Š-stem at times infringed upon the province of D (*cf.* *ʾmṣ*).

ḥṭʾ	2	*kpr*	2	*dky*	2	*ḏky*	2	Lv. 6.19
ḥṭʾ	2	—	—	*nṭr*	2	—	—	Gn. 31.39

In each example BH-2 is denominative in origin but different in meaning, first 'bring a sin-offering, atone' then 'bear the loss of something'. In the first case SP-2 and AS-2 are factitives, thus are probably employed independent of the D-stem as such. However, TO-2 is associated with a transitive B-stem; its use here in D could indicate a conformity to the original (though mistaken). In the second example only SP-2 translates directly; the case is much like that of TO-2 above.

ḥyy	2	*qym*	2	*ḥyy*	4	*ḥyy*	4	Gn. 7.3

The general meaning is 'keep alive'. While TO-2 paraphrases BH-2, SP and AS translators clearly regard the Š-stem of the root as equivalent.

(Table I, continued)

BH		TO		SP		AS		
ḥly	2	*mrʿ*	4	*ʾty*	4	*mrḍ*	4	Dt. 29.21

The general meaning is 'weaken'. TO and AS here equate Š-stems associated with B-statives, the BH D-form having similar association. The Š-form of SP is one element in a paraphrase.

ḥll	2	*ḥll*	4	*ṭwš*	2	—	—	Gn. 49.4
ḥll	2	*ḥll*	2	*ṭnf*	2	*bḍl*	1	Lv. 21.6
ḥll	4	*bṭl*	2	*bṭl*	2	*bḍl*	1	Nu. 30.3
ḥll	4	*šry*	2	*šry*	1	*bdʾ*	8	Gn. 9.20

The general meaning is 'profane'. The BH-2 forms are paralleled by both TO-2 and TO-4 forms, as well as by the SP-2 factitives 'make illicit' and 'make impure'. Though the D- and Š-stems are clearly equivalent in TO, the fact that TO (as well as SP) does not employ the same form to translate BH-4 might indicate that the translators did not see BH-2 and -4 as equivalent. AS, on the other hand, uses the same B-stem 'sacrifice' to translate both BH forms.

ḥlp	4	*ḥlp*	2	*ḥlp*	2	*bdl*	2	Lv. 27.10
ḥlp	4	*šny*	2	*ḥlp*	1	*bdl*	1	Gn. 35.2

All mean 'replace'. In the first example TO and SP (employing the same root) as well as AS present a D-form as translation for BH-4. In the second, TO persists in this (though with change of root), while SP and AS this time choose D-stems of the same roots they had used as D, suggesting a not-too-clear distinction between the two stems.

ḥlṣ	2	*šlp*	2	*šmṭ*	1	*ḫlʿ*	1	Lv. 14.40

The meaning is 'despoil, carry off', only TO following BH in stem.

ḥlq	2	*plg*	2	*plg*	2	*qsm*	2	Gn. 49.7
ḥlq	1	*zmn*	2	*plg*	2	*bṭṭ*	1	Dt. 4.19

The meaning is 'divide'. The AS translations might indicate conformity to the BH choices, however SP recognizes no difference between BH-1 and -2 for this root. In the second example TO paraphrases as 'appoint'.

ḥmd	1	*ḥmd*	2	*rgg*	1	*hwy*	1	Ex. 20.17

The use of TO-2 to translate a root found only once as D in BH (Ct. 2.3) suggests that, while Hebrew denominalized a noun 'warmth' as a B-stem stative 'be warm, desire', Aramaic developed a D-stem denominative 'feel warmth, desire'. This exemplifies what we have called the 'association' of two verbal forms, without implying the 'derivation' of one from the other; it also shows how two stems might emerge with the 'same' meaning, but by different routes.

ḥml	1	*rḥm*	2	*rḥm*	2	*rṭy*	1	Dt. 13.9

The D-stem 'love' in TO and SP is regularly associated with the root employed, thus is not relevant to the usage of BH-1 'spare' or AS 'pity'.

ḥmš	2	—	—	—	—	—	—	Gn. 41.34

The translations do not render at all the denominative concept of 'dividing into five' found in BH.

(Table I, continued)

BH		TO		SP		AS		
ḥnn	1	*rḥm*	2	*rḥm*	2	*r'f*	1	Gn. 33.11
ḥnn	1	*rḥm*	5	*rḥm*	2	*r'f*	1	Gn. 43.29

The general meaning is 'favor, love', though AS translates 'pity'. Once again the D-forms of TO and SP are regularly associated with *rḥm*.

ḥnk	1	*ḥnk*	1	*ḥdt*	2	*dšn*	1	Dt. 20.5

The meaning is 'dedicate'. SP employing a factitive D-stem (which occurs elsewhere in BH and TO) in a somewhat unusual and specialized way. AS-1 has a clear connection with the BH D-denominative from *dšn* (above) and is either a B-stem denominative or a back-formation from a D-form.

ḥpś	2	*blš*	1	*bṣ'*	1	*ftš*	2	Gn. 44.12

The general meaning is 'search'. TO- and SP-1 do not distinguish between BH-2 and a possible BH-1 (occurring elsewhere). AS *ftš* is regularly employed in D.

ḥpš	2-P	*ḥrr*	5	*ḥrr*	5	*ʿtq*	1-S	Lv. 19.20

All mean 'be free(d)'. The BH, TO and SP D-stems reflect the regular usage for the given roots, and all are undoubtedly factitive in origin. AS employs the kind of stative B-stem with which the other forms may originally have been associated.

ḥṣy	1	*plg*	2	*plg*	2	*qsm*	1	Gn. 32.8

All mean 'divide'. Again we see how certain stems have become associated with certain roots or root-concepts in Aramaic. Nothing in the context would otherwise account for this translation of BH-1.

ḥrm	4	*gmr*	2	*ḥrm*	4	—	—	Nu. 21.2

The BH-4 denominative 'devote to destruction' is paralleled by SP-4. Possibly TO translates with D to avoid ambiguity, since TO-4 of this root could equally well mean 'consecrate'.

ḥšb	2	*ḥšb*	2	*ḥšb*	1	*ḥṣb*	1	Lv. 25.27
ḥšb	1	*ḥšb*	2	*ḥšb*	1	*ḥsb*	1	Gn. 38.15

The examples cited, all forms meaning 'reckon, regard', once more demonstrate greater regularity in stem-usage among the translations than in the original, as well as the meaninglessness of the BH distinction between B- and D-stems for later scholars, where both are transitive.

ḥšq	2	*kbš*	2	—	—	—	—	Ex. 38.28

BH-2 'make joined' is translated by TO-2 'make pressed'. TO preserves the stem of BH, though the B-stem of this root is more common elsewhere.

ṭbl	1	—	—	*ṣbʿ*	2	*ǧms*	1	Dt. 33.24

Only SP employs the D-stem for the meaning 'immerse'. A doubtful case.

ṭbʿ	2-P	*ṭbʿ*	5	*ṭbʿ*	1	*ǧrq*	1	Ex. 15.4

Only TO preserves the more elaborate form of BH-2 'be made to sink', the translators of SP and AS apparently feeling that the B-stem intransitive was sufficient to convey the full meaning of BH-2.

(Table I, continued)

BH		TO		SP		AS		
ṭhr	2	*dky*	2	*dky*	5	*ṭhr*	1-S	Lv. 13.6

BH, TO and SP are parallel factitives 'make pure'. AS changes subject.

ṭm'	2	*s'b*	2	*ṭmy*	2	*njs*	2	Gn. 34.5

All mean 'defile' and may be construed as parallel factitives.

ṭmn	1	*ṭmr*	2	*ṭmr*	1	*dfn*	1	Ex. 2.12

All mean 'hide', TO again considering the D-stem congruent with a transitive B-stem.

ṭrp	2-P	*qṭl*	1-P	*tbr*	1-P	*frs*	8	Gn. 37.33
ṭrp	1	*qṭl*	1	*tbr*	1	*dqq*	1	Dt. 33.20

The general meaning is 'tear apart', variously paraphrased. Strangely, neither TO-2 nor SP-2 is used here, although the D-stem is regularly associated with the roots employed. If conformity to BH is involved, the connection of the *pu''al* with D is brought into question.

ybm	2	*ybm*	2	*ybm*	2	—	—	Gn. 38.8

The same D-stem denominative 'act as levir' appears in the original and in those translations which seek to give a precise rendering. The lack of such in Arabic may arise from the want of an equivalent term.

yd'	1	*rby*	2	*yd'*	1	*šrf*	2	Ex. 33.12

The D-stem factitives employed in TO 'make increase' and AS 'make illustrious' present amplifications of the idea contained in BH- and SP-1, thus are not directly comparable with it.

yḥm	2	*yḥm*	2	*ḥmy*	1	*wḥm*	5	Gn. 30.41

The meaning is 'be in heat, breed' and the forms are denominative throughout. However while BH can express the concept either by the B-stem stative 'be hot' or by the D-stem as here, SP expresses it only in the stative, the D-stem being used in the causative sense 'bring (another) into heat'. Thus, to the SP translator BH-1 and -2 are 'the same' and are translated thus, though they may have had different origins.

ykḥ	4	*zmn*	2	*tyb*	2	*wqf*	2	Gn. 24.14

The general meaning is 'summon'. BH-4 is translated throughout by the D-stem, possibly because the concept involved is of a type usually expressed in BH by a D-stem of factitive origin. We may note also that while Saadia uses the D-stem here, the normal usage in modern Arabic would be the Š-stem: an illustration of the Š-stem's intrusion into the function of D.

yld	2	*yld*	4	*yld*	4	*qbl*	3	Ex. 1.16
yld	2-P	*yld*	8	*yld*	8	*wld*	1-P	Gn. 6.1

The distinction was made in BH between the D-stem denominative 'assist at a birth' and the Š-stem causative 'cause to bear, beget'. TO and SP merge the two concepts in the Š-stem, thus must employ that stem to translate both BH forms. In the second example the use of the B-stem and its reflexive throughout the translations strengthens the view that BH-2 in the passive is not properly part of the D-stem, but of the B.

(Table 1, continued)

BH		TO		SP		AS		
ysr	2	*'lp*	2	*'lp*	2	*'db*	2	Dt. 4.36
ysr	2	*rdy*	1	*rdy*	4	*'db*	2	Lv. 26.18
ysr	2	*lqy*	4	*rdy*	1	*'db*	2	Dt. 22.18

The meaning is 'discipline'. Only AS preserves the D-stem factitive of BH, though this may be reflected in TO and SP of the first example.

yʿd	1	*qym*	2	*nsb*	1	*zwj*	2	Ex. 21.9

One encounters here idioms of the various languages, pertaining to the taking of a wife; comparison of stem usages is of little value.

yṣg	4	*dʿṣ*	2	*dʿṣ*	1	*wḍʿ*	1	Gn. 30.38

The general meaning is 'set, fix (in place)'. Since the root of BH-4 is found only in this stem and no cognates are known which can illuminate its original meaning, the most one can do here is to note that the TO translator did not regard use of D as incongruent with the Š-stem.

yrd	1	*kbš*	2	*kbš*	1	*hdd*	1	Dt. 28.52
yrd	4	*prq*	2	*rkn*	4	*fḍl*	2	Nu. 1.51

In the first example the subject of BH-1 'go down' becomes the object of the Aramaic and Arabic forms. The example illustrates only the tendency of the earlier Aramaic dialect to use the D-stem of a transitive verb where SP finds a B-stem sufficient. The second example shows TO's concomitant disposition to employ D for a causative function filled in SP usually by Š, as is usual in Arabic.

yry	4	*pny*	2	*hzy*	8	*dll*	1	Gn. 46.28
yry	4	*'lp*	2	*'lp*	2	*dll*	1	Ex. 4.12

In the first example the precise meaning of BH-4 is unclear, but the general meaning must be contained in the translations, as they agree fairly well. In the first example TO-2 seems not to be directly related to the root, but to be a denominative in the sense of 'show one's face', since SP-8 'be seen' and AS-1 'show' would support this. The first BH-4 thus seems to mean 'appear', whereas the second means 'teach', translated in Aramaic by the D-stem, customary for this concept.

yrš	2	*ḥsn*	4	*'kl*	1	*qrḍ*	1	Dt. 28.42
yrš	4	*trk*	2	*'bd*	4	*qrḍ*	1	Nu. 32.21

In the first example the use of TO-4 for BH-2 'take possession' indicates that the latter was probably regarded by the TO translator as equivalent to BH-1 of the same root, since in both Hebrew and Aramaic the B- and Š-stems of the respective roots are interchangeable. Thus D- and Š-stems would also have to be similar in meaning. The fact that this is the sole occurrence of BH-2 may indicate that it is purely a literary device. In the second example, use of TO-2 for BH-4 'take possession from' has no discernable purpose.

kbd	2	*yqr*	2	*yqr*	2	*krm*	4	Ex. 20.12
kbd	4	*yqr*	2	*ʿby*	2	*ṯql*	2	Ex. 8.11

The general meaning of the first example is 'honor', of the second 'make heavy'. TO and SP do not preserve the specialization of BH. which uses a different stem for each meaning. Aramaic instead uses D for both concepts, apparently construing both 'be heavy' and 'weigh heavily' as aspects of the same stative adjective, and making both transitive in the D-stem, as would normally be expected.

(Table I, continued)

BH		TO		SP		AS		

The situation is somewhat different in Arabic, since the meaning of the root varies in the two examples, *i.e.* 'be noble' and 'be heavy' respectively. The use of Š for 'honor' is merely another example of Arabic's tendency to overlap D and Š usages.

kbs	2-P	*ṣbf*	8	*ḥll*	5	*ġsl*	1-P	Lv. 13.58
kbs	1	*ḥwr*	2	*ḥll*	2	*ġsl*	1	Ex. 19.10
kbs	1	*ṣbʿ*	2	*ḥll*	2	*ġsl*	1	Lv. 11.25

The general meaning is 'cleanse', except for TO-2 of *ḥwr* 'make white'. The alternation is between B- and D-stems and their reflexive/passives; in no way do the translations correspond to BH originals, as is usual when we deal with transitive verbs in BH-1.

khn	2	*šmš*	2	*khn*	2	*ʾmm*	1	Ex. 28.1

The BH meaning is 'act as priest'. SP is the only exact translation, and is likewise a denominative. Though TO also has a D-stem denominative for its translation 'perform a service', this is unrelated to BH.

kzb	2	*kdb*	2	*dgl*	2	*kḏb*	1	Nu. 23.19

The meaning is 'tell a lie'. Similar D-stem denominatives are found throughout Hebrew and Aramaic here. Arabic, however, employs the D-stem of this root in an estimative sense, 'think someone a liar', and denominalizes in the B-stem (possibly a back-formation from D).

kḥd	2	*ksy*	2	*ṭšy*	2	*ktm*	1	Gn. 47.18

The general meaning is 'hide'. Although TO and SP use roots other than that of BH, their use of the D-stem (optional) may reflect BH influence.

kḥš	2	*kdb*	2	*kpr*	1	*jḥd*	1	Gn. 18.15

The meaning is 'deny, tell a lie'. BH and TO seem to use the D-stem in the estimative sense 'declare something a lie, deny', while SP and AS employ the more direct B-stem 'deny'.

kly	2	*ḥšk*	2	*gmr*	2	*šḫṣ*	1	Lv. 26.16
kly	2-P	*kll*	10	*šlm*	1-S	*kml*	1-S	Gn. 2.1

The BH-2 factitive is used in the double meaning 'bring to an end' and 'make complete'. Only SP-2 duplicates the first of these, while TO-2 'make dark' and AS-1 'be glazed' introduce more vivid terminologies, arising from the fact that the object (AS subject) is 'eyes'. In the second example, SP and AS employ simple B-stem statives 'be whole', while TO employs the Š-stem passive instead of the BH D-form.

ksy	2	*ksy*	2	*ksy*	2	*ġṭw*	2	Gn. 9.23
ksy	2-P	*ḥpy*	5	*ksy*	5	*ġṭw*	2	Gn. 7.19

All mean 'cover', and the D-stem is employed throughout, indicating a probable association of this verbal concept with the stem.

kʿs	2	*rgz*	4	*rgz*	4	*ġḍb*	4	Dt. 32.31

The general meaning is 'make discontent, agitated'. The BH D-factitive is not carried over into the translations, Aramaic and Arabic both employing the Š-stem for this purpose, usually associated with D in Aramaic.

(Table I, continued)

BH		TO		SP		AS		
kpl	1	*ʿwp*	1	*ʾʿp*	2	*ṯny*	1	Ex. 26.9

The meaning is 'double'. The reason for SP use of a D-form is unclear.

kpr	2	*kpr*	2	*ḥsy*	2	*ğfr*	10	Ex. 29.36
kpr	2-P	*kpr*	5	*ḥsy*	5	*ğfr*	10-P	Ex. 29.33

The meaning is 'atone'. The BH- and TO-2 denominatives, the SP-2 factitive and AS-10 denominative represent idiomatic developments, though the first two probably have a common origin.

krt	4	*qṣṣ*	2	*ʾbd*	4	*qṭʿ*	1	Lv. 26.30

BH-4 'cause to be cut off' is paraphrased throughout the translations. The use of TO-2 rather than TO-1 of the root may reflect the translator's sense that D and Š served comparable functions.

kšp	2	—	—	—	—	—	—	Ex. 7.11

The BH-2 denominative 'practice sorcery' has no counterpart elsewhere.

ktt	1	*špp*	1	*dqq*	2	*brd*	1	Dt. 9.21

The general meaning is 'crush'. The reason for the use of SP-2 is unclear, since the root occurs in B with the same meaning.

lhṭ	2	*yṣy*	4	*yqr*	4	*sṭʿ*	1	Dt. 32.22

BH-2 'devour' is translated by TO-4 'cause to end', SP-4 'burn', and paraphrased by AS-1 'spread (an odor)'. No comparison is possible.

lḥk	2	*yṣy*	4	*rʿy*	1	*lḥs*	1	Nu. 22.4
lḥk	1	*lḥk*	2	*rʿy*	1	*lḥs*	1	Nu. 22.4

The use of TO-2 'lick up' to translate BH-1 but not BH-2 in the same verse shows how little the alternation of BH-1 and -2 for transitive verbs meant for the translator. SP-1 'gnaw away' and AS-1 'lick' show the same thing. It seems likely that the two forms were employed in BH merely for the stylistic purpose of variety in expression. TO-4 'cause to end' likewise serves the purpose of varying terminology.

lmd	2	*ʾlp*	2	*ʾlp*	2	*ʿlm*	2	Dt. 4.1

All mean 'teach', and all employ D-factitives from stative verbs.

lqḥ	2-P	*brʾ*	8	*nsb*	8	*ʾḫḏ*	1	Gn. 3.19
lqḥ	1	*dbr*	2	*dbr*	2	*ḫrj*	4	Gn. 24.7
lqḥ	1	*qbl*	2	*qbl*	2	*qbl*	1	Gn. 4.11
lqḥ	1	*qrb*	2	*nsb*	1	*ʾḫḏ*	1	Gn. 15.9

The BH meaning is 'take', subjected to a number of modifications or specializations in the translations. The first example again suggests to us that the *puʿʿal* may not be considered exclusively as part of the D-stem. The other three examples show, in SP and TO use of the D-stem, how the vividness of D-stem factitive-denominative forms serves the stylistic purpose of varying the more simple and direct language of the BH original 'take'.

(Table I, continued)

BH		TO		SP		AS		
lqṭ	2	*lqṭ*	1	*lqṭ*	1	*jmʿ*	1	Gn. 47.14
lqṭ	2	*lqṭ*	2	*lqṭ*	1	*lqṭ*	1	Lv. 19.9

BH-2 'gather' clearly exercises no influence over the stem employed by the translators, nor is TO consistent in its use of the root.

mʾn	2	*srb*	2	—	—	*ʾby*	1	Gn. 37.35

The general meaning is 'refuse, hold rejected'. TO-2 may reflect the influence of BH-2, while AS again chooses the more direct B-form.

mgn	2	*msr*	1	*šlm*	4	*slm*	4	Gn. 14.20

The general meaning is 'deliver up', paraphrased in SP and AS as 'bring to an end, make complete'. BH-2 seems to be an original denominative 'make an offering (of something)' with no counterpart in the translations.

mhr	1	*qym*	2	*nsb*	1	*mhr*	1	Ex. 22.15

The context refers to the taking of a bride for a price, BH-1 meaning 'obtain for a marriage-price', exactly duplicated by AS-1. Both would seem to be denominatives. TO-2 is best taken as a specialized use of the stem, but it might also be a denominative from 'contract'.

mwr	4	*ḥlp*	2	*ḥlp*	2	*bdl*	2	Lv. 27.10
mwr	4	*ʿbr*	2	—	—	—	—	Lv. 27.10

The BH root occurs only in Š, as 'exchange', thus its origin is obscure. TO- and SP-2 'make succeed', TO-2 'make pass over' and AS-2 'make to replace' seem to be based on the assumption that BH-4 is the causative of a root meaning 'replace', for D is used here in a causative sense.

mḥṣ	1	*qṭl*	2	*ʾbd*	4	*whn*	4	Nu. 24.17

The precise manings vary from BH-1 'smash' to AS-4 'cause to languish', thus direct comparison is difficult. Both Aramaic dialects use their standard expressions for 'destroy' without regard to the BH form.

mkr	1	*zbn*	2	*zbn*	2	*byʿ*	1	Gn. 25.31

All mean 'sell'. TO- and SP-2 is determined by the idiom of the Aramaic language, which developed the concept of 'sell' not independently, but in association with 'buy', *i.e.* 'make buy' (as in German), whereas Hebrew and Arabic evolved a separate terminology for 'sell'. The D-stem of *zbn* might also be thought of as a denominative 'make a purchase'.

mlʾ	2	*mlʾ*	2	*mly*	1	*mlʾ*	1	Gn. 44.1
mlʾ	2	*šlm*	4	*šlm*	2	*kml*	4	Gn. 29.27

BH-2 means first 'make full, fill' then 'make full, complete'. Only TO-2 preserves BH usage of D. In the second example Aramaic and Arabic have no parallel usage of the D-stem, and revert to their standard usage to express the concept 'finish', although SP-2 would normally be SP-4.

mll	2	*ʾmr*	1	*ʾmr*	1	*qwl*	1	Gn. 21.7

The BH-2 denominative 'talk' had no counterpart in the other languages.

(Table I, continued)

BH		TO		SP		AS		
m‘l	1-S	*šqr*	2	*‘ly*	4	*nkṯ*	1	Lv. 5.15

The TO-2 factitive 'make false, defraud' is here parallel with BH-1 stative 'be unfaithful', as well as with SP-4 denominative 'do an injustice', a situation which often occurs, thus emphasizing the nominal aspect of the D-stem.

mṣ’	1	*‘r‘*	2	*mṭy*	1	*ṣwb*	4	Dt. 31.17

BH-1 'find', TO-2 'bring into contact', SP-1 'touch', AS-4 'direct' are too variant in meaning for comparison.

mry	1	*srb*	2	*mrmr*	1	*ḫlf*	3	Nu. 20.24
mry	4	*srb*	2	*mrmr*	1	*ḫlf*	3	Dt. 1,26

BH-1 and -4 both have the general meaning 'be disobedient', any difference between them apparently going unrecognized in the translations. TO use of the D-form 'decline' instead of the available B-form has no justification in the BH text, and exemplifies the standardization of vocabulary in Aramaic as opposed to Hebrew.

mrq	2-P	*mrq*	8	*mrq*	8	*jrd*	1-P	Lv. 6.21

The meaning is 'scour', translated in AS as 'denude'. Once again, the B-stem translations cast doubt on whether the *pu‘‘al* is part of D.

mšḥ	1	*rby*	2	*mšḥ*	1	*msḥ*	1	Ex. 28.41

The contextual meaning is 'smear'; the TO-2 'make increase' is one element in a paraphrase of the original sentence.

mšš	2	*mšš*	2	*mwš*	2	*jss*	2	Gn. 31.37

All mean 'touch'. Arabic *jss* usually occurs in the B-stem.

n’ṣ	2	*rgz*	4	*rgz*	4	*‘ṣy*	1	Nu. 14.11

BH-2 estimative 'treat as contemptible' is paraphrased by TO/SP 'agitate' and AS-1 'disobey'. The Arabic Š-form is associated with an intransitive active verb 'shake', the Hebrew D-form with a stative.

nbl	2	*rgz*	4	*ṣḥy*	2	*sqṭ*	4	Dt. 32.15

The BH-2 estimative/denominative 'treat with scorn' is paralleled by SP-2 'treat with contumely'. TO-4 'cause to tremble' and AS-4 'cause to decline' are again associated with intransitive active verbs.

ngḥ	2	*qṭl*	2	*dqr*	1	*nṭḥ*	1	Dt. 33.17

The general meaning is 'push, gore', translated into TO as 'kill'. TO-2 is probably not dependent upon the BH stem, since the root occurs much more often in the D- than in the B-stem in TO.

ng‘	2	*’ty*	4	*mḥy*	2	*bly*	1	Gn. 12.17
ng‘	4	*qrb*	2	*’ḥd*	1	*qdm*	2	Ex. 4.25

The BH-2 denominative 'send a plague upon' is exactly paralleled by SP-2 but paraphrased by TO-4 'cause (a plague) to come' and AS-1 'afflict'. In the second example, the uses of TO-2 and AS-2 are idiomatic, and only approximate BH-4 'cause to touch, reach' and SP-1 'seize on'.

(Table I, continued)

BH		TO		SP		AS		
ngš	4	*qrb*	2	*qrb*	2	*qdm*	2	Gn. 27.25

The existence of factitive/denominative D-forms in the translations contrasts with the BH-4 causative of a transitive verb 'cause to approach, bring near'. These usages are parallel, but did not originally overlap, as happened during the later development of the West Semitic languages. The difference between Š and D is basically that between 'cause to do' and 'cause to be', respectively.

ndr	1	*qym*	2	*ndr*	1	*ndr*	1	Gn. 28.20

The meaning is 'vow', TO-2 representing either a specialized use of the stem for this root or a denominative 'contract for' (*cf. mhr*).

nhg	2	*dbr*	2	*bdr*	2	*bdd*	2	Dt. 4.27
nhg	1	*dbr*	2	*dbr*	2	*swg*	1	Ex. 3.1

The general meaning is 'drive', paraphrased in the first example by SP/AS 'scatter'. Only AS seems to reflect the alternation of B- and D-stems in BH, but even this may result from the fact that the D-stem of *bdd* is the more common usage connected with this root in Arabic.

nhl	2	*dbr*	2	*dbr*	1	*swq*	1	Ex. 15.13

The general meaning is 'lead'. BH-2 may have influenced the choice of stem in TO, but the origin of the BH form is obscure, and its use is undoubtedly the outcome of some process of specialization, if it is not a denominative.

nwḥ	4	*ʾsr*	2	*ḥbš*	2	*wḍʿ*	1	Lv. 24.12

The translators paraphrase BH 'cause to settle down' as 'bind' in Aramaic and as 'place' in Arabic. The Aramaic texts substitute a factitive D-stem for the causative Š-stem of BH. While they are independently preserved, this indicates a narrowing-down of the ground between the stem-types and a recognition of their common qualities.

nws	4	*ʿrq*	2	*ʿrq*	4	*ḥrb*	2	Dt. 32.30

The general meaning 'cause to flee' is translated by AS-2 as 'lay waste'. BH-4, the causative of an intransitive active verb, is paralleled by SP-4 but TO employs the D-form of the same root for the same purpose. It is possible that TO-2 may be an original denominative 'put to flight' which for all practical purposes is equivalent to 'cause to flee'. This is the type of parallelism which could have led to overlap in stem usage.

nwʿ	4	*ʾḥr*	2	*ṭʿy*	4	*tyh*	2	Nu. 32.13

The general meaning is 'cause to wander, stray', paraphrased by TO-2 as 'delay'. BH- and SP-4 once again are causatives of an intransitive active B-stem, while TO- and AS-2 'make lost' are D-factitives. Thus, the compatibility of the two stems for the translators is demonstrated.

nḥy	1	*dbr*	2	*ybl*	4	*syr*	2	Ex. 13.17
nḥy	4	*dbr*	2	*dbr*	2	*syr*	2	Gn. 24.48

The general meaning is 'lead'. AS-2 'make to travel' shows the D-stem infringing upon the normal function of Š as causative of an active verb. On the other hand, BH-4 here seems to infringe upon the normal role of D as factitive of a transitive B-stem participle ('make led'), and this is also true of the SP-4 form 'cause to be led'.

(Table I, continued)

BH		TO		SP		AS		
nḥl	2	*ḥsn*	4	*yrt*	4	*qsm*	1	Nu. 34.29

The BH-2 denominative 'give possession (water rights) to' is translated by denominatives of Š, TO 'give possession' and SP 'give as inheritance'. AS-1 is simply 'divide'.

nḥm	2	*nḥm*	2	*byy*	2	*‘zy*	2	Gn. 5.29

The meaning 'give comfort, consolation' is preserved throughout, always as a denominative of the D-stem.

nḥš	2	*nhš*	2	*nḥš*	2	*ṭyr*	5	Lv. 19.26
nḥš	2	*bdq*	2	*nḥš*	2	—	—	Gn. 44.5

In the first example the D-stem denominative 'perform sorcery (with a snake)' is preserved throughout, in AS as 'perform sorcery (with birds)'. In the second, TO-2 'make tested (by sorcery)' is of the factitive type, and seems in context to be used almost as a play on words.

nky	2-P	*lqy*	1-S	*’bd*	1	*‘ṭb*	1-S	Ex. 9.31
nky	4	*qṭl*	2	*qṭl*	1	*qtl*	1	Gn. 36.25
nky	4	*lqy*	4	*ngd*	2	*ḍrb*	1	Dt. 25.2

BH-2 'be smitten' is ambiguous, since it is the sole occurrence of the root apart from the Š-stem. If it is part of D one may speculate that this came about by analogy with other verbs which were equivalent in meaning in the D- and Š-stems. In any case, BH-2 does not affect the translations, which are various kinds of stative B-stems.

nkr	2	—	—	*rwm*	10	*nkr*	1	Dt. 32.27

BH-2 is an original factitive-estimative 'regard as unknown, misconstrue', the force of which is somewhat dissipated in AS-1 'be ignorant'. SP-10 'be proud' is an interpretation rather than a translation.

nsy	2	*nsy*	2	*nsy*	2	*mḥn*	8	Gn. 22.1

All mean 'test'. Hebrew and Aramaic seem to have an original D-stem denominative, AS the reflexive of an original B-stem denominative, as 'test oneself'.

nsk	1	*nsk*	2	*nqy*	2	*ršš*	1	Ex. 30.9
nsk	4	*nsk*	2	*nsk*	1	*ršš*	1	Gn. 35.14

All mean 'pour'. The two examples provide a classic case of the confusion among the stems which existed in West Semitic. Most interesting is the use of TO-2 to translate BH-4, used where one would normally expect to have BH-2.

n‘r	2	*šnq*	2	*ṭrf*	1	*ġrq*	2	Ex. 14.27

BH-2 'shake off' is translated by TO-2 'choke', SP-1 'strike' and AS-2 'immerse'. Despite this variation in meanings, the translations seem to prefer to use the D- rather than the possible B-stem.

npl	1	*mgr*	2	*rmy*	4	*wq‘*	1	Gn. 49.17

The noun 'rider' is the subject of both BH-1 and AS-1 'fall', but the object of TO-2 and SP-4, both of the latter being used as causative of an intransitive verb, thus 'make to fall'.

(Table I, continued)

BH		TO		SP		AS		
nṣl	2	—	—	*npṣ*	2	*nsf*	10	Ex. 3.22

SP-2 'cast down' seems to be influenced in stem choice by BH-2 'despoil', while AS employs the reflexive of Š in a specialized sense.

nqb	1	*prš*	2	*prš*	1	*byn*	2	Gn. 30.28

BH-1 'designate' is paralleled by SP-1 'explain'. There seems to be no reason other than customary usage for the translation of TO-2. AS-2 is an example of D-stem use for causative function, common in Arabic.

nqy	2	*zky*	2	*zky*	2	*br'*	2	Ex. 20.7
nqy	2	*slḥ*	1	*zky*	2	*br'*	2	Ex. 34.7

BH-2 'make exempt' is paralleled by TO/SP-2 'make pure' and AS-2 'make guiltless'. The D-stem factitive is preserved throughout, except for the TO-1 paraphrase 'forgive'. The uniformity of stem-usage in concepts and expressions of this type give us the surest indication that we are dealing with the original meaning of D in such cases.

nqr	2	*ʿwr*	2	*ʿwr*	2	*qlʿ*	1	Nu. 16.14

TO- and SP-2, factitive 'make blind', conform to BH-2 'bore out' only coincidentally. AS-1 'pluck out' is closer to the original in meaning.

nś'	1	*slḥ*	2	*šql*	1	*ḥml*	1	Lv. 10.17
nś'	1	*qbl*	2	*šrr*	1	*qbl*	1	Ex. 23.1
nś'	1	*šḥr*	2	*dbr*	1	*sẖr*	1	Nu. 16.15
nś'	4	*qbl*	2	*šql*	1	*ḥml*	1	Lv. 22.16

The use of TO-2 throughout the four examples, as contrasted with the use of B in SP and AS, symbolizes effectively the TO translator's preference for this stem, either for stylistic reasons or because its use was more common in this relatively early dialect. One would assume that in later Aramaic and Arabic the stem would tend to drop out of common use for verbs of transitive action, as grammarians and speakers of the language lost an awareness of the characteristics which originally distinguished it from the B- and Š-stems, and as the functions of the three stems began to overlap. Incidentally, the translations of BH-4 'cause to bear' are the result of a change of subject.

nśg	4	*ʿrʿ*	2	*drk*	4	*drk*	4	Lv. 26.5

The precise origins of BH-4 'overtake' and of TO-2 'meet, bring into contact' are unclear, making any comparison of them futile.

nšk	2	*nkt*	2	*nkt*	2	*ḥrq*	4	Nu. 21.6
nšk	1	*nkt*	2	*nkt*	2	*ldǧ*	1	Nu. 21.9

All mean 'bite'. AS-4 employs the Š-stem for the same function performed elsewhere by D; however, in this case, exceptionally, it is Š which is associated with a stative B-stem, while the D-form is associated with a transitive B-stem. Note also that the Aramaic translations do not recognize any distinction between the B- and D-stems in the BH original, though the two examples occur within a few verses of one another.

nšk	4	*rby*	2	*rby*	2	*ʿyn*	3	Dt. 23.20

The BH denominative 'give interest' is translated by the TO/SP factitive 'make great, increase' and by the AS-3 denominative 'make money'. All three forms are clearly idiomatic indigenous usages.

(Table I, continued)

BH		TO		SP		AS		
nšl	1	*trk*	2	*ʼbd*	4	*ṭḥṭḥ*	1	Dt. 7.22

The general meaning is 'drive away', paraphrased as SP-4 'destroy' and AS-1 'break'. Only TO has the D-stem, as often with verbs of destruction.

nšq	2	*nšq*	2	*nšq*	2	*qbl*	2	Gn. 31.28
nšq	1	*nšq*	2	*nšq*	2	*qbl*	2	Gn. 48.10

All mean 'kiss'; no difference between BH-1 and -2 can be seen.

ntḥ	2	*plg*	2	*pšḥ*	2	*ʻḍḍ*	1	Ex. 29.17

The meaning is 'cut up'. BH-2 seems to be denominative, while Aramaic 'dissect' is associated with a transitive B-stem.

ntn	1	*mny*	2	*šlṭ*	4	*wly*	2	Gn. 41.41
ntn	1	*qym*	2	*qwm*	4	*jʻl*	1	Gn. 38.9

The first example refers to 'give rule', the second to 'give an offering', and the translations attempt a clarification of the original BH verb 'give'; thus the diversity of stems would be expected. AS-2 employs the D-stem as 'put in charge', used the same way as Š in SP-4 'cause to rule'.

ntṣ	2	*trʻ*	2	*ʻqr*	1	*qlʻ*	1	Dt. 12.3
ntṣ	1	*trʻ*	2	*ʻqr*	1	*nqḍ*	1	Ex. 34.13

BH 'pull down' is translated by TO 'break', SP 'overturn' and AS 'pluck out' (1) and 'pull down' (2). The translations do not distinguish between BH-1 and -2, though most roots involved occur in both stems.

ntr	2	*qpṣ*	2	*nbr*	1	*wṭb*	1	Lv. 11.21

The general meaning is 'leap, jump'. The fact that both the BH and TO roots occur everywhere else in the B-stem suggests that TO perhaps reflects BH influence in choice of stem.

swg	4	*šny*	2	*šny*	2	*zyğ*	4	Dt. 19.14

The general meaning is 'reverse'. BH-4 and AS-4 are associated with active B-stems, TO- and SP-2 with statives. Thus each here preserves its distinct function, though the two functions are in parallel usage.

skn	4	*ʼlp*	2	—	—	*ʻwd*	2	Nu. 22.30

BH-4 'be accustomed to' may have a denominative origin as 'have a custom' since it does not stand in a causative relationship to the B-form 'be of use'. Similarly, both TO-2 and AS-2 are associated with B-stem statives, 'be accustomed', but neither can be construed as a factitive 'make accustomed' unless one assumes that D is used here as a reflexive 'accustom oneself'. The alternative would be to explain these D-forms as denominatives from nouns no longer in currency, as 'have the custom'.

slp	2	*qll*	2	*hpk*	4	*zyf*	1-S	Ex. 23.8

A BH-2 denominative 'make (something) a lie, subvert' is translated by TO-2 'ruin', SP-4 'destroy' and AS-1 'be bad' (with change of subject). TO use of the D-stem is normal for verbs of this meaning, and is unconnected with BH usage.

(Table I, continued)

BH		TO		SP		AS		
spq	1	*śpq*	1	*ṭrp*	2	*ṣfq*	2	Nu. 24.10

All mean 'clap'. This example is unique, in having the D-forms in the two later texts, as opposed to the B-forms of the earlier.

spr	2	*šʿy*	5	*šʿy*	5	*qṣṣ*	1	Gn. 24.66

The usage in SP/TO-5 factitive 'make oneself pleasant' is idiomatic and independent of BH-2 'recount' as far as stem usage is concerned, though all four forms refer to 'conversing'.

stm	2	*ṭmm*	1	*tmm*	1	*sdd*	1	Gn. 26.15

All mean 'stop up, clog', no translation preserving the BH D-form.

str	4	*slq*	2	*hpk*	4	*ḥjb*	1	Dt. 31.17

BH-4 'conceal' is translated by TO-2 'remove', SP-4 'destroy' and AS-1 'cover'; the meanings vary too much for comparison.

ʿbd	2-P	*plḥ*	8	*dbr*	8	*flḥ*	1	Dt. 21.3

The BH *puʿʿal* 'be worked' seems to belong to the B-stem, as suggested by TO- and SP-8, reflexives of B. On the other hand, BH could be the passive of a denominative 'be made a slave, enslaved'.

ʿbr	4	*ʿbr*	4	—	—	*qrb*	2	Lv. 18.21

The general meaning is 'devote (to sacrifice)', the AS D-stem 'bring near' merely paraphrasing the original, as 'present (for sacrifice)'.

ʿwd	4	*shd*	4	*shd*	2	*nšd*	3	Gn. 43.3

BH- and TO-4 and SP-2 are all denominatives 'act as witness, give testimony'. Since TO-2 and SP-4 also occur for *shd*, with the same meaning, the shift of stems is not significant. AS-3 is probably also denominative in origin, as 'give an oath'.

ʿwp	3	*prḥ*	2	*prḥ*	1	*ṭyr*	1	Gn. 1.20

All mean 'fly'. If the text has been correctly transmitted, TO-2 is an anomaly, since the normal translation as a factitive or causative is inappropos. Perhaps it is the remnant of an older Stem III in Aramaic (as with Hebrew pôlel), the long vowel of the first syllable being natural instead of the result of compensatory lengthening.

ʿwr	2	*ʿwr*	2	*ʿwr*	2	*ʿmy*	4	Ex. 23.8

All mean 'blind'. AS-4 here assumes a normal function of the D-stem.

ʿzb	1	*rḥq*	2	*šbq*	1	*trk*	1	Dt. 31.17

The general meaning is 'abandon', the TO-2 form representing a specialized and idiomatic use of the factitive 'make distant'.

ʿll	5	*ḥyk*	2	*bzḥ*	2	*rwǧ*	6	Nu. 22.29

BH-5 'deal wantonly' is translated by TO/SP-2 'laugh' and AS-6 'delude (someone)'. Despite the differences in roots and precise meanings, a denominative/factitive sense is preserved throughout.

(Table I, continued)

BH		TO		SP		AS		
‘md	1	*šmš*	2	*qwm*	1	*wqf*	1	Gn. 18.8
‘md	4	*qwm*	2	*qwm*	2	*bqy*	4	Ex. 9.16

In the first example TO-2 ‘render (religious) service’ states explicitly what is expressed idiomatically as ‘stand’ in the other texts. In the second, the Aramaic translations use the D-stem in a manner exactly parallel to the use of Š in Hebrew.

‘nw	2	*sgp*	2	*sgp*	2	—	—	Nu. 30.14
‘nw	2-P	*‘nw*	5	*mkk*	5	—	—	Lv. 23.29
‘nw	2	*‘nw*	2	*ṣ‘r*	2	*‘ḏb*	2	Gn. 16.6

The general meaning is ‘afflict’, with slight variations in some translations. This is one of the best examples of the persistence of a D-stem ‘type’ in the West Semitic languages, the ‘type’ here being factitive, and associated with a stative B-stem.

‘ny	1	*‘ny*	2	*‘ny*	2	*jwb*	3	Ex. 15.21

The meaning is ‘sing’, originally the denominative ‘make a response’ as represented in TO/SP-2 and AS-3. The D-stem of the root occurs elsewhere in Biblical Hebrew, so BH-1 here may be a back-formation.

‘nn	2	*‘nn*	2	*slq*	4	*ğym*	2	Gn. 9.14

The meaning is ‘raise (a cloud)’, the SP-4 causative ‘cause to go up’ eliminating the redundancy created by the D-stem denominative ‘make a cloud’, found elsewhere with the direct object ‘cloud’; at the expense, however, of the picturesqueness of language which is so often a concomitant of the D-stem.

‘qb	1	*ḥkm*	2	*nkl*	1	*‘qb*	1	Gn. 27.36

The B-stem denominative of BH-1 ‘seize at the heel’ is preserved in AS-1, but paraphrased by a D-factitive in TO-2 ‘make wise, outwit’.

‘qr	2	*tr‘*	2	*‘qr*	2	*ql‘*	1	Gn. 49.6

TO-2 ‘break’ may reflect the stem-usage of BH-2 factitive ‘make sterile’ (exactly paralleled by SP), especially since, like AS-1 ‘pluck out’ it does not parallel BH in meaning.

‘ry	2	*npṣ*	1	*npṣ*	1	*frğ*	2	Gn. 24.20
‘ry	4	*gly*	2	*gly*	1	*‘ry*	2	Lv. 20.18

In the first example AS-2 ‘make empty’ duplicates BH-2, both being factitives associated with stative B-stems ‘be empty’, while TO and SP employ active B-stems meaning ‘empty’. In the second, AS-2 is seen by the translator as equivalent to BH-4 ‘lay bare, abandon’. More interesting is the diverse use of BH-2 and -4, the former apparently having been specialized as ‘make empty’, the latter as ‘make bare’. Arabic, by using two different roots, avoids this necessity, and can employ the D-stem in its factitive for both roots without confusion. This is illustrative of the richness of the Arabic vocabulary as compared with that of Hebrew and Aramaic. TO-2 ‘uncover, make bare’ exemplifies the way in which the D- and B-stems are recognized, rightly or wrongly, as being equivalent in function.

‘rl	1	*rḥq*	2	*šbq*	1	*ḥrm*	2	Lv. 19.23

BH ‘leave uncircumcised’ is translated by TO ‘make alien’. SP ‘desert’ and AS ‘make unlawful’, use of the D-stem being idiomatically determined.

(Table I, continued)

BH		TO		SP		AS		
‘rk	1	*sdr*	2	*‘bd*	1	*ṣqq*	3	Gn. 14.8

The general meaning is ‘order, arrange’, paraphrased in SP as ‘perform’. BH-1 and TO-2 probably represent the denominalization of a noun ‘order, row’ in different stems – a common phenomenon.

‘śr	2	*‘śr*	2	*‘sr*	2	*‘šr*	2	Dt. 14.22

All mean ‘divide into ten, tithe’. Again the unanimity of usage indicates that we deal here with a basic and original function of the D-stem.

‘tr	1	*ṣly*	2	*ṣly*	2	*šf‘*	1	Gn. 25.21

The general meaning is ‘entreat, plead’. TO/SP-2 ‘pray’ seems to be an original factitive ‘make aware’ or causative ‘make listen’.

p’r	2	*ply*	2	*ply*	2	*qṣy*	10	Dt. 24.20

The BH-2 denominative ‘strike with a bough’ is not paralleled in the translations; TO/SP-2 ‘seek after’ cannot be related in stem-usage.

pg‘	1	*‘r‘*	2	*pg‘*	1	*wfy*	3	Gn. 28.11

The general meaning is ‘meet’. TO-2 factitive ‘bring into contact’ seems to be an idiom of this dialect, but it is a typical D-stem circumlocution, with its correspondent elegance of expression and ambiguity.

pgš	1	*‘r‘*	2	*pg‘*	1	*jw’*	1	Gn. 32.18

The comments made about *pg‘* apply to this root as well.

pwṣ	4	*bdr*	2	*bdr*	1	*bdd*	2	Gn. 11.8

BH-4 ‘cause to disperse’ is translated as ‘scatter’. BH-4 is causative of an intransitive B-stem, while TO-2 and AS-2 are factitives associated with a transitive B-stem (found in SP-1). Thus each stem preserves its original function.

pl’	2	*prš*	2	*prš*	1	*ṣwǧ*	2	Nu. 15.3
pl’	4	*prš*	2	*prš*	1	*ṣwǧ*	2	Nu. 6.2

BH-2 and -4 seem to share a common denominative/factitive construction ‘do something unusual, make different’, their similarity apparently reflected in the translations, which do not distinguish between them.

pll	2	*sbr*	2	*sbr*	1	*rjw*	8	Gn. 48.11

The general meaning is ‘expect’. TO-2 ‘conclude’ may reflect the influence of BH-2, despite the difference in their origins and roots.

pny	2	*pny*	2	*tqn*	2	*njl*	1	Gn. 24.31

The general meaning is ‘clarify, disclose’. SP-2, associated with a transitive B-stem, may reflect the influence of BH-2, though the latter is factitive in origin, associated with a stative B-stem.

(Table I, continued)

BH		TO		SP		AS		
pṣl	2	*qlp*	2	*qlp*	1	*qsr*	2	Gn. 30.37

The general meaning is 'split', though paraphrased by AS-2 as 'force'. Although TO-2 'shell' is parallel to BH-2 in stem usage, it may have a denominative rather than a factitive origin as in BH, which is associated with a stative B-stem. In this case SP-1 would exemplify the D-stem denominative which in use has dropped back at least partially into the B-stem. AS-2 may reflect the influence of the BH stem.

pqd	2-P	*mny*	8	*mny*	8	*ʿdd*	1-P	Ex. 38.21
pqd	1	*mny*	2	*pqd*	1	*šyʾ*	1	Nu. 27.16

The general meaning is 'count, look after'. In the first example, the *puʿʿal* again seems to belong to the B-stem represented in the translations. In the second the use of TO-2 is arbitrary, and does not represent the regular use of this root in TO.

prd	4	*prš*	2	*prš*	1	*frq*	2	Dt. 32.8

All mean 'separate'. BH-4 is the causative of an intransitive B-stem 'separate', while TO-2 is a factitive associated with a transitive B-stem 'separate' (seen in SP-1), and AS-2 falls in the same category. BH-4 here performs a function often associated with D; however, the D-form of this root has been specialized as 'go apart, make a separation'.

prm	1	*bzʿ*	2	*ṣry*	2	*mzq*	2	Lv. 10.6
prm	1	*bzʿ*	2	*prm*	2	*mzq*	2	Lv. 13.45

All mean 'rend, split'. There is no way to explain the uniform use of D in the translations, except by reference to a general disposition to use the stem for verbs of 'dividing' in these later dialects.

prʿ	4	*bṭl*	2	*bṭl*	2	*jḏb*	1	Ex. 5.4

TO/SP-2 'abolish, make at an end' is used as parallel to BH-4 'cause neglect, cause to be loose'. It is in such cases that the dividing line between D-stem factitive and Š-stem causative becomes blurred.

prq	2	*prq*	2	*prq*	2	*fkk*	1	Ex. 32.2

All mean 'split, separate'. The Aramaic translations preserve the BH D-stem, as might be expected for a root with this meaning. In BH, however, the B-stem of the root is more often used.

prš	2-P	*prš*	8	*pšq*	5	*fsr*	2-P	Nu. 15.34

All mean 'explain'. In this case the puʿʿal seems to be an authentic D-form, since the D-stem is commonly associated with this root in the active, as well as with roots similar in meaning in the other languages. TO failure to employ the D-stem is unusual, since that would be the common usage for this dialect.

pth	2	*šdl*	2	*šdl*	2	*ḫdʿ*	1	Ex. 22.15

All mean 'deceive'. TO/SP-2 reproduces the factitive sense of BH-2, lost in AS, as 'make simple'.

ptḥ	2	*šry*	2	*šry*	1	*ḥll*	1	Gn. 24.32

All mean 'loosen, open'. TO may reflect BH influence, lost elsewhere.

(Table I, continued)

BH		TO		SP		AS		
ptl	2-P	*šny*	5	*ptl*	2-P	*qlb*	5	Dt. 32.5

All mean 'be twisted'. BH-2 here is actually a pilpel formation, and might be construed as an adjective rather than as a verbal form. The translations seem to prefer the latter interpretation; the use of D in them connotes a link between the D-stem and the so-called 'reduplicated' stems, in meaning if not in origin.

ptr	4	*pšr*	1	—	—	*fsr*	2	Gn. 40.8

All mean 'interpret'. The use of the D-stem in AS is an indigenous development, the root occurring in this stem alone.

ptt	1	*bṣʿ*	2	*ptt*	1	*ṭrd*	1	Lv. 2.6

The general meaning is 'crumble, break', paraphrased in AS-1 as 'reject'. The use of D in TO once more points up the connection of the stem with verbs of destruction in this dialect.

ṣbʾ	1	*ḥyl*	2	*ḥyl*	5	—	—	Nu. 4.23

BH-1 'wage war' is a B-stem denominative, TO-2 and SP-5 D-stem denominatives 'use force (for oneself)', thus no parallelism of stem exists.

ṣdq	4	*zky*	2	*zky*	2	*zky*	2	Ex. 23.7

All mean 'justify, purify'. BH-4 has taken over what one would normally regard as a function of D, which in BH, however, has been specialized as a declarative/estimative 'regard (someone) as righteous'. The translators clearly saw BH-4 as factitive, and used D as the most suitable translation.

ṣwh	2	*pqd*	2	*pqd*	2	*ʾmr*	1	Gn. 2.16
ṣwh	2-P	*pqd*	5	*pqd*	5	*ʾmr*	1-P	Lv. 8.35

All mean 'order, command'. BH has only the D-stem of this root, probably an original denominative 'give a command'. TO and SP, however, have equivalent B-stems, thus may be following BH usage here.

ṣḥq	2	*ḥyk*	2	*gḥk*	2	*lʿb*	1	Gn. 21.9
ṣḥq	1	*ḥyk*	2	*gḥk*	1	*ḍḥk*	1	Gn. 18.12

In the first example BH, SP and TO alike use the D-stem as a causative 'make laugh, jest with', while AS paraphrases as 'play with'. In the second, where the indicated meaning is 'laugh', TO retains the D-stem, although its causative use is inappropriate here. The only feasible explanations of the TO usage here are (1) that it represents an original denomiantive 'give a laugh' which became merged with the D causative, or (2) that the D-stem here is intensive, *i.e.* means 'laugh violently'.

ṣʿq	1	*ṣwḥ*	4	*bgn*	2	*ṣrḫ*	1	Ex. 5.8

All mean 'cry out'. All four forms may be original denominatives, 'give a cry' which became associated with different stems in the various languages and dialects, in TO with the D-stem.

ṣpy	2	*ḥpy*	1	*qrm*	1	*ġsy*	2	Ex. 36.34

All mean 'overlay, cover'. BH-2 is a denominative 'plate' with no counterpart in TO or SP. AS-2 probably reflects the influence of BH, and could be either a denominative 'make a covering for' or a factitive 'make covered' associated with the root's transitive B-stem.

(Table I, continued)

BH		TO		SP		AS		
ṣr‘	2-P	—	—	*qrb*	2-P	—	—	Ex. 4.6

Both mean ‘made leprous’. BH-2 is exactly paralleled by SP-2, but is paraphrased elsewhere by descriptive phrases, pointing up the factitive-denominative nature of the D-stem, both factitive and denominative being types of linguistic shorthand, replacing long phrases.

qbṣ	2	*knš*	1	*knš*	2	*jm‘*	1	Dt. 30.3

All mean ‘gather’. Only SP reflects the BH original in stem usage.

qbr	2	*qbr*	2	*qbr*	1	*dfn*	1	Nu. 33.4
qbr	2-P	*qbr*	8	*qbr*	8	*qbr*	1-P	Gn. 25.10

All mean ‘bury’. In the first example no consistency of stem-usage is seen. In the second, the *pu‘‘al* might seem to be associated with B as its passive, but the general inconsistency of stem-usage for the root makes this uncertain.

qdm	2	*‘r‘*	2	*qrb*	2	*lqy*	5	Dt. 23.5

All mean ‘meet’, and all might be regarded as factitive in function, with the possible exception of AS-5, which might be viewed as the reflexive-causative of a B-form ‘meet’, thus ‘have oneself meet’.

qdš	2	*qdš*	2	*qdš*	2	*qds*	2	Gn. 2.3

All mean ‘sanctify’ and all are D-stem factitives.

qwy	2	*sbr*	2	*sky*	2	*rjw*	1	Gn. 49.18

The general meaning is ‘wait for, expect’. Both BH-2 and SP-2 occur principally in D as factitive, associated with the transitive B-stems which also occur for these roots. TO-2 ‘hope’ involves a slight shift in meaning, and may be an original denominative ‘have hope’.

qwm	4	*qwm*	2	*qwm*	4	*ṭbt*	4	Nu. 30.14

The meaning here is ‘make stand’, paraphrased in AS as ‘cause to be firm’. TO-2 employs the D-stem as a causative equivalent to the Š-stem of BH (and SP), while AS-4 employs Š for a function associated with D.

qwṣ	1	*rḥq*	2	—	—	—	—	Lv. 20.23

BH-1 ‘loathe’ is translated by the TO idiom regularly employed to express this concept.

qll	2	*qll*	4	*ṣḥy*	4	*štm*	1	Ex. 22.27

The general meaning is ‘curse, vilify’. The TO translator here regards the Š-stem causative of a stative verb as in practice equivalent to the D-stem factitive associated with the stative B-forms. Thus both are originally ‘make light’. AS and SP do not possess this figurative phrase.

qn’	2	*qn’*	2	*ṭnn*	1	*ḥsd*	1	Gn. 26.14
qn’	4	*qn’*	4	*ṭnn*	4	*kyd*	1	Dt. 32.21

BH-2 and -4 seem to be parallel denominatives, specialized as ‘feel jealousy’ and ‘induce jealousy’ respectively, and have an exact counterpart in TO. SP-4 is, however, the causative of a B-stem denominative, as seen here, which also has associated with it a D-stem factitive ‘make jealous’. The latter might be expected here, but the BH text may have influenced the choice of Š. Once again, Arabic eschews circumlocutions.

(Table I, continued)

BH		TO		SP		AS		
qṣy	4	*qlp*	2	*qlp*	1	*qšr*	1	Lv. 14.41

BH-4 seems to be an Š-stem denominative 'put an end to'; while TO-2 may also be denominative in origin (see *pṣl*) it is independent of BH.

qṣʿ	4	*qlp*	2	*qlp*	2	*qšr*	1	Lv. 14.41

This BH form was apparently regarded by the translators as equivalent to the Š-stem of the preceding verb.

qṣṣ	2	*qṣṣ*	2	*psq*	1	*qṣṣ*	1	Ex. 39.3

All mean 'cut off', again a verb of division, represented in the D-stem only in the earlier versions.

qrʾ	1	*ṣly*	2	*qrʾ*	1	*dʿy*	1	Gn. 12.8
qrʾ	1	*rby*	2	*qrʾ*	1	—	—	Ex. 31.2

The general meaning is 'call', paraphrased by TO twice, as a more specific 'make persuaded', associated with a transitive B-stem, and 'make great', associated with a stative B-stem. These two examples show how D can be used to produce a more colorful mode of expression.

qrb	1	*qrb*	2	*qrb*	2	*qdm*	5	Lv. 16.1

BH and AS mean 'approach, come near to', while TO- and SP-2 are factitives 'bring near', the latter being used because the verb acquires an object in these two texts. Thus the shift from B to D is a concomitant of a shift from intransitive to transitive. The D-stem reflexive of AS, of course, has an implicit object, thus is practically equivalent to the intransitive B-stem.

q̱ry	4	*zmn*	2	*ṭyb*	2	*wqf*	2	Gn. 24.12

BH-4 'cause to approach' is translated by D-stem factitives throughout: TO 'make prepared', SP 'make ready' and AS 'make present'. The D-stem is here regarded by the translators as functionally equivalent to the Š of BH, which in fact has infringed on a D function in this example.

qrʿ	1	*bzʿ*	2	*ṣry*	1	*ḥzq*	2	Gn. 37.29

The general meaning is 'tear, rend', paraphrased by AS-2 as 'pierce'. There is no discernable reason for the use of TO-2 and AS-2, unless one attributes the usage to the category of meaning in which the root falls.

qšy	2	*qšy*	2	*ḥsn*	1	*ṣʿb*	1	Gn. 35.16
qšy	4	*qšy*	4	*qšy*	2	*ṣʿb*	2	Ex. 7.3

In the first example the BH-2 denominative 'have difficulty, severe labour' is a form used interchangeably with BH-4, which also can be used to refer to a difficult childbirth. The D-stem, of which this is the sole BH example, may result in this case from an effort to specialize the concept in this stem, in order to distinguish it from the normal meaning of the Š-stem 'make hard', seen in the second example. This may already have happened in TO, which employs the D-stem both here and in Gn. 35.17, where BH uses Š; on the other hand TO employs the Š-form in the second example along with BH. No such process was taking place in Syriac, since we see SP-2 in a typical use of D, as a factitive associated with a stative B-stem – a function taken by Š in both BH and TO; while in the first example SP employs a specific verb 'labor hard'. Finally, AS uses D in a manner similar to that of SP, but here it is associated with a D-stem stative 'be difficult, hard'.

(Table I, continued)

BH		TO		SP		AS		
qšr	2-P	*bkr*	2-P	—	—	—	—	Gn. 30.41

Though both forms are D-stems, BH-2 'make vigorous' is a factitive, TO-2 'beget the first-born' a denominative in origin; TO represents a significant modification in meaning. Both are idiomatic expressions, here independently employed.

rbb	1	*nqm*	2	*sgy*	1	*kṭr*	1	Gn. 49.23

The general meaning is 'increase, be many'. The TO D-stem denominative 'take vengeance' must arise from misunderstanding or reinterpretation.

rgl	2	*ʾll*	2	*gšš*	1	*rwm*	1	Nu. 21.32

Both BH-2 'set foot upon, spy out' and TO-2 'act as a spy' seem to be denominative, but are unrelated in usage here.

rwḥ	4	*qbl*	2	*rwḥ*	4	—	—	Gn. 8.21

TO-2 'receive' is unrelated to BH/SP 'smell' in function.

rwʿ	4	*ybb*	2	*ybb*	2	*jlb*	2	Nu. 10.7

All mean 'shout' and are probably denominatives of their respective stems, although AS-2 may be a factitive associated with the transitive B-stem 'attract', idiomatic and figurative in usage.

rwq	4	*zrz*	2	*zyn*	2	*jrd*	2	Gn. 14.14

TO-2 and SP-2 factitives 'arm (troops)' are paraphrases of BH-4 'cause (an army) to pour forth', while AS-2, originally a factitive 'make denuded' is used idiomatically as 'send (troops)'. Thus this is not a true example of confusion between D and Š.

rḥb	4	*pth*	4	*rwḥ*	2	*wsʿ*	4	Dt. 12.20

BH, TO and AS Š-forms are causatives of intransitive B-stems, as 'cause to widen, open', while SP-2 is a factitive associated with a stative B-stem as 'make wide'. The translator thus equates the two constructions.

rḥm	2	*rḥm*	2	*rḥm*	2	*rḥm*	1	Ex. 33.19

All mean 'love'. We seem to have here an original D-stem denominative, which in AS has fallen back into the B-stem.

rḥp	2	*nšb*	2	*rḥp*	2	*ḥbb*	1	Gn. 1.2

BH-2 'hover aloft' is exactly paralleled by SP-2; in both languages the D-stem is regularly associated with this root. Since TO-2 'blow' is likewise intransitive, and since it could as well have been in the B-stem, it may reflect BH influence.

rḥṣ	1	*qdš*	2	*šwg*	4	*g̃sl*	1	Ex. 30.19

The general meaning is 'rinse, wash', paraphrased in TO as 'sanctify'. SP use of the Š-stem is inexplicable.

(Table I, continued)

BH		TO		SP		AS		
rmy	2	*šqr*	1	*nbl*	1	*rtb*	4	Gn. 29.25

The general meaning is 'deceive', but is translated by AS-4 'prepare'. The BH-2 factitive 'make loose', used figuratively, is not reproduced in the Aramaic translations, and is probably indigenous to Hebrew.

rnn	1	*šbḥ*	2	*šbḥ*	1	*rnn*	4	Lv. 9.24

All four forms mean 'rejoice, give praise', and all are probable denominatives in origin. The use of two different stems for each of the two roots involved demonstrates how denominative verbs developed independently in the West Semitic languages.

rʿy	1	*ʾḥr*	2	*rʿy*	1	*tyh*	1	Nu. 14.33

The general meaning is 'graze', paraphrased in TO-2 as 'be after, linger', paralleled in AS-1 'wander about'.

rpʾ	2	*šlm*	2	—	—	—	—	Ex. 21.19

Again, TO-2 provides a figurative idiomatic usage, seeing BH-2 'heal' as 'make whole'. Thus it employs D independently of BH.

rqḥ	1	*bsm*	2	*bsm*	2	*ʿtr*	5	Ex. 30.33
rqḥ	1	*bsm*	2	*bsm*	2	*ʿtr*	2	Ex. 30.25

The general meaning is 'mix ointment, perfume'. All four forms seem to be denominatives, independently developed in each language. The BH form might have been expected to be in D, and probably is a back-formation.

rqʿ	2	*rdd*	2	*rqq*	4	*rqq*	4	Ex. 39.3

The general meaning is 'flatten'. BH- and TO-2 are factitives associated with transitive B-stems; SP- and AS-4 are causatives which apparently serve the same function, since they are also associated with transitive B-stems. The line between Š and D is not clear here.

ršʿ	4	*ḥyb*	2	*ḥwb*	4	*ẓlm*	1	Ex. 22.8

The general meaning is 'condemn (as guilty)'. Here we see the Š-stem being used in a function, the estimative-declarative, usually associated with D, as in TO here. This clearly was recognized by the TO translator, while the SP translator followed BH in choice of stem.

śyḥ	1	*ṣly*	2	—	—	*ṣlw*	2	Gn. 24.63

BH-1 'be concerned (with something)' is paraphrased by TO/AS denominative 'offer a prayer (for something)'.

śym	1	*šwy*	2	*śwm*	1	*jʿl*	1	Gn. 4.15

The general meaning 'put, place' is paraphrased by TO-2 'join'. The reason for the use of the D-stem here is obscure, since a B-form exists for the root with the same meaning, and there is nothing in the context to call for a figurative usage.

(Table I, continued)

BH		TO		SP		AS		
śkl	2	*ḥkm*	4	*ḥlp*	4	*ḥkm*	4	Gn. 48.14

TO/AS-4 represents a misunderstanding of the root, and a translation of the BH form as 'make wise'. BH-2 seems to be a factitive related to a stative concept something like 'be crossed' (which does not exist independently). SP recognized the meaning, but had no similar expression, thus employed the causative of an intransitive stem as an equivalent 'cause to change'.

śmḥ	2	*ḥdy*	2	*ḥdy*	2	*frḥ*	2	Dt. 24.5

All mean 'make happy' and are factitives associated with stative B-forms.

śn'	1	*rḥq*	2	*sny*	2	*šnw*	1	Dt. 16.22
śn'	2	—	—	—	—	—	—	Nu. 10.35

All mean 'hate'. TO-2 represents the customary TO idiomatic expression for verbs of disliking. BH-2 is not translated anywhere, directly. It can be explained only as a denominative 'feel hatred' or, if desired, as an intensive.

śrṭ	1	*ḥbl*	2	*ḥrṭ*	1	*ḫdš*	1	Lv. 21.5

The general meaning is 'slit', used of tattooing. TO paraphrases this as 'wound', used in D, probably because of the association with cutting.

śrp	2-P	*yqd*	10	*yqd*	1-S	*ḥrq*	4-P	Lv. 10.16

All mean 'be burned'. The translations offer circumlocutions of BH-2, in the B- and Š-stems, regarded as equivalent to the original.

š'l	1	*š'l*	2	*š'l*	2	*š'l*	3	Gn. 43.7

All mean 'ask'. The Hebrew and Aramaic forms occur in coordination with the infinitive absolute, BH-1 and TO-2 with that of the B-stem, SP-2 with that of the D-stem. The root occurs in D only twice in BH, but in Aramaic B- and D-stems exist as truly alternative usages, as with Stems I and III in Arabic. Such examples as this suggest that, where alternatives do exist, the choice of a translator may be dependent upon extra-linguistic factors and seem arbitrary.

šbʻ	4	*qwm*	2	*ymy*	4	*ḥlf*	2	Gn. 24.3

The meaning is 'cause (someone) to swear an oath', found in the expected Š-stem in BH and SP. TO-2 may be explained as a denominative 'give an oath (to someone)', which provides an alternative to use of the causative. However, AS-2 is directly parallel to BH-4, the causative of the B-stem (itself a probable denominative), as shown by the fact that AS-2 also takes a direct object as 'cause (someone) to swear'. This clarly shows the overlap in use of these stems in Arabic, and gives an indication why early Arab grammarians linked D and Š.

šbṣ	2	*rmṣ*	2	*ʻbd*	1	*wšy*	2	Ex. 28.39
šbṣ	2-P	*rmṣ*	2-P	*'ḥd*	4-P	*ʻyn*	2	Ex. 28.20

The general meaning is 'ornament, embellish'. BH-2 'ornament' is translated by TO-2 'use a pointed tool, etch' and AS-2 'embellish' (1) and 'make in the form of a flower' (2), but paraphrased in SP-1 'work' and SP-4 'cause to be grasped'. Although the D-stem occurs everywhere except in SP, no two uses are directly parallel in meaning, the fact that all may be denominatives undoubtedly being coincidental.

(Table I, continued)

BH		TO		SP		AS		
šbr	2	*tbr*	2	*tbr*	2	*ksr*	2	Ex. 9.25

Not only in this example, but elsewhere in the Pentateuch where this root occurs, the translations follow BH-2 'break' in employing a D-form. However, at least in TO, no D-form occurs as translation of a BH B-form. The same statements cannot be made about any other frequently-occurring root. This may indicate a substantive difference in usage between the two stems, or it may be the result of the connection of the root with the concepts of destruction and division. The latter explanation would be more consistent with our observation of other roots in this table.

šbt	4	*bṭl*	2	*bṭl*	2	*ʿṭl*	2	Ex. 5.5

The meaning is 'cause to rest, make cease'. In the translations, the D-stem is clearly regarded as equivalent in function to the BH Š-form.

šgʿ	2-P	*šṭy*	8	—	—	—	—	Dt. 28.34

Both mean 'be demented'. BH-2 seems to be a true passive of a D-stem factitive, as 'made furious'. TO-8 is the only stem associated with this root in Targumic Aramaic; Syriac has a B-stative 'be stupid'.

šḥṭ	1	*qṭl*	2	*nks*	2	*qtl*	1	Nu. 14.16

The general meaning is 'slaughter, sacrifice'. The TO- and SP-2 forms must represent a dialectal preference, reflected in other verbs of destruction. In any case it is unrelated to the BH stem usage.

šṭp	2-P	*šṭp*	8	*šwg*	10	*g̃sl*	1-P	Lv. 6.21

All mean 'be rinsed, washed'. BH-2 may again not be truly part of the D-stem, since no corresponding active form occurs.

šyr	1	*šbḥ*	2	*šbḥ*	2	*sbḥ*	2	Ex. 15.1

The translations are D-stem denominatives 'give praise', and paraphrase the BH D-stem 'sing'.

šyt	1	*śwy*	2	*śwm*	1	*jʿl*	1	Gn. 3.15

All mean 'put, place'. The TO-2 form is considered under *śym*.

škb	1	*škb*	1	*ʿṣr*	2	*ḍjʿ*	3	Gn. 34.7

The general meaning is 'lie (with a woman)'. SP-2 factitive 'make pressed, rape' is a figurative use, while AS-3 seems to reflect the specialization of one stem to express a specific aspect of the root meaning, which again is 'lie'.

škl	2	*tkl*	4	*gym*	2	*ṯkl*	1	Gn. 31.38

The general meaning 'be bereaved (of a child), undergo a miscarriage' is borne by denominatives of various stems in BH, TO and AS. The SP-2 translation 'make disappear' probably results from a misunderstanding.

škm	4	*qdm*	2	*qdm*	2	*drj*	2	Gn. 19.2

BH-4 'do early' is unclear in origin. TO/SP-2 represents idiomatic Aramaic usage 'be previous, act beforehand', while AS-2 'make rise' may reflect a misunderstanding of the BH text.

(Table I, continued)

BH		TO		SP		AS		
škn	2	*šry*	4	*šry*	4	—	—	Nu. 14.30

TO/SP-4 'cause to dwell' is here regarded as the equivalent of BH-2 'make settled', both in meaning and in function.

škr	4	*rwy*	2	*rwy*	4	*skr*	4	Dt. 32.42

Here and elsewhere, Š- and D-stems alternate both among and within the various languages and dialects of West Ṣemitic as 'make drunken', a testimony to their functional equivalence in some situations.

šlb	2-P	*šlb*	2-P	—	—	—	—	Ex. 26.17

Both mean 'be joined (with a crossbar)' and are D-stem denominatives.

šlḥ	2	*šlḥ*	2	*šdr*	1	*ṭrd*	1	Gn. 3.23
šlḥ	2	*gly*	4	*šdy*	1	*ṭrd*	1	Lv. 18.24
šlḥ	1	*šlḥ*	2	*šdr*	1	*b'ṯ*	1	Gn. 37.14
šlḥ	4	*gry*	2	*šdr*	2	*ṭlq*	4	Lv. 26.22

All mean 'send', the variety of the expressive means illustrating well the overlap of stem-functions both within the BH text and in its translations.

šlm	2	*šlm*	2	*prʿ*	1	*kfʾ*	3	Gn. 44.4

The original meaning is a factitive 'make complete, repay', a figurative and idiomatic use paralleled by AS-3 'make return, repay'.

šlš	2	*tlt*	2	*tlt*	2	*ṯlṯ*	2	Dt. 19.3

The D-stem denominative 'divide into three' is preserved throughout, suggesting an original function of the D-stem.

šmʿ	1	*qbl*	2	*šmʿ*	1	*qbl*	1	Gn. 3.17

TO-2 factitive 'receive', asosciated with a transitive verb (*cf.* AS), is a paraphrase of BH-1 'hear'.

šnn	2	*tnn*	2	*tny*	1	*ḥky*	1	Dt. 6.7

The meaning is 'repeat, relate'. TO-2 preserves the D-stem of BH, but such a usage seems to have been unnatural to the SP translator.

ššʿ	2	*prq*	2	*štp*	1	*fṣl*	1	Lv. 1.17

All mean 'divide'. As one would expect, BH and TO employ the D-stem.

šqd	2-P	*ṣyr*	2-P	*qbʿ*	1-P	*lwz*	2-P	Ex. 25.33

AS-2 is interesting, insofar as it offers an exact parallel to the BH-2 denominative 'made in the shape of an almond', whereas the TO and SP translators, not having a precise equivalent available, were forced to approximate the original meaning. Such an example is important because it demonstrates the carefulness of even the latest translator to provide the most exact possible translation of the original text. This implies that one can feel confidence that any important aspect of the original text within the understanding of the translators will be preserved insofar as is possible, and, conversely, that any aspects not so preserved are of relatively small importance.

(Table I, continued)

BH		TO		SP		AS		
šqṣ	2	*šqṣ*	2	*ṭm'*	2	—	—	Lv. 11.11

All three forms are D-stem factitive-estimative forms, 'regard as unclean, loathesome, impure', associated with stative B-stems.

šqr	2	*šqr*	2	*dgl*	1	*nkṯ*	1	Lv. 19.11
šqr	1	*šqr*	2	*dgl*	2	*ğdr*	1	Gn. 21.23

All mean 'deceive'. TO does not attempt to preserve the BH-1 and -2 variation, while SP reverses the BH use of the stems. Clearly, all the Hebrew and Aramaic forms are denominatives, probably original in D, but entering into B through back-formations.

šrt	2	*šmš*	2	*šmš*	2	*ḫdm*	1	Gn. 39.4

All mean 'perform a service, serve'. The BH, TO and SP roots occur only in the D-stem, and thus are probably original denominatives. This is an example of parallel but independent development within two or more languages.

t'y	2	*kwn*	2	*tḥm*	1	*ḥdd*	4	Nu. 34.7

BH-2, which is probably an original denominative 'draw a line', does not seem to influence the stem choice of TO. The origin of the TO form is unclear *vis-à-vis* the Hebrew-Arabic root *kwn*, but it may perhaps be best described as an original factitive 'make firm, fixed', associated with a stative B-stem.

twr	1	*'ll*	2	*gšš*	1	*rwm*	1	Nu. 13.2

All mean 'spy'. TO-2 is an idiomatic usage (see *rgl*).

tll	4	*šqr*	2	*dgl*	2	*sḫr*	1	Gn. 31.7

TO-2 'make foolish, cheat', a factitive, fills a function parallel to that of BH-4 'cause to act foolishly'. SP is a denominative 'tell a lie'.

tmk	1	*s'd*	1	*smk*	2	*snd*	4	Ex. 17.12

All mean 'grasp, support'. The reason for use of SP-2 is obscure.

t'b	2	*rḥq*	2	*dḥq*	1	*krh*	1	Dt. 23.8

BH-2 is a denominative-estimative 'regard (something) as an abomination', while TO-2 reflects the usual means of expressing dislike in this dialect.

Even a casual perusal of the examples listed in the preceding pages will show that even where a degree of consistency exists in the employment of the D-stem, *e.g.* for factitive expressions or verbs of destruction, such consistency is at best imperfect. However, in a number of cases both the original authors and their translators appear to be arbitrary and spontaneous in their choices of stem. Thus with *š'l* the root remains a constant factor, yet no pattern of use is discernable; this is much more the case with a root such as *šlḥ*, for which a number of roots and stems (but always with the same meaning) are employed in the translations. Nevertheless, as we have pointed out, the Arabic translation of the D-stem of *šqd* 'make almond-shaped' exemplifies the translators' effort to provide the most precise verbal equivalent possible for the original, within the limits of their own languages, whether from pietistic or scholarly motives (or both). From these disparate elements of seeming arbitrariness and seeming carefulness revealed by this survey of forms, we may conclude that in cases where the stem usage may appear inconsistent, the distinctions among the stems were in fact regarded as linguistically insignificant by the author or translator, and that, on the other hand, agreement in usage is not necessarily significant for our purposes.

The conscious or subconscious attitude that stem-differences were often of little importance for accurate translation could have arisen from any one of two or three possible conditions: (1) two or more physically distinct forms had originally the same meaning; (2) two or more forms had distinctive origins AND meanings; (3) certain roots and/or concepts followed several independent lines of development indigenous to various languages and dialects of West Semitic. Such 'idiomatic' usage (including the specialization of forms which we have frequently noted) often precludes the possibility of exact parallels between text and translation, and even operates against perfect consistency within a single document.

The first of these three possibilities, while it seems to run counter to general linguistic principles, may have some relevance to our problem. First, as we have already suggested, Stems II and III almost certainly represent alternative phonetic developments of an original single form, while their later distinctiveness of meaning, where such exists (almost exclusively in Arabic), represents accretion of specialized functions (semantic in Arabic but phonetic in Hebrew, in connection with certain 'weak' roots) to the individual forms. Thus it should not disturb us to find a root used in Stem II in the original text but in Stem III in translation, or *vice-versa.* While the phonetic relationship of Stem IV to II and III is by no means as obvious, there is even a possibility that there was an original morphological link among the three which could account for some of the ambiguity surrounding the choice of one of the three over the others. The fact that we are dealing here with three languages (and four dialects) obviously implies that, whatever the Common Semitic origin of a form or forms, individual languages might well be expected often to express the same concept by different means. Yet, more remarkable than the discrepancies we have found is the broad area of agreement between text and translations which our survey has revealed. This measure of agreement underlies the likelihood that, for instance, whenever a Hebrew D-stem possessed a significance not present in its corresponding B-stem it would be treated by the translators in a manner different from that employed for B. If there is no common point of origin for these two or three stems, then the second and third possibilities come to the fore, both of which explain the differences in stem-usage among the four texts as the result of popular usage, which tended on the one hand to break down the distinctive semantic aspects of two or more stems within an individual language when their general meanings were similar, and which, over a group of languages, tended to associate specialized meanings with certain roots and stems in an unsystematic manner, and in the process often relegated the non-specialized meaning to another stem construed as roughly similar in function. It is easily seen that the latter phenomenon is to a degree contingent on the former, the blurring of the line dividing two stems.

Of course, in order to speak of the D-stem either as overlapping or as being overlapped in function *vis-à-vis* other stems, it is necessary to point to an original clear identity of that stem itself, some standard use by comparison with which other uses may be said to be aberrant. Is any such identity indicated by our examples? We have seen many cases in which one or more translations followed the Hebrew text in employing the D-stem. What we must ask is, (1) is this merely a superficial echo of a sacred text, or does it reflect a unique meaning of the D-stem which the translators felt could be expressed only by an equivalent D-stem in their own languages, and (2) why was the D-stem rather than some other employed in the original text.

A positive statement in answer to these questions is particularly needed because of the negative conclusion we have already drawn on the basis of these examples, that there is no basis for any claim that there was an original plurative or intensive force in the D-stem, and very little basis for any claim that such a connotation evolved from the original meaning, whatever that was. As far as the plurative aspect is concerned, the evidence is unambiguous. For instance, the claim has been advanced that when a verb in the B-stem means 'kill' the corresponding D-stem either will have the plurative meaning 'kill many', *i.e.* 'massacre', or will be regularly used where the object (or subject) is more than one person or thing. The example cited under *hrg* (B-stem) shows the Aramaic translation to be *qṭl* (D), the Arabic *qtl* (B). The subject and object of the verb (Cain and Abel) are both singular, yet the stem-usage varies as just stated. Moreover, we have noted that in Targumic Aramaic at least, *qṭl* is regularly used in the D-stem, regardless of the Hebrew form it translates. This suggests that the reason for the Aramaic choice has nothing to do with B- and D-stem *per se*, but arises from a heightening or consolidation in this dialect of a general West Semitic tendency to express verbal concepts related to destruction in the D-stem. Throughout our examples, verbs with a plural object or subject will occur in the D-stem in Hebrew, but in the B- or Š-stem in the translations, and *vice-versa.* On the basis of such evidence, attribution to the D-stem of a plurative function must appear to be a linguistic rationalization which arose out of the felt need to explain the existence of the two or three forms which otherwise would seem to have the same meaning – an embarassing situation for linguists.

In the final analysis, the designation of 'linguistic rationalization' must also, at least so far as the present examples indicate, be applied to the 'intensive' interpretation of the D-stem. The evidence of this chapter certainly does not support the existence of any connection between gemination and intensity of action. Not only does the B-form translate an original D-form many times, but even more to the point, the

D-form is not infrequently employed to translate an original B. Although Hebrew and Targumic Aramaic, it is true, share the use of the D-stem more often than not, the lengthy list of exceptions which would be appended to any description of this as a pattern would lead us to suspect that in many cases the use of the same stem in translation is meaningful not semantically, but only stylistically, as an effort to imitate as closely as possible the original text. Even this motive seems to have carried little weight for the Syriac and Arabic translators.

Moreover, any attempt to determine the specific semantic significance of the B- and D-stems of transitive verbs occasions problems even within an individual language; one wonders whether Western scholars in making such an attempt may have been influenced by their own languages. For instance, the original pairs *ṯabar*/*ṯabbar* and *qatal*/*qattal* are perhaps cited so frequently because there exists in many Indo-European languages a distinction between 'break' and 'shatter', between 'kill' and 'massacre'. But if one applies the same semantic pattern to the pairs *šalaḥ*/*šallaḥ* or *kanaš*/*kannaš*, he is forced to translate the D-forms as 'gather eagerly' or 'gather many', 'send enthusiastically' or 'send a crowd'. Such translations are almost obviously untenable; the barest survey of forms will confirm their inappropriateness. Thus, the examples cited under *šlḥ*, to which many others could have been added, clearly demonstrate that neither the original author(s) nor the translators saw any difference in usage between B and D (and even Š) forms of this root. Likewise, an example such as that cited for *zbḥ*, wherein only Targum Onkelos employed the D-stem, would seem to indicate either that the translator read something into the original text, or that he saw no difference in use between the two stems, or that D had become the stem regularly associated with this root in his dialect. One of the two last possibilities would seem more likely to be correct. It may be said, that more D-forms among our examples are what we may call the *šlḥ*/*zbḥ* type than the *ṯbr*/*qtl*, *i.e.* there is no neat way of attributing an intensive-plurative connotation to them. At times it seems that a semantic distinction possible in the Indo-European languages has been read back into Semitic, or at least that scholars have generalized concerning the D-stem on the basis of atypical rather than typical B/D pairs.

Far more consistent with the evidence is the observation made by a number of scholars, that the predominant function of the D-stem is that of transitivization, *i.e.* it is factitive when associated with a stative B-stem, *e.g.* 'be whole/make whole', and causative when associated with an intransitive or transitive B-stem, *e.g.* 'go/cause to go' or 'remember/remind' respectively, in the latter case being what is usually called 'doubly transitive'. This is a more meaningful categorization of the stem, from the standpoint of descriptive grammar. However, it orients the D-stem primarily toward those functions in which it is directly paralleled by and overlapping the Š-stem (including the denominative), and is inevitably accompanied by a non-analytical approach to those D-stems which have traditionally been described as 'intensive', those which manifest no other conceivable difference in meaning between B and D forms. Furthermore, it implies for the 'doubly transitive' or causative D-stems an importance which they do not truly have in the total scheme of the stem (except in Modern Arabic), as a result of the desire to depict this group and the factitives as parallel. Thus the stem is given a causative orientation which inevitably does violence to the requirements of historical and comparative grammar, insofar as origins are not considered, and the problem of assigning the same function to two stems (whether B and D or Š and D) is disregarded.

For it is clear that in the example *šālaḥ/šillaḥ/hišlīḥ* neither a plurative nor an intensive nor a causative function distinguishes the D-usage from that of B and Š. Moreover, our examples have amply demonstrated that the three stems were often used interchangeably in the original text and in the translations. The inference might well be drawn, that the D-stem had no distinctive identity, that it performed no function which could not be as well and as appropriately performed by one of the other two. The D-stem might seem to be a parasite, drawing its meanings from the provinces of other stems; the D-stem would be a semantic redundancy, maintaining its relationship with some roots purely by virtue of capricious, idiomatic usages. The increasing use of the B and Š stems which we noted in Arabic as opposed to the Aramaic translations, and in the Syriac as opposed to the Targumic translation, suggests an element of truth in such a view.

If this did happen, however, our knowledge of general linguistics assures us that it must be a secondary development and reflect an accretion of new functions to the D-stem, since it is improbable that two forms evolved that performed the same original function. Yet, to say this is not to say that two forms could not have come to be used in approximately the same way in colloquial speech, and that such use could not have enlarged the purview of a particular stem. In fact, that almost certainly did occur. The original confusion among the stems which arose from their approximately parallel usages must have served as the basis for a process of analogical extension, in this case employing false analogies which tended to break down even further the original distinctions among them. Finally at a later date usage would tend to avoid duplication of function; roots would tend to become associated with either B OR D in a dialect, and either D OR Š would become the standard means for expressing causation.

The Aramaic translations suggest that the breakdown of clearly definable functions for the stems of an individual language may have been an outgrowth of dialect variation. In many cases our examples show a root used in the D-stem in Targum Onkelos (usually paralleling the Hebrew original), while the Syriac translator used the same root in the B-stem. Even if one allows for the possibility that some Peshiṭṭa B-forms have been inaccurately transmitted and are actual D-forms, the frequent employment of the Syriac B-stem for the Hebrew/Targumic D-stem, in addition to indicating that the translator sensed no special semantic overtones in the geminated stem, suggests that he tended to associate root and stem according to the usage most natural to his own dialect. Some roots which, if one may judge from Targum Onkelos, were found primarily in the D-stem in the early stages of Aramaic as in Hebrew, seem to have fallen back into the D-stem in Syriac, probably because the two stems had in practice ceased to be sharply distinguished from one another. One can well imagine that a similar process had taken place within Hebrew and Arabic; that, particularly in the former, the variation among the stems of a specific root resulted from a collation of dialect practices, and a corresponding loss of clear identity for the individual stem.

Much the same thing may be said of the use of the Š-stem in Syriac, where Targum Onkelos like Hebrew has the D-stem. In this case, though, the dissimilarity of the consonantal structure of the two stems makes the case much less ambiguous. Apparently the line of demarcation between the two stems became blurred in practice, until at least in some cases it was possible to use them interchangeably. In any case, the tendency to use Š where Hebrew uses D (or vice-versa) is strongest in the Arabic version, less strong in the Peshiṭṭa, and least noticeable in Targum Onkelos. This may indicate, in the case of such roots as *rqʿ*, *sbʿ*, *sḥṭ*, either (1) increasing loss of awareness as to the meaning of the original forms, or (2) breakdown of the stem distinctions within an individual language, Aramaic or Arabic, as it came to maturity and developed dialect variations which were assimilated into the mainstream of the idiom.

Somewhat different in import is the connection which the translators often seem to feel between Stems II and III (*cf. šʾl*, *ʿll*, *mry*, *ḥbq*) or between the D-stem and the reduplicated stems (*cf. ptl*, *mry*, *gll*), for these evolved from the same impulse which produced the D-stem, and thus are akin to it in feeling and intent, unlike Stems I and IV, which have only an indirect relationship with Stem II in origin but have become intertwined with it in use.

The crux of the problem, insofar as it arises from Sibawaihi's statement concerning the common identity of Stems II and IV, lies in a definition of what constitutes the causative aspect of the D-stem. For, as we have seen, even the Targumic translator, who seems to have made a conscious effort to adhere to the stem-usage of Hebrew, makes a partial identification of the D-stem with causative overtones of Š, frequently using the former where Hebrew uses the latter. In the other translations use of the Š-stem is virtually on a par with use of D. Although this may assist in disestablishment of the claims for a plurative-intensive D-stem, it complicates our search for an alternative explanation. Faced again with the improbability that two stems evolved to fill the same semantic and syntactic purpose, we might say tentatively that the semantic difference between D and Š is embodied in the respective phrases 'cause to be' and 'cause to do', and the syntactic difference by the fact that D-forms are more likely to govern a single object, the Š-forms a double object. Thus the D-stem would not have been thought of as 'doubly transitive'. These distinctions can be seen in the Syriac and Arabic tranlations BH *ntn* (B), used here as 'give rule'. The Syriac Š-stem of *slṭ* means 'cause (someone) to rule (something)', the Arabic D-stem of *wly* 'make (someone) powerful'. In the former two direct objects are possible, in the latter the object of the power must be expressed by a prepositional phrase such as 'over (someone)'.

Such distinctions are paralleled to a degree in the denominatives associated with the two stems. A D-stem denominative, typically, will relate originally to the inducement of a personal state or action by means of associating oneself with the condition or object embodied in the relevant noun, *e.g.* 'act as a priest', 'feel jealousy' or 'feel warmth'. On the other hand, a typical Š-stem denominative will refer to the inducement of a state or action external to oneself, by associating the condition or object with another person or creature, *e.g.* 'cause jealousy (in someone)', 'make (someone) feel warmth', 'lay a saddle upon (some animal)'. Thus, in general D-stem denominatives are intransitive, taking an object only through the mediation of a prepositional phrase, while those of Š are transitive, taking and acting upon direct objects. Of course, there are also numerous denominatives of the B-stem in all the Semitic languages, most of which seem to be of the D-stem type, *i.e.* they concern the subject's performance of the action implicit in the relevant noun, *e.g.* Hebrew *ndr*, in the B-stem 'take an oath', translated by Targumic *qym*, in the D-stem 'make a covenant'. Whether this means that the B-stem denominatives are back-formations from the D-stem, or whether the two are parallel developments employing triliteral and quadriliteral structures respectively, is a moot point.

What is certain, is that the denominative aspects of the three stems became, almost inevitably, confused with one another, as in Hebrew *qšy* and *pl'*, used both in D and Š to mean 'have severe labour' and 'perform a wonder' respectively, or in Aramaic *shd*, used in Targum Onkelos in Š, in Syriac in D, but both meaning 'act as a witness, give witness to'. It is at least possible, even if one does not wish to distinguish between 'types' of denominatives, to suppose that the common exercise of a denominative function by the three stems was the means by which the three came to infringe upon one another's functions of other sorts. The D-stem thereupon became, on the one hand, indistinguishable from the causative Š-stem both in practice and in grammatical theory, and on the other, distinguished from the B-stem in grammatical theory alone, by the assertion of a plurative-intensive connotation, an assertion which became much tortured in its application to specific instances. In the face of such confusion, any attempt to categorize the D-stem as distinctive may seem to be presumptuous. However, since general linguistics assures us that the stem's very existence bears witness to its original uniqueness, such an attempt must be made.

On the basis of the material in this chapter, we may claim a factitive/denominative origin for the stem. Lest this in itself seem to be too obvious yet also too ambiguous, we define the stem thus:

The D-stem denotes and embodies the process by which one person (the subject) brings another person or some other entity (the object) into a state of being implicit in the nominal form (noun or adjective) to which the verbal form is related. The D-stem itself is not derivable from any other stem, nor dependent upon the existence of any other for its own existence; rather, like most elementary verbal forms, it is directly derivable from a nominal form, and constitutes one of the several alternate and coordinate stems of the Semitic verbal system. Finally, it is quadriliteral in structure; this structure is integral to its function and is to some extent an outcome thereof.

The gemination of the second radical, then, while it undoubtedly came to assume morphological significance, originated as one of several devices for extending a triconsonantal root to quadriconsonantal proportions. Other such devices are seen in such forms of relatively rare and specialized occurrence as Hebrew *paʿlel* and *pilpel*; Aramaic *qawtal* and *qaytel*; Arabic *iqtalla* (Stem IX) and the Arabic type represented by *ṭaḥṭaḥa* 'smash', associated with *ṭwḥ* 'perish'. The widespread use of the geminated middle radical as opposed to these other devices, may have come about from nothing more profound than its greater simplicity. In this regard we may note that, among the roots covered in this chapter, very few of those with a 'weak' middle radical were found in the D-stem, while Š-stems were common in such cases. The implication is, that one reason for the use of Š where one would expect D may have been the practical difficulty in speech of doubling a weak radical, so that as in the B-stem they tended to disappear or to be avoided. Human laziness in speech is widely recognized as an important factor in the historical development of any language.

We are now to lay before the reader two other bodies of material which have bearing upon the validity of our definition above. These are to be surveys of D-forms found in the Old Testament and the Qurʾan, including one example at least from each root which occurs the D-stem. The use of the stem in these two documents, each with its special problems, will be discussed. In a final chapter we will select relevant material from all chapters, for the validation of various hypotheses concerning the meaning and function of the D-stem.

V

THE D-STEM IN BIBLICAL HEBREW

The purpose of this chapter is to survey and comment upon the roots of Biblical Hebrew which occur in the D-stem, and to draw from them a general impression of the function(s) of that stem in Old Testament texts. An integral part of this survey has been classification of the existent D-forms, first into the two broad categories of Transformative and Non-transformative, then into five sub-classes based upon the relationship of the D-form to other existent forms of the root, both verbal and nominal. In outline, this classification is:

I. D-stems Transformative (Total 344).

A. Associated with B-stems Durative Stative, *e.g. šālēm* 'be whole'/*šillēm* 'make whole' (39).

B. Associated with B-stems Perfect Stative, *e.g. lāmaḏ* 'learn'/*limmēḏ* 'teach' (52).

C. Associated with B-stems Transitive, *e.g. qāḇar* 'bury'/*qibbēr* 'bury' (203).

II. D-Stems Non-transformative (Total 110).

A. Associated with Nominal Forms, *e.g. dāḇār* 'word'/*dibbēr* 'speak' (71).

B. Associated with B-stems Intransitive, *e.g. hālaḵ* 'walk'/*hillēḵ* 'walk' (39).

In the listing each root will be immediately followed by the citation of relevant data, and sometimes by an analytical statement. The data include (1) the meaning of the root's B-stem, if any, or the meaning of the B-stem of the same root in a cognate language, wherever relevant, (2) enumeration of the D-forms with their meaning(s), plus the citation of at least one textual reference, (3) mention of the Š-form, if any, along with its meaning, (4) citation of forms of the same root as it occurs in Arabic, where this serves to illuminate the situation in Hebrew, and (5) miscellaneous data from Biblical Hebrew or its cognate language wherever pertinent.

This classification itself, and many of our later comments on it, have been inspired principally by Götze's article, "The So-Called Intensive of the Semitic Languages,"[1] and by two articles of Rundgren, "Das althebräische Verbum: Abriss der Aspektlehre"[2] and "Das Verbalpräfix *yu-* im Semitischen und die Entstehung der factitiv-

[1] Götze, "The So-Called Intensive", 1-8.

[2] Rundgren, *Das Althebräische Verbum.*

kausativischen Bedeutung des D-Stammes."[3] Although their arguments, based principally upon Akkadian forms, cannot be perfectly applied to Biblical Hebrew, and though neither offers any completely satisfactory explanation of the place of forms in Groups II-A and II-B (usually referred to as denominatives and cursives, respectively) in the general scheme of the D-stem, nevertheless the three articles, taken together, are indispensable to an understanding of the (essentially) transformative nature of the stem in Biblical Hebrew.

Rundgren comments, "Im D-Stamm wird ein non-transformatives Semantem in ein transformatives verwandelt."[4] Taken by itself, this remark might seem to involve no more than updating of the terminology in such a traditional statement as that of O'Leary, namely, "... it commonly happens in all the Semitic languages that an intransitive verb becomes transitive when it is put in the intensive."[5] As such, it would concern only those D-forms in our Groups I-A and I-B (usually referred to as causatives). In his earlier article, however, Rundgren was more precise as to what he meant by transformative and non-transformative. A form such as Akk. *kašid* is described by him as a "possessive denominative" meaning 'he has *kšd*', *i.e.* 'he is a conqueror', expressing a situation analogous to that of *damiq* 'he has *dmq*, is good'. He sees this as neutralization of the transformative active value of *kašādum* 'he conquers'. The interpretation of *kašid* as a perfect stative 'he has conquered and thus possesses', which he imputes (apparently) to Götze, he regards as a later development of the possessive denominative by a back-formation, a development which gave the form an essentially active (or transitive) significance.

Parallel to this 'pure' possessive-conditional type is Hebrew *qāṭal-* (in its various combinations) 'have *qṭl*', which in itself has a neutral value and thus can assume various functions within the language in various contexts. With the personal prefixes and suffixes it assumes active temporal value and may take an object; with the particle *wᵉ* it can mean 'and has killed' when following another perfect or in a context of past action, or 'and will kill' when following an imperfect or in a context of future action. According to Rundgren, that which both *kašid* and *qāṭal* embody is verbal content extra terminos, in which only initium actionis is relevant; the content is neutral.

All verbs in their stative aspect are non-transformative sememes. Thus *paris*, for instance, cannot mean 'he decided', but can appear only as a condition, thus must be realized as a passive 'be decided'. The linguistic function of the verb is secondary, and may be regarded as "die Realisierung des ... neutralen Werts der Form in besonderem Sprechakten zu verstehen",[6] that is, as lexicon in its broadest sense. For us, this is helpful in understanding how a root *ʿzb* comes to be used in Arabic *ʿazaba* as

[3] F. Rundgren, "Das Verbalpräfix yu- im Semitischen und die Entstehung der factitiv-kausativischen Bedeutung der D-Stammes", in *Orientalia Suecana* 13 (1964), 99-114.
[4] Rundgren, "Das Verbalpräfix yu-", 109.
[5] L. de O'Leary, *Comparative Grammar of the Semitic Languages* (London, 1923).
[6] Rundgren, *Das althebräische Verbum*, 92.

a stative 'be distant, escape', but in Hebrew *'azab̲* as an active-causative 'relinquish'; or how Hebrew *mālē'* can mean both 'be full' and 'fill', *bākā* both 'weep' and 'beweep'. The meanings which we associate are a function of lexicon, the use which we make of various forms, as opposed to what we may scientifically view as their place in a schema of oppositions and aspects.

It is, of course, lexicon with which Götze is primarily (and rightfully) concerned in his article, toward which Rundgren takes a rather deprecatory and condescending attitude when he suggests that Götze's distinctions between durative, perfect and passive statives rests upon a confusion of Language with the words of a particular dialect/language, stating that "Der Akk. Stative stellt eine einheitliche Kategorie im System der Langue dar, und Begriffe wie 'durativ', 'perfektiv' und 'passiv' sind daher nicht relevant, da diese sich als sekundäre Realisationen der Kategorie in besonderen Semantemen und in besonderen Sprechakten ergeben."[7] These last are, however, Götze's principal concern. His distinction of three types of stative is not designed to provide abstract linguistic categories, or even to describe the origins of the forms in Proto-Semitic, but to show how the general concept 'stative' was varied in the practice of the Akkadian language, and how it corresponded to various types of D-stems.

To us, the three types of stative which Rundgren himself actually mentions, *i.e.* *damiq* 'is good', *kašid* 'is a conqueror (of), conquers' and *paris* 'is decided', seem very close to Götze's three categories (see page 18). It would perhaps be accurate to say that Götze describes three lexical entities within what Rundgren describes as one linguistic entity, the non-transformative sememe (stative). Moreover, Rundgren's description of this stative as a possessive-denominative, taken with the reference in his later article to the D-stem as factitive-causative, suggests that a reasonable interpretation of the D-stem would be 'make s.o. possessed of *dmq*' or 'cause s.o. to have *kšd*'. It seems to us that the two men are not so far apart at this point. The possession of verbal content extra terminos may be worked out semantically to denote the presence of a quality (durative), the completed performance of an action (perfective) or the state resultant from the action of another (passive); the associated D-stems may denote respectively the attribution of a quality to someone, the anterior stimulation of someone to activity, or the subjection of someone to the activity of another. All involve the transformation of some person or thing other than the subject.

Thus we are willing to say with Rundgren, that the D-stem serves a single transformative function *vis-à-vis* Götze's three categories of stative, and that these are indeed part of a larger linguistic unit, without being willing therefore to discard these categories as an accurate and useful scheme for sorting out the complexities of stative and D-stem alike, in Hebrew as well as in Akkadian. This accounts for our designation of this category of D-stem in Biblical Hebrew (over 75% of the total number) as Transformative, while its three sub-categories reflect the tripartite division of Götze (from which Rundgren himself did not escape).

[7] Rundgren, "Das Verbalpräfix yu-", 109.

Rundgren constantly reminds us that our thinking must not be confined by the meanings which were attributed to the forms of a language, which often are employed capriciously and are subject to distortion from their original function. He thus reassures us, when the two forms of the same root, such as the B- and D-stems, or the D- and Š-stems, do not form the neat pair or opposition which our familiarity with the general situation might lead us to expect. Moreover, he gives substance to what we have felt instinctively and have already suggested elsewhere, that the D-stem is not derived from any other verbal stem either consciously or unconsciously, therefore need not conform to any ironclad concept of its 'correct' relationship to some other stem; rather, the three basic alternate stems arose independently, then came to be associated in more or less regular ways, but also to overlap in their functions, through lexicalization and through a striving toward literary style. Götze gives us the means for discerning the nature of the associations which evolved, the means of introducing order into what is otherwise a scene of linguistic confusion. However, we need not be concerned if the actual forms associated with some stems behave unpredictably. The over-arching general pattern will become transparent to anyone who surveys with us the existent forms, given in the list which follows. At the conclusion of the individual sections of this list we shall pause to comment further on elements of Götze's categorization and Rundgren's linguistic analysis as they apply to Biblical Hebrew.

TABLE II

Part I. *D-Stems Transformative*

Section A. *Associated with B-stems Durative Stative*

'dm: 'be red, ruddy' (once, Lam. 4.7). D four times in pass. pple., twice as 'a tanned skin', *i.e.* 'that which has been made red' (Ex. 25.5), twice as 'reddened' (Nah. 2.4); once in reflexive as 'show o.s. red, be red' (Pr. 23.51). The Š-stem occurs once as 'be red', perhaps 'have redness' (Is. 1.18). As in the Indo-European languages, no clear line can be drawn between noun and adjective, or between adjective and stative verb, in reference to colors.

'ḥr: 'remain' (once, Gn. 32.5), *cf.* Syr. and MHb *'ḥr* 'be behind'. D fourteen times as 'hesitate, delay (to do)' (Gn. 34.19), used reflexively as 'make s.o. late', once as 'delay s.o.' (Gn. 24.56). Š once as 'hesitate' (II Sam. 20.5). D and Š might be construed as denominative in origin, from *'āḥar* 'behind, after', if one takes the prepositions as original nouns. The fact that the root is used predominantly in the D-stem (*cf.* Akk. *uḫḫuru* 'remain behind', Ar. *'aḫḫara* 'delay') supports this possibility.

'lm: no B, but *cf.* Ar. *'alima* 'be in pain', suggesting an original meaning 'be constricted'. D once as 'bind (into sheaves)' (Gn. 37.7).

'lṣ: no. B, but *cf.* Syr. *'lṣ* 'be narrow'. D once as 'press hard upon' (Jd. 16.16).

'mṣ: 'be firm, strong'. D nineteen times as 'strengthen' (Dt. 2.30). Š twice as 'feel strong' (Ps. 27.14).

b't: no B, but *cf.* Aram. *b'ēth* 'be timid'. D eleven times as 'terrify' (Job 18.11). Stem III of Ar. *baġata* shares meaning of the B, 'surprise'.

(Table II, continued)

bṣr: no B, but *cf.* Ar. *baẓira* 'be inaccessible, unspeakable'. D twice as 'make impregnable (a wall)' (Is. 22.10).

br': no B, but *cf.* Ar. *bari'a* 'be free, cleared'. D twice as 'make clear' (Jos. 17.15).

bśr: no B, but *cf.* Ar. *bašara/baššara* 'be happy/bring good news'. In the absence of a clear B-stem in other cognate languages, one may assume a similar development behind BH D-form 'bring good news' or 'announce', occurring twenty times (I K. 1.42).

gbr: 'be superior, prevail'. D three times as 'make superior' (Zec. 10.6), once in reflexive as 'show o.s. superior' (Is. 42.13). Š three times as 'prevail'. Ar. *jabbara* is used as a specialized 'set bones', but its reflexive means 'show one's own strength'.

glḥ: no B, *cf.* Ar. *jalaha* 'be bald'. D sixteen times as 'shave' (Nu. 6.9), three times in reflexive as 'have o.s. shaved' (Lv. 13.35).

grw: no B, *cf.* Ar. *jaru'a* 'be bold'. D three times as 'make bold, incite' (Pr. 15.18), seven times reflexive as 'strive' (Pr. 28.4). *Cf.* Ar. *jarra'a* 'embolden', *tajarra'a* 'dare'.

dmy: 'be like'. D thirteen times as 'liken, compare' (Ps. 50.21), once reflexive as 'liken o.s. to s.o.' (Is. 14.14). The usage here is estimative.

dšn: 'be fat(ty)'. D six times as 'make fat' (Ps. 23.5). D is also used as a denominative 'clear away the fat ashes' (Ex. 27.3), thus this is a conglomerate form.

zhm: no B, *cf.* Ar. *zahima* 'be foul, stink'. D once as 'think s.o. loathsome' (Job 33.20).

zky: 'be blameless, clean'. D three times as 'cleanse' (Ps. 73.13), once in reflexive as 'cleanse o.s.' (Is. 1.16). Š occurs in estimative meaning 'regard as blameless' (Mic. 6.11).

zny: 'be unfaithful, fornicate'. D once in passive as 'made unfaithful' (Ez. 16.34), used in an impersonal sense. Ar. *zaniya* has no D-form.

ḥbr: 'be united'. D ten times as 'join' (Ex. 26.6), three times reflexive 'join o.s. to' (Dan. 11.23), once in *ethpa''el* with same meaning (II C. 20.35).

ḥdy: 'be joyful, rejoice'. D once as 'make joyful' (Ps. 21.7).

ḥdt: no B, cf. Ar. *ḥaduṯa* 'be new'. D ten times as 'renew' (I Sam. 11.14), once reflexive as 'renew o.s.' (Ps. 103.5) – an Š reflexive in Arabic.

ḥzq: 'be strong'. D frequent as 'strengthen' (Ps. 147.13), in reflexive 'show o.s. strong' (II C. 13.21). Š has principal meaning 'seize', occurs occasionally as 'strengthen' (Dan. 11.1).

ḥyy: 'be alive, live'. D common as 'keep alive, give life to' (Gn. 12.12). Š occurs often with this meaning. While both stems occur in Arabic also, Š is the more common in that language.

ḥkm: 'be wise'. D five times as 'make wise' (Ps. 119.98), three times reflexive as 'show o.s. wise' (Ex. 1.10). Š once as 'make wise' (Ps. 19.8).

ḥly: 'be ill, weak'. D twenty times as 'make sick, weaken' (Dt. 29.21; Is. 14.10), twice reflexive as 'show o.s. weak' (II Sam. 13.2). Š four times with the same meaning (II C. 18.33).

(Table II, continued)

ḥmm: 'be warm'. D once in active as 'warm' (Job 39.14), once reflexive as 'warm o.s.' (Job 31.20). Ar. *ḥumma/ḥammama* is a precise counterpart.

ḥnn: 'be gracious, favorable'. D once as 'make s.th. gracious' (Pr. 26.25), frequent in reflexive as 'make o.s. gracious (to s.o.)' or 'make favor for o.s.' (Hos. 12.5).

ḥrb: 'be dry, dried up'. D twice in passive as 'dry up' (trans.) (Jd. 16.17), a meaning more often found in Š (II K. 19.24).

ḥrp: no B, *cf.* Ar. *ḫarifa* 'be feeble-minded'. D once as 'confuse' (Ps. 57.4).

ḥšq: 'be attached to'. D once as 'join together' (Ex. 38.28), twice in pass. pple, as 'joints', *i.e.* 'those joined together' (Ex. 27.17).

ḥtt: 'be shattered, frightened'. D once as 'frighten' (Job 7.14), Š occurring both as 'shatter' (Is. 9.3) and 'frighten' (Jer. 1.17).

ṭhr: 'be pure'. D common as 'cleanse, purify' (Lv. 13.13).

y'š: no B, *cf.* N 'despair of (min)', Ar. *ya'isa* 'give up hope (min)'. The original meaning seems to be 'be hopeless'. D once as 'make s.th. despair' (Ecc. 2.20), a meaning found in Arabic in the Š stem.

ybš: 'be dry'. D three times as 'dry up' (Nah. 1.4), found more commonly in Š (Ps. 38.6).

yg': 'be weary'. D twice as 'make weary' (Ecc. 10.15), a meaning also found twice in Š (Mal. 2.17); once as 'torture' (II Sam. 5.8).

yḥd: 'be united with, one with'. D once as 'unite' (Ps. 86.11).

yḥm: 'be hot, in heat'. D once as 'bring into heat' (Gn. 30.41), three times as 'be in heat, conceive' (Ps. 51.7). Both stems may be denominatives independently evolved, *cf.* Ar. *waḥam* 'desire'.

ypy: 'be beautiful'. D once as 'beautify' (Jer. 10.14). Ar. *wafiya/waffā* is similar, 'be perfect/perfect'.

yr': 'be afraid, fear'. D five times as 'frighten' (II Sam. 14.15).

yšn: 'be asleep'. D once as 'put to sleep' (Jud. 16.19).

yšr: 'be straight, smooth'. D nine times as 'straighten, smoothe' (Is. 40.3, Ps. 119.128), once as 'go straight' (Pr. 15.21), once in pass. pple. as 'that which is evenly applied, foil' (I K. 6.35).

kbd: 'be heavy, honored'. D common as 'honor' (Pr. 13.18). Š has this meaning twice (Is. 8.23), but normally means 'make heavy'. This illustrates the specialization of meaning in different stems. However D reflexive serves both as 'make o.s. heavy' and 'make o.s. honored' (Nah. 3.15, Pr. 12.9), probably an indication that both meanings were originally subsumed under the D-stem, and that the Š-form was a secondary development which could not be extended to a reflexive form, Hebrew having no regular stem for this purpose.

kby: 'be quenched, go out'. D nine times as 'quench (a light)' (II Sam. 14.17).

kly: 'be complete, finished'. D common as 'finish' (Gn. 18.33). For Ar. *kll* 'be tired', the corresponding meaning is found in Š.

(Table II, continued)

---

k'ś: 'be angry, discontent'. D twice as 'irritate, grieve' (Dt. 32.21), but the stem regularly associated with this meaning is Š (II K. 23.26).

lbš: 'be clothed'. D four times as 'make clothed' (I K. 22.10). Š also occurs frequently in this meaning (Gn. 3.21). Arabic uses D regularly.

ml': 'be full'. D common as 'fill, complete' (Ex. 35.25). However, B is sometimes employed as transitive 'fill' (Gn. 1.22), as with Ar. *ml'* when it has the vocalization *mala'a*. The latter form is far more common in Arabic than is the Š causative associated with the stative *mali'a*. Thus one Arabic stem serves basically the same function as two in Hebrew, this being made possible by the distinction in vocalization, not so highly developed as a morphological device in Hebrew. This is surely a major reason why Arabic often employs the B-form of a root where Hebrew must employ an alternate stem, and why the D-stem in Arabic comes to have a more widespread strictly causative meaning than in Hebrew.

mrr: 'be bitter'. D three times as 'make bitter' (Gn. 49.23), once serving an adverbial function in the phrase 'make bitter with (b^e) weeping'. The same meaning occurs a number of times in Š, while a reflexive 'embitter o.s.' occurs in the form *hiṭmarmar* (Dan. 8.7).

nbl: 'be stupid'. D four times as 'treat s.o. as foolish' (Dt. 32.15).

nkr: no B, *cf.* Akk. *nakāru* 'be a stranger', Ar. *nakara* 'not know'. D four times as 'make unknown' (Jer. 19.4) or 'misconstrue' (Dt. 32.27), in reflexive three times as 'show o.s. as a stranger' (I K. 14.5). Š occurs as 'inspect, recognize (strange things)', a type of estimative usage. The Arabic D and Š forms have similar uses, meaning 'disguise' and 'deny' respectively.

nqy: no B, *cf.* Ar. *naqiya* 'be clean'. D fifteen times as 'cleanse' (Joel 4.21), as with Ar. *naqqā*.

skl: no B. *cf.* Ar. *šakula* 'be confused, vague'. D twice as 'make foolish, confused' (II Sam. 15.31), Š twice as 'behave foolishly' (Gn. 31.28), possibly a denominative connected with *sekel* 'folly'.

slp: no B, *cf.* Ar. *salafa* 'be over, past'. D seven times as 'bring to an end, pervert, overthrow' (Job. 12.19).

'bṭ: no. B, *cf.* Ar. *'abiṭ* 'silly', suggesting a root meaning 'be vague, ambiguous'. D once as 'change, make haphazard (one's paths)' (Joel 2.7).

'wd: no B, but cognate Syr. and Ar. D-stems 'accustom' suggest a root meaning 'be fixed, sure, accustomed'. D once as 'capture' (Ps. 119.61); Š frequent as 'repeat, admonish, make customary' (Gn. 43.3), also as a denominative 'bear witness'.

'wy: 'do wrong'. D here seems to reflect an independent evolution, occurring twice as 'make crooked' (Lam. 3.9), *cf.* Ar. *'awiya* 'be bent'. Š appears both as causative 'pervert' (Job 33.27), *cf.* Ar. *'awwaya* 'mislead', and as denominative 'do wrong' (II Sam. 7.14).

'wt: no B, but the root is apparently a dialect variant of the preceding. In this case D carries the meaning 'mislead', occurring eight times (Ecc. 7.13). However, the passive occurs once as 'made crooked' (Ecc. 1.15), the reflexive once as 'bend o.s.' (Ecc. 12.3).

'wr: no B, *cf.* Ar. *'awira/'awwara* 'be blind/blind s.o.' D five times as 'make blind' (Ex. 23.8).

'zz: 'be strong'. D once as 'strengthen' (Pr. 8.28). Š twice as 'show (one's face) as strong' (Pr. 7.13). Arabic likewise uses both stems as 'strengthen'.

(Table II, continued)

ʿlp: no B, *cf.* Aram. *ʿlp* 'be obscure, faint', and BH N-stem 'become faint'. D in passive only, once as 'be made obscure, covered' (SS 5.14), three times as 'made faint, faint away' (Is. 51.20), *cf.* Ar. *ğallafa* 'cover'. Reflexive once as 'cover o.s.' (Gn. 38.14), twice as 'faint' (Am. 8.13).

ʿnw: 'be afflicted, downcast'. D frequent as 'afflict, humble' (Dt. 22.24), once in reflexive as 'humble o.s.' (Gn. 16.9). Š occurs once with this meaning (Is. 25.5). Ar. *ʿaniya/ʿannā* 'be worried/torment' is parallel.

ʿpl: no B, *cf.* Ar. *ğafala* 'be negligent, heedless'. D once in passive as 'made careless' (Hab. 2.4). Š once as denominative 'show carelessness in' (Nu. 14.44).

ʿry: no B, *cf.* Ar. *ʿariya* 'be naked, free'. D eight times as 'uncover' (Is. 3.17) or 'empty' (Gn. 24.20), once in reflexive as 'make o.s. naked' (Lam. 4.21). Š three times as 'uncover, empty' (Is. 53.12).

ʿšr: 'be rich'. D once in reflexive 'think o.s. rich, pretend to be rich' (Pr. 13.7). Š occurs as 'make rich' taking the factitive function.

ʿtd: no B, *cf.* Ar. *ʿatuda* 'be ready'. D once as 'make ready, prepare' (Pr. 24.27), once reflexive 'be made ready, destined' (Job 15.28). In Arabic, Š takes the factitive function.

pšḫ: no B, *cf.* Akk. *pašaḫu* 'become quiet', *upaššaḫu* 'let lie fallow'. This is clearly paralleled in the one D form 'make fallow' (Lam. 3.11).

pty: 'be foolish'. D frequent as 'make foolish, deceive' (Jd. 14.15).

ṣdq: 'be righteous'. D five times as 'justify, think righteous' (Ez. 16.51), a meaning found equally often in Š.

qdš: 'be holy'. D common as 'sanctify' (Lv. 20.21), in reflexive 'show o.s. to be holy' (Ez. 38.23). Š occurs in a related, estimative meaning 'treat as holy' (Ex. 28.38). The equivalent Arabic D-form *qaddasa* incorporates both factitive and estimative functions.

qll: 'be light'. D frequent as 'make light (of), curse' (Lv. 20.9). Š also occurs as 'make light', in the literal rather than the figurative sense (Jon. 1.5), but also can occur as 'treat with contempt, regard as little' (II Sam. 19.44).

qṣr: 'be small, short'. D once as 'shorten' (Ps. 102.24), a meaning found once in Š (Ps. 89.46). Arabic *qaṣura/qaṣṣara* is parallel.

qrb: 'be near'. D eight times as 'bring near' (Is. 41.21), a meaning more often found in Š (including the specialized meaning 'bring an offering') (Ex. 28.1). Arabic *qrb* regularly employs D for 'bring near'.

qšy: 'be hard, severe'. D once as 'find s.th. hard' *i.e.* 'have hard (labour)' (Gn. 35.16). In the next verse the same meaning occurs in the Š-stem, a clear case of an author's effort for variety. Š occurs elsewhere as 'make difficult' (Dt. 2.30) and also in a reflexive sense as 'make o.s. difficult, be stubborn' (Dt. 10.16). Arabic *qasā* 'be harsh' uses both D and Š for 'harden'.

rby: 'be much, numerous, many'. D four times as 'make numerous' (Jd. 9.29) and 'make great, bring up (children)' (Lam. 2.22). Š is far more common in the meaning 'make much, many'. Arabic *rbw* 'grow, increase' uses D as 'bring up', Š as 'increase s.th.', paralleling Hebrew.

rwḥ: 'be large', used figuratively as 'feel relief'. D once in pass. pple. as 'made large, spacious' (Jer. 22.14). The Š-form 'smell' is unrelated.

(Table II, continued)

rḥq: 'be far'. D four times as 'make far-off, send away' (Is. 6.12), also found more commonly in Š.

rkk: 'be soft, timid'. D once in pass. pple. as 'made soft' (Is. 1.6), Š occurring once as 'make timid' (Job 23.16). Specialization may be present.

rṣy: 'be pleased with, favorable to'. D once as 'seek to make favorable' (Job 20.10), once in reflexive as 'make o.s. pleased with, reconcile o.s. to' (I Sam. 29.4).

ršš: no B, *cf.* Ar. *raṯṯā* 'be ragged, torn', Akk. *rašāšu* 'be smelted'. D once as ***pôlel*** 'shatter' (Jer. 5.17), once in passive 'be shattered' (Mal. 1.4).

śbʿ: 'be satisfied'. D twice as 'satisfy' (Is. 7.10), a meaning more commonly expressed in Š (Is. 58.10). Arabic regularly employs D for 'satisfy'.

śgb: 'be high, inaccessible'. D seven times as 'make high, protect' (Ps. 20.2).

śkl: no B, *cf.* Ar. *šakala/šakkala* 'be ambiguous/diversify'. D once as 'confuse, exchange' (Gn. 48.14).

śmḥ: 'be joyful'. D frequent as 'make joyful' (Dt. 24.5), Š occurring once with this meaning (Ps. 89.43).

šgʿ: no B, *cf.* Ar. *šaju'a* 'be bold', Akk. *šēgū* 'be furious'. D five times in pass. pple. as 'be infuriated, maddened' (I Sam. 21.16), twice in reflexive as 'show o.s. mad' (I Sam. 21.16).

škl: 'be bereaved (of a child)'. D frequent as 'bereave (a woman of her children)' (Gn. 42.36). Arabic *ṯkl* employs Š for this meaning.

škr: 'be drunken'. D four times as 'intoxicate' (Jer. 51.7), Š three times with the same meaning. (Jer. 48.26).

šlm: 'be whole, complete'. D common as 'make whole, fulfill' (Jd. 1.7). Š has a similar but specialized meaning 'perform' (Is. 44.26), and also a denominative meaning 'make peace' (Jos. 10.1). Ar. *sallama* 'keep intact' shows a similar meaning.

šny: 'be different, change'. D nine times as 'change, pervert' (Jer. 2.36), once in reflexive as 'disguise o.s.' (I K. 14.2).

špr: no B, *cf.* Syr. *špr*, 'be beautiful', Ar. *safara* 'shine'. D once as 'polish, make beautiful' (Job 26.13).

tqn: 'be straight'. D twice as 'make straight' (Ecc. 12.9). Ar. *tqn* has Š as 'make perfect'.

Section B: *Associated with B-stems Perfect Stative*

'bd: 'perish'. D frequent as 'destroy' (Nu. 33.52), once as 'let s.th. go as lost, think of s.th. as having perished' (Ecc. 3.6). Š also occurs as 'destroy', but less often.

'lp: 'learn'. D three times as 'teach' (Job 15.5), paralleled by Ar. *'alifa/'allafa* 'be familiar with, accustom s.o. to s.th.'

'ny: no B, *cf.* Ar. *'anā* 'mature, come near (the time of s.th.)'. D once as 'cause to occur' (Ex. 21.13), twice in passive as 'caused to occur, befall' (Pr. 12.21), once in reflexive as 'bring o.s. to an event, seek a quarrel against s.o.' (II K. 5.7). Ar. has D as reflexive 'be patient'.

(Table II, continued)

'šr: 'walk (ahead)'. D six times as 'lead (aright)', *i.e.* 'cause to walk straight' (Is. 1.17), *cf.* Ar. *'aṯṯara* 'influence, induce'.

bly: 'wear out'. D five times as 'wear out (trans.)', used figuratively as 'enjoy' (Is. 65.22) and 'oppress' (I C. 17.9). Ar. *baliya* 'be worn out' has its causative in Š.

bl': no B, *cf.* Ar. *balaġa* 'have an effect on s.o., go far in s.th.' D twice as 'confuse, confound', *i.e.* 'make to go far' (Is. 3.12), *cf.* Ar. Stem III 'overdo, exaggerate'; once reflexive as 'be confused' (Ps. 107.27). This D form may also be a denominative from *bela'* 'confusion'.

b'r: 'burn, blaze up'. D frequent as 'kindle, burn up' (Ex. 35.3), also found several times in Š (Jd. 15.15).

g's: 'shake, tremble'. D four times in reflexive as 'cause o.s. to shake', the *hithpôlel* also occurring twice with this meaning (Jer. 25.16).

dbq: 'adhere, cleave'. D twice in passive as 'made to cleave, joined' (Job 38.38). This meaning is more often expressed in Š, active and passive. The D form of Arabic *dbq* is not a factitive but a denominative of *dibqun* 'birdlime'.

dbr: no B, *cf.* Ar. *dabara* 'turn one's back, pass'. D twice as 'cause to turn way' (SS 5.6), once as 'destroy' (II C. 22.10), *cf.* Ar. *dabbara* 'direct'. Š twice as 'cause to turn back'.

ḥlp: 'pass on'. D three times as 'change, alter' (Gn. 41.14), this meaning being found more often in Š (Is. 9.9).

ḥsr: 'lack, diminish'. D twice as 'made to lack' (Ecc. 4.8). Š once with the same meaning (Is. 32.6).

ḥqh: no B, *cf.* MHb 'imitate'. D twice in passive as 'carved', *i.e.* 'made to imitate, represent' (I K. 6.35).

ṭb': 'sink down'. D once in passive as 'be sunk' (Ex. 15.4). Š three times as 'cause to sink' (Pr. 8.25).

ṭpḥ: no B, *cf.* MHb 'extend, stretch out', Ar. *ṭafaḥa* 'run over'. D once as 'spread out (the heavens)' (Is. 48.13).

ygy: no B, *cf.* Ar. *wajiya* 'feel pain'. D once as 'grieve s.o., cause s.o. to feel pain' (Lam. 3.33), a meaning more common in Š (Is. 51.23).

yd': 'know'. D once as 'make s.o. know' (Job 38.12), twice reflexive as 'make o.s. known' (Gn. 45.1). Š frequent, both as 'make s.o. know s.th.' (Gn. 41.39) and 'make s.th. known' (Ex. 18.6). This is a case of the D-stem's serving as alternate to Š, its reflexive serving for Š also.

yld: 'bear, bring forth (a child)'. D nine times in pres. pple. 'midwife', *i.e.* 'one who helps bring forth' (Ex. 1.15), while Š occurs as 'engender'. D may have evolved here solely as alternative usage for a specialized meaning. However, if this is so, the fact that Arabic makes a similar distinction in some cases suggests a common origin of the usage.

yšb: 'sit'. D once as 'set' (Ez. 25.4), normally expressed in Š (II C. 23.20).

lmd: 'learn'. D common as 'teach' (Ecc. 12.9).

mgr: no B, *cf.* Syr. mgr 'fall'. D once as 'hurl (to the ground)' (Ps. 89.45). Biblical Aramaic has D once as 'overthrow' (Ezra 6.12).

(Table II, continued)

mlṭ: no B, *cf.* N-stem 'save o.s., escape'. D common as 'rescue, let escape' (II Sam. 19.6; II K. 10.24), in reflexive once as 'leap forth', *i.e.* 'let o.s. escape' (Job 41.11). Š occurs as 'deliver (a child)' (Is. 31.5).

nbt: no B, *cf.* Aram. *nbt* 'rise'. D once as 'make (the eyes) rise', *i.e.* 'look at' (Is. 5.30), the meaning of the frequent Š-form. In this case D is a stylistic variant of Š.

nhl: no B, *cf.* Ar. *nahila* 'drink', BH *nahlal* 'watering place'. D eight times as 'lead, take care of' (Ex. 15.13), *i.e.* 'make drink, lead to drink', associated originally with the image of the herder, then generalized. In three occurrences (Ps. 23.2; Is. 40.11; Is. 49.10) the original image is retained; elsewhere the context is that of drink.

nḥl: 'inherit, get possession of'. D four times as 'give possession of s.th.' (Nu. 34.29), seven times reflexive as 'take possession of' (Nu. 33.54). The meaning 'give possession' is more common in Š. Arabic *naḥala* 'give as a donation' shows Hebrew D meaning associated with B.

nḥt: 'go down'. D three times as 'press down, settle' (II Sam. 22.35), a meaning also found once in Š (Joel 4.11).

nšy: 'forget'. D once as 'make s.o. forget' (Gn. 41.51), the same meaning occurring twice in Š (Job 39.17) as in Arabic *'ansā*.

sbb: 'turn about, encompass'. D once as 'make turn', *i.e.* 'change (the course of events)' (II Sam. 14.20). This seems to be a stylistic variant of the more common Š-form, possibly because this context calls for a figurative use.

s'r: 'move violently'. D twice as 'cause to move violently', *i.e.* 'scatter' (Zec. 7.14), once in *pôlel* with the same meaning.

sbl: 'bear'. D once in pass. pple. as 'caused to bear, pregnant' (Ps. 144.4).

'bd: 'work'. D twice in passive as 'caused to work, enslaved' (Dt. 21.3). The second of these meanings might also be construed as a denominative 'made a slave' (Is. 14.3). The causative is normally expressed in Š, but Arabic expresses 'subjugate' in D.

'br: 'pass by, over, beyond'. D once as 'cause (a chain) to pass over' (I K. 6.21), once as 'cause s.o. to pass beyond, excite s.o. sexually' (Job 21.10), eight times in reflexive as 'cause o.s. to pass beyond (the limits of rationality)' (Ps. 78.21). Š is common, used literally, as opposed to the figurative uses of D.

'dr: no B, *cf.* Ar. *ğadira* 'deceive', BH N-stem 'be missed', suggesting a root meaning 'fail, be lacking'. D once as 'make fail' (I K. 5.7).

'nn: no B, *cf.* Ar. *'anna* 'take shape'. D once as 'cause to take shape, make appear' (Gn. 9.14), ten times in *pôlel* as 'cause to take shape' (Lv. 19.26) with specific reference to the spirits of the dead, or as a denominative 'raise a cloud', *i.e.* 'raise a ghost'. The regular D-form may be employed to avoid confusion with the specialized meaning of the *pôlel*.

plṭ: 'escape'. D frequent as 'deliver, save' (Ps. 18.49), Š twice with the same meaning (Mic. 6.14).

pny: 'turn, avert'. D eight times as 'cause to turn away, clear out' (Zep. 3.15), roughly the same concept being expressed in Š (Jer. 48.39), *cf.* Ar. *fanā/'afnā* 'be consumed/wear out'.

ṣhl: 'cry aloud, whinny'. D once as 'make cry out' (Is. 10.30).

(Table II, continued)

ṣḥq: 'laugh'. D six times as 'make s.o. laugh, jest with s.o.' (Gn. 21.9). The corresponding meaning in Arabic is expressed by Š.

ṣʿy: 'stoop, incline'. D once as 'make to incline, tilt' (Jer. 48.12).

qwm: 'arise, persist, be valid'. D eleven times as 'establish, confirm' (Is. 13.6), five times as *pôlel* 'raise up' (Is. 44.6). Š far more common, with both D meanings. D reflexive four times as 'rebel', *i.e.* 'raise o.s. up against s.o.' (Ex. 40.17).

qṭr: no B, *cf.* Akk. *qatāru* 'rise, go up (odor or smoke)', in D 'cause to go up'. D frequent as 'cause (a sacrifice) to go up (in smoke)' (II K. 17.11). Š is also frequent with the same meaning (Ex. 29.18). A possibly intentional distinction between the two stems is that D is used principally in reference to sacrifice to a foreign god, Š in reference to the worship of Jahweh. If intentional, this is an interesting specialization.

qrr: no B, *cf.* Ar. *qarra* 'settle down'. D once as 'make come down, destroy (city walls)' (Is. 22.5).

rwy: 'drink deeply'. D four times as 'drench, saturate' (Pr. 5.19), indicating that the B-stem meaning is probably a secondary development from an original 'be wet, watered'. Š also occurs as 'drench' (Is. 55.10). Ar. *rawwā* has the literal meaning 'cause to drink'.

rpd: 'spread out'. D twice as 'spread out (trans.)' (SS 2.5).

rpy: 'sink down, decline'. D four times as 'weaken, let droop' (Job 12.21), once as reflexive 'let o.s. sink, become idle' (Jos. 18.3). Š is frequent as 'abandon' (Jos. 1.5).

rtḥ: no B, *cf.* MHb 'boil (intr.)' D twice as 'boil (trans.)' (Is. 24.5). Š also occurs with this meaning (Job. 41.23).

śḥq: 'laugh, play'. D frequent as 'make laugh' (Jer. 15.17), also in a denominative sense as 'make sport, be glad' (Jer. 30.19).

škn: 'dwell, settle down'. D seven times as 'make dwell' (Nu. 14.30). Š has the same meaning six times (Gn. 3.34), *cf.* Ar. *'askana*.

šmʿ: 'hear'. D twice as 'cause to hear, assemble' (I Sam. 15.4), a figurative use, as opposed to the literal Š-form. Ar. *sammaʿa* is also literal

šśʿ: 'separate'. D three times as 'separate (trans.)' (Lv. 1.17).

šś': B, *cf.* Eth. *ss'* 'walk along'. D once as 'lead, make walk' (Ez. 39.2).

t'r: 'turn, incline (a border-line) (intr.)' D once as 'outline (a shape)', *i.e.* 'cause (a line) to turn' (Is. 44.13), once in passive as 'caused to incline' (Jos. 19.13).

Groups I-A and I-B are best commented upon jointly, since they have a number of features in common, and since in fact it is often difficult to distinguish them. They have traditionally, however, been described as intransitives (I-A) and transitives (I-B), the basis for this classification being the rudimentary principle that transitive verbs may take a direct object. These are also the two categories, the D-stems of which have usually been described as 'causative', the transferral into the D-stem presumably having turned the intransitives into transitive-factitives (e.g. *yāšar* 'be straight'/*yaššara* 'straighten'), and the transitives into double transitive-causatives (*e.g. lāmad* 'learn'/*limmēd* 'teach'). Finally, these are the categories of which Götze remarked, "The causative-factitive force of the form is customarily said to be an outgrowth of the intensive force. But nobody has ever been able to demonstrate in a satisfactory manner how this development should have been possible."[8]

Götze has pointed to only one of the problems inherent in this classification. The principal problem is, that the intransitive-transitive distinction will not stand up under scrutiny. In the first place, such concepts as 'learn' and 'inherit', while they 'take an object' in the Indo-European languages, are not construed as transitive verbs of the order of 'smash' or 'build', rather as intransitive verbs which define the relationship of one person *vis-à-vis* another person or some object. As such they point to the state or condition of the person, as 'be aware of' or 'become possessor of' (*cf.* Rundgren's definition of *kašid* as 'be conqueror of'). Some action at a specified time may be involved, but the main reference is to the condition resulting from that action. The same situation obtains in the Semitic languages. The principal difference between these verbs (I-B) and those of I-A, is that the latter refer to some general condition or quality of a person ('is healthy, pretty, foolish'), which while it partially defines his relationship to other persons cannot be construed as the outcome of a particular action on his part. They are general states of mankind.

In the second place, such concepts as 'wear out', 'perish', 'sit' and 'pass on' are also found in I-B. These verbs do not take an object, therefore are not classifiable as 'transitive' even in the most rudimentary definition of that term. These verbs, it can easily be seen, likewise denote a state or condition of the subject, in this case resulting not from the subject's relationship to an object or person, but from some process he has undergone or movement he has made. It is clear that they could be verbalized as 'be worn out', 'be extinct', 'be seated' and 'be past', yet they have more in common with such a concept as 'learn' than with one such as 'be whole', as they imply the conclusion of an activity which had some beginning, and not merely an indeterminate general condition. At the same time they are distinguished from so-called 'cursives' (Group II-B), which generally describe an action or event in process, without reference to its initiation or termination.

The verbs of I-A are differentiated from the others by more than their indeterminate nature, which has led them to be called 'neuter' verbs. These are the forms parallel to the Akkadian permansive type of which Götze writes, "Forms like Akkadian šalim ... are obviously of nominal origin; they are nothing else but the predicative form of adjectives, the status absolutus of šalmum, ... etc.".[8] The line between a stative verb 'be heavy' and an adjectival phrase consisting of an implicit copulative plus adjective 'heavy' and a possessive denominative 'have weight' is at best blurred,

[8] Götze, "The So-Called Intensive", 3.

even in Indo-European languages, and distinctions are more a matter of opinion than analysis. It is probably not without significance in this regard, that in Biblical Hebrew a number of the roots which have an associated adjective (*e.g. ḥdš, skl, ʿwr*) have no B-stem though a D-form does exist. This is typical Hebrew economy of vocabulary (as opposed to Arabic generosity, which permits both nominal and verbal forms in these cases), and implies an identity of function. No comparable situation exists for the verbs of I-B, unless we would describe *lamid* as a possessive denominative or a nominal sentence, as Rundgren suggests.

What the three types of verb have in common, however, is that in their B-stem the roots are employed in non-transformative sememes, *i.e.* they denote conditions rather than actions. In the corresponding D-stems the roots are used in transformative sememes, *i.e.* one person puts another into the condition expressed in the B-stem. Thus in B the first person (A) is the subject of a state or completed activity, while in D (A) becomes the auxiliary by whom a second person (B) becomes the subject of the same state or completed activity, even while he himself is the object of (A)'s initiating action. In other words, the force of the verb shifts from the subject of the sentence to its object. This distinction will be important for us when we review Group I-C. It may also be noted here, that in the context of Hebrew it is possible for the D-stem to refer not only to an actual transformation of the object, but also to a hypothetical transformation, as 'call s.o. good' or 'think s.o. foolish' (usually referred to as 'declarative' and 'estimative' usages, respectively). These occur almost exclusively, as might be expected, with the verbs of Group I-A.

A final question connected with these two groups arises from the existence within them of a sizable number of Š-forms with meanings either identical with or similar to those of the D-forms of the same root. Approximately a third of the roots in I-A and half of those in I-B have such Š-forms serving a transformative function. One would 'normally' expect the D and Š forms to mean 'cause s.o. to be in a condition' and 'cause s.o. to perform an action' respectively. This distinction will be seen in Group I-C, where the D-stem will have a meaning parallel to that of B, while the Š-stem will stand in a causative relationship to B. This 'normal' situation is reflected in one striking example from Group I-B, the root *yld*. The D-stem occurs in the active participle as 'midwife', *i.e.* 'one who assists s.o. to have borne', while the meaning of the Š-forms is 'engender', *i.e.* 'cause s.o. to bear', used of the progenitor. The former refers to a completed action, the latter to the institution of an activity. For the most part, however, the existence of the two forms has no such rationale, particularly in the verbs of I-B. One may note, however, that the majority of the Š-forms referred to in this group are connected with verbs of motion, such as 'pass on' (*ḥlp*), 'pass beyond' (*ʿbr*) and 'turn' (*sbb*). It may well be that the Š-form in such cases referred originally to initium actionis and the D-stem to terminus actionis, such a distinction being lost in practice.

Another distinction between the two stems, particularly prominent in Group I-A, is that although the general meaning may be the same, the semantic function may be different for each. Thus the D-forms in a number of cases will have a figurative use, as opposed to a literal use of the Š-form, *e.g. qll* (D 'make light of', Š 'lighten'); *kbd* (D 'honor', Š 'make heavy' in most occurrences); and from I-B *šmʿ* (D 'assemble', Š 'cause to hear'). In several cases, particularly where the D-stem is common in a factitive meaning, Š will serve an estimative function, *e.g. qdš* (D 'sanctify', Š 'treat as holy'); *zky* (D 'purify', Š 'regard as blameless'). Other types of specialization also occur, as noted under the roots involved. In all, some kind of specialization characterizes fifteen of the thirty cases in I-A where both stems occur, and one must assume that an Š-form was occasionally used in the normal function of D when this served to clarify the lexicon, since it must have been felt that there was some common ground between the two stems (see the later discussion under Group II-A). Perhaps more noteworthy than this (relatively) small area of overlap between the two stems is the general strictness with which their originally distinctive functions have been retained, as opposed to the considerable breakdown of function noted in Syriac and Arabic in Chapter IV. The function of Š in relation to D will be further discussed later in this chapter as well.

Section C: *Associated with B-stems Transitive*

'hb: 'love'. D sixteen times in pres. pple. as 'lover, friend', *i.e.* 'one who make s.o. loved' or 'one who gives love to s.o.' (Hos. 2.9). In the case of Arabic *habba* D is used as a causative.

'zn: no B, *cf.* Ar. *wazana* 'weigh'. D once as 'weigh' (Ecc. 12.9), used figuratively of 'weigh (proverbs)'. This stem may also be a denominative, as 'give weight (to proverbs)', used figuratively.

'zr: 'gird, enclose'. D six times as 'gird' (Is. 45.5), twice in reflexive as 'gird o.s.' (Is. 8.9). Despite the similar meaning, B is used in reference to girding oneself, D in reference to girding another (except in the reflexive). Arabic *'azara/'azzara* 'surround/cover, wrap up' suggests that the two stems may originally have been separate in meaning in Hebrew, then have taken on specialized aspects of the same meaning. In any case, for such a root as this the distinction between 'do s.th.' and 'have s.th. done' has practical significance.

'ḥz: 'cover', used of Solomon. D once as 'cover', used of Jahweh (Job 26.9).

'kl: 'eat, consume'. D four times in passive as 'be eaten, consumed', a figurative use for 'be destroyed' (Ex. 3.2). Ar. *'akkala* is causative.

'sp: 'gather'. D eight times as 'bring in', used primarily in the sense of giving aid or comfort to another person, bringing him from need into fulfillment (Jd. 19.15, Is. 52.12).

'sr: 'bind'. D once in passive as 'be bound' (Is. 22.3).

'rr: 'curse'. D once as 'curse' (Gn. 5.29), four times as 'make accursed' (Nu. 5.18), as though associated with a stative B-stem.

bhl: no B, *cf.* MHb *bahûl* 'precipitated' and Bib. Aram. *bhl*, with a B reflexive 'hurry', *i.e.* 'move o.s. quickly'. The BH N-stem 'be dismayed' and D 'dismay', occurring seven times (Ps. 2.5), represent an indigenous development of a related meaning. D occurs three times as 'hasten' (Ecc. 5.1), referring back to the original B 'hurry s.th. along', as does the one D passive 'be hurried' (Est. 8.14). The N-stem is mediopassive, referring to one's being moved quickly; D is the vehicle for the root concept here.

bzz: 'plunder'. D once in passive as 'be plundered' (Jer. 50.37).

bhn: 'test, investigate'. D twice in passive as 'be tested' (Is. 28.16).

bky: 'weep, beweep'. D twice as 'make s.o. wept for, beweep' (Ez. 8.14). By contrast, Arabic *bakkā* means 'cause to weep'.

bl': 'swallow'. D thirteen times as 'make swallowed up, engulf, destroy' (Is. 49.19), the figurative use being concentrated in this stem. The Arabic D-form is again used as a causative.

blq: 'lay waste, ruin'. D once in passive as 'be laid waste' (Nah. 2. 11).

bṣ': 'cut off'. D seven times, both as 'cut off' (Ez. 38.12) and as the figurative 'finish, fulfill' (Lam. 2.17).

bqr: no B, *cf.* MHb 'scrutinize', Ar. *baqara* 'split open'. D eight times as 'attend to, bestow care on' (Ez. 34.12). The stem might also be construed as a denominative associated with *baqqarah* 'care'.

bqš: no B, *cf.* MHb 'seek'. D extremely common as 'seek for, search' (Gn. 31.7). In such a case one could well assume that the meaning was first associated with D, and that the MHb B-stem is a secondary form.

brr: 'purge'. D once as 'purify' (Dan. 11.35), a meaning which also occurs in Š (Jer. 4.41). *Cf.* Ar. *barrara* 'exonerate, justify'.

bšl: 'boil' (once: Ez. 24.5). D twenty times as 'boil' (I K. 19.21), and seems to be the original stem. Š once as 'make ripe', associated with the other B-stem meaning 'grow ripe'. Apparently both 'boil' and 'ripen' evolved from some original concept such as 'be edible, palatable'.

btq: no B, *cf.* Akk. *batāqu* 'cut off'. D once as 'slaughter' (Ez. 16.40).

btr: 'cut apart' (once: Gn. 15.10), *cf.* Ar. *batara* 'cut off'. D once, in the same verse. One of the two stems was probably used for variety.

g'l: no B, but this seems to be a dialect variant of *g'l* 'loathe, abhor', since the N-stem of both is 'be loathesome, polluted'. D four times as 'pollute' (Ezra 2.62), twice in reflexive as 'pollute o.s.' (Dan. 1.8). As frequently happens, D seems more closely related to N than to B.

gd': 'cut off, break'. D nine times as 'break' (Ps. 107.16).

gdp: no B, *cf.* Ar. *qadafa* 'hurl, slander', the latter a figurative use. D five times as 'revile' (II K. 19.6), *cf.* Ar. *jaddafa*, which has the same meaning.

gly: 'uncover, reveal'. D frequent in this meaning (Jer. 49.10), often referring to the disclosure of something other than a physical object, *e.g.* in the sense of 'laying open' or 'betraying'. Ar. *jalā* is alike in B and D.

gm': no B, *cf.* Aram. *gm'* 'swallow'. D once as 'swallow up (the ground)' (Job 39.24). The Š-form means 'cause to drink'.

gnb: 'steal'. D five times as 'steal' (II Sam. 15.6), twice reflexive as 'steal o.s. (away)' (II Sam. 19.4).

grd: no B, *cf.* Ar. *jarada*/*jarrada*, both 'peel, scrape off'. D once as reflexive 'make o.s. scraped clean' (Job 2.8).

gr': 'deduct, diminish s.th.'. D once as 'draw up (the waters)' (Job 36.27), *i.e.* 'make the waters diminished (by evaporation)'.

grš: 'drive out'. D frequent in this meaning (Ex. 2.17).

gšš: no B, *cf.* Ar. *jassa* 'touch, handle'. D once as 'touch' (Is. 59.10).

dḥy: 'push'. D once in passive as 'be pushed (down)' (Ps. 36.13).

dk': no B, *cf.* BH *dwk* 'crush'; Ar. *dakka* 'beat down' and *dakkaka* 'mix'. D frequent as 'crush' (Ps. 72.4), twice in reflexive as 'be crushed' (Job 5.4). Apparently D was the regular stem for this root in Hebrew, perhaps by displacement of B through the association of D with verbs of destruction. The root also occurs as *dky*.

dly: 'draw up (water)'. D once, used figuratively as 'draw up (the soul from Sheol)' (Ps. 30.2).

dqr: 'wound, transfix'. D three times in passive as 'wounded (by a sword)' (Lam. 4.9).

hrg: 'slay'. D twice in passive as 'be slain' (Is. 27.7).

hry: 'conceive'. D once in passive as 'be conceived' (Job 3.3).

hrs: 'tear down, overthrow'. D twice as 'destroy' (Ex. 23.24).

zbḥ: 'slaughter, sacrifice'. D frequent in this meaning (Hos. 12.12). Arabic *ḏabaḥa* likewise has the same meaning in both stems.

zqq: 'filter, refine'. D five times with these meanings (Mal. 3.3).

zrb: no B, *cf.* Syr. *zrb* 'press'; Ar. *zarbun* 'enclosure'. D once in passive as 'be pressed together' (Job 6.17), *cf.* Akk. *zurrubu* 'press'.

zry: 'scatter', usually 'winnow'. D frequent as 'scatter', most commonly in the sense of 'spread out s.th.' (Lv. 26.33). In this case it seems to be B which has assumed the more specialized meaning. Arabic *ḏarā* 'winnow' is the same in both stems.

zr': 'sow'. D once in passive as 'be sown' (Is. 40.24).

zrq: 'throw'. D twice in passive as 'be thrown (upon)' (Nu. 19.13).

ḥb': no B, *cf.* N-stem 'hide o.s., be hidden'. D once in passive as 'be hidden' (Job 24.4), ten times in reflexive as 'hide o.s.' (Gn. 3.8). Š also occurs as 'hide s.th.' (Jos. 6.17).

ḥbl: 'act corruptly', which seems to be an idiomatic use derived from an original 'destroy', *cf.* Akk. *ḫabālu*, Ar. *ḫabala*, Syr. *ḥbl*, all 'destroy'. D seven times as 'destroy, ruin' (Is. 13.5).

ḥbq: 'embrace'. D nine times as 'embrace' (Gn. 33.4), as opposed to the three occurrences of B.

ḥbš: 'bind on, saddle'. D once as 'bind up (a wound)' (Ps. 147.3), once figuratively as 'dam up (a stream)' (Job 28.11). Arabic *ḥabasa* means 'obstruct' in both stems.

ḥwy: no B, *cf.* perhaps Ar. *waḥā* 'reveal'. D five times as 'reveal, inform' (Ps. 19.3). The same use of D occurs in Bib. Aramaic, which also employs the Š-form of the root in this meaning.

ḥṭb: 'cut'. D once in passive as 'be cut' (Ps. 144.12).

ḥll: no B, *cf.* Akk. *ḫalālu*, Ar. *ḫalla* 'pierce'; MHb 'hollow out'. D once as 'be pierced (by the sword)' (Ez. 33.26).

ḥlṣ: 'draw off, strip'. D primarily as 'deliver, rescue' (II Sam 22.20), perhaps a specialization of B. However Ar. *ḫalaṣa/ḫallaṣa* 'be free/deliver' suggests that B is the secondary development in this case, a transitive counterpart of an original stative 'be free'.

ḥlq: 'divide'. D frequent as 'divide, apportion' (Jos. 13.7).

ḥnq: no B, *cf.* Ar. *ḫanaqa* 'strangle (s.o.)'; BH N-stem 'strangle o.s.' (II Sam. 17.23). D once as 'strangle' (Nah. 2.13).

ḥpy: 'cover'. D five times as 'cover' in the specialized sense of 'overlay (with metal)' (II C. 3.5).

ḥpś: 'search for'. D ten times as 'search for' (Gn. 31. 35), six times in reflexive as 'disguise o.s.', *i.e.* 'make o.s. searched for' (I Sam. 28.8).

ḥṣb: 'hew, cut'. D once in passive as 'be hewn' (Is. 51.1).

ḥṣṣ: 'divide' (pple. only), *cf.* MHb 'separate (trans.)' D once in passive as 'be severed, cut off' (Job 21.21), once in active pple. with meaning uncertain, but presumably 'those who divide (in the watering-places)' (Jd. 5.11). Arabic *ḫaṣṣa* means 'divide' in both stems.

ḥqq: 'decree, enact'. D once in pass. pple. 'decreed' (Pr. 31.5), seven times in *pôlel* as 'command' (Jd. 5.14). A comparison with Arabic *ḥaqqa/ḥaqqaqa* 'be true/effect' suggests that the BH B-form may be secondary.

ḥqr: 'search out'. D once in this meaning (Ecc. 12.9).

ḥšb: 'account, devise s.th.' D seventeen times in these meanings (Lv. 25.27), once in reflexive as 'account o.s. (as s.th.)' (Nu. 23.9).

ṭlʾ: 'patch'. D once in passive as 'be patched, spotted' (Jos. 9.5).

ṭʿn: no B, *cf.* Ar. *taʿana* 'pierce'. D once in passive as 'pierced' (Is. 14.19).

ṭpḥ: no B, *cf.* perhaps Akk. *ṭuppū* 'bring up, raise'. D once as 'raise (a child)' (Lam. 2.22).

ṭrp: 'tear, rend'. D three times in passive as 'be torn' (Gn. 37.33). Š occurs as 'let tear, cause to devour' (Pr. 30.8).

ydy: 'shoot', probably original 'cast' (*cf. ydd* 'cast a lot'). D twice as 'cast, cast down' (Lam. 3.53).

ysd: 'establish, found'. D frequent as 'establish, appoint' (I K. 16.34). Š occurs twice with this meaning (Ezra 3.11).

ysr: 'admonish' (pple. only). D frequent as 'correct, chastise' (I K. 12.11), once in reflexive *nithpaʿʿel* as 'have o.s. admonished' (Ez. 23.48). D undoubtedly has precedence here, and is probably a dialect variant of the D-form of *yšr* (q.v.) 'straighten', retained side-by-side in the language with a specialized meaning.

yṣr: 'form'. D once in passive as 'be formed' (Ps. 139.16).

kbs: 'cleanse, rinse'. D much more frequent as 'cleanse' (Gn. 49.11), yet the existence of Akk. *kabāsu* 'tread down' and Ar. *kabasa* 'squeeze' indicates a Common Semitic B-stem for the root. The Arabic root has the same meaning in both stems.

kbš: 'subdue'. D once as 'subdue' (II Sam. 8.11).

kḫd: no B, *cf.* N 'be hidden'. D twelve times as 'hide' (Jos. 7.19). Š occurs as 'cause to disappear, efface' (II C. 32.21), seemingly associated with an intransitive B-form. This might mean that D is also causative, but would not explain N. Probably the root, like many others, possessed both transitive and intransitive aspects.

kns: 'collect, gather'. D three times as 'gather' (Est. 4.16), once reflexive as 'wrap o.s. up' (Is. 28.20).

ksy: 'cover'. D much more common as 'cover' (Gn. 9.23), also in reflexive 'dress o.s.' (Gn. 24.65), *cf.* Ar. *kasā/takassa* 'dress s.o./dress o.s.'

kpr: 'cover (with s.th.)' (once: Gn. 6.14), *cf.* Ar. *kafara* 'cover'. D is common as 'atone, appease' (Gn. 32.21), *cf.* Akk. *kapāru/kuppuru* 'wipe off/expiate'. D may be a specialization of the root meaning, which ceased to be employed because of the religious associations of D, or may be a denominative from such a noun as *kōfer* 'reparation'.

krt: 'cut'. D twice in passive as 'be cut' (Ez. 16.4). Š frequent as 'cut off, destroy'. In this root, B and Š are both used figuratively, while D is used literally.

ktb: 'write'. D twice as 'write' (Is. 10.1). Arabic uses the D-form of this root as 'cause to write', while it seems here to be used for the purpose of exalted speech or distinctive phraseology.

lhṭ: 'devour, consume'. D nine times in this meaning (Joel 1.19).

lḥk: 'lick up' (once, as infinitive: Nu. 22.4). D six times as 'lick up' (Nu. 22.4). The B-form may well be an incorrectly vocalized D-form, for Ar. *laḥika* 'stick' suggests that D was an original factitive.

lṭš: 'sharpen'. D once in passive as 'be sharpened' (Ps. 52.4).

lqḥ: 'take'. D common in passive as 'be taken' (Gn. 3.23).

lqṭ: 'gather'. D frequent as 'gather', most often in the specific sense 'glean' (Is. 17.8), or in reference to other forms of food-gathering. Ar. *laqaṭa* likewise has the meaning 'gather' in both stems.

lqq: 'lick up, lap'. D twice as 'lap' (Jd. 7.6).

mgn: no B, *cf.* Phoen. *mgn* 'offer'; BH *māgén* 'shield'. D three times as 'give freely, deliver over' (Gen. 14.20).

mdd: 'measure'. D twice as 'measure' (Ps. 60.8), once in *hithpôlel* as 'stretch o.s. upon', *i.e.* either a denominative 'make o.s. the measure for' or a reversion to the meaning of Ar. *madda* 'stretch' (I K. 17.21).

mny: 'count, number'. D ten times as 'appoint, ordain' (Jon. 2.1). Either D is a specialization of the B meaning or, as suggested by the cognate noun *mānāh* 'portion', both stems are secondary developments from an original 'separate'. Biblical Aramaic makes the same distinctions of stem.

mʿk: 'press'. D once in passive as 'be pressed' (Ez. 23.3).

mrṭ: 'polish'. D five times in passive as 'be polished' (I K. 7.45).

mrq: 'clean'. D once in passive as 'be cleaned' (Lv. 6.21). Š also occurs once as 'scour' (Pr. 20.30).

mšk: 'draw, drag'. D three times in passive as 'be drawn out' (Pr. 13.12).

mšš: 'feel, touch'. D five times as 'feel', used particularly in the sense of 'search through s.th.' (Gn. 31.34). Š occurs as 'cause to feel' (Jd. 16.26).

n's: 'despise'. D fifteen times as 'despise' or 'make despised', *i.e.* 'regard as despicable' (Nu. 14.11), once reflexive in *hithpô'el* as 'be despised' (Is. 52.5).

ngy: 'gore'. D six times as 'push (with horns), gore' (Dt. 33.17), once reflexive as 'push o.s. against' (Dan. 11.40).

ng': 'touch, injure'. D four times as 'strike' (Gn. 12.17). Š frequent as 'cause to touch'.

ndy: no B, *cf.* Akk *nadû* 'throw'. D twice as 'cast out, exclude' (Is. 66.5).

ndḥ: 'thrust, impel'. D once in passive as 'be thrust' (Is. 8.22). Š is frequent as 'scatter' (Dt. 30.1), N as 'be scattered' (Dt. 22.1).

nhg: 'drive away, lead'. D ten times with these meanings (Gn. 31.26).

nṭš: 'abandon, forsake'. D once in passive as 'be abandoned' (Is. 32.14).

nky: no B, *cf.* N 'be smitten'. D once in passive as 'be smitten' (Ex. 9.31). Š also means 'smite' in both active and passive forms.

nkl: 'cheat, deceive'. D once as 'beguile' (Nu. 25.18), once reflexive as 'make o.s. a cheat (toward)' (Ps. 105.25), a quasi-denominative usage.

nsk: 'pour'. D once as 'pour' (I C. 11.18).

n'r: 'shake, shake off'. D three times as 'shake off' (Ex. 14.27), once reflexive as 'shake o.s. free' (Is. 52.2).

npṣ: 'shatter'. D ten times as 'shatter' (Jer. 48.12). Ar. *nafaḍa* also has the same meaning in both stems.

nṣḥ: no B, *cf.* Ar. *naṣaḥa* 'advise, guide'. D frequent, principally in the active pple. as 'direct, oversee' (Ezra 3.8).

nṣl: no B, *cf.* Ar. *naṣala* 'get rid of', BH N-stem 'be delivered, escape'. D three times as 'strip off' (Ex. 3.22), once as 'deliver' (Ez. 14.14), once reflexive as 'strip o.s. of s.th.' (Ex. 33.6). Š is common as 'deliver' (Ex. 5.23). This may suggest that the original root meaning was stative 'be free(d)', in which case D is a factitive 'make o.s. free of s.th.', both D and Š developing specialized variations of this.

nqp: no B, *cf.* Aram. and MHb 'strike (off)'; Ar. *naqafa* 'smash (the head)'. D once as 'strike down (thickets)' (Is. 10.34).

nqr: 'bore out, hollow', *cf.* Ar. *naqara* 'dig'. D four times as 'dig' (Is. 51.1).

nqš: no B, *cf.* N-form 'be ensnared' (Dt. 12.30). D twice as 'ensnare' (Ps. 107.11), once reflexive 'snare for o.s.' (I Sam. 28.9). The stem could as well be a denominative 'set a snare for'.

nś': 'lift up, accept'. D twelve times as 'lift, carry' (Amos 4.2), nine times in reflexive as 'lift o.s. up' (Nu. 23.24). Š is 'cause to carry'.

nšk: 'bite'. D twice as 'bite' (Jer. 8.17).

nšl: 'clear away'. D once as 'clear away' (II K. 16.6).

nšq: 'kiss'. D five times as 'kiss' (Gn. 31.28).

ntḥ: no B, *cf.* Ar. *nataḥa* 'hew out'. D eight times as 'cut up' (Ex. 29.17).

ntq: 'take off, draw away'. D eleven times as 'tear apart' (Jd. 16.9). Š three times as 'draw away' (Jos. 8.6), in the specific sense of separating one group of combatants from another.

sbk: 'interweave, entangle'. D once in passive as 'be interwoven' (Job 8.13).

sgr: 'shut up, close in'. D four times as 'deliver up (into the power of s.o.)', a specialized figurative use of the root meaning (I Sam. 17.46). Š occurs with both the B and the D meanings.

sḥw: no B, *cf.* N-stem 'be scraped away' (Pr. 2.22); Ar. *saḥā* 'scrape'. D once as 'scrape away' (Ez. 26.4).

skr: no B, *cf.* Akk. *sekēru*, Ar. *sakara* 'dam up'; BH N-stem 'be stopped up' (Ps. 63.12). D once as 'deliver up' in the sense 'seal into slavery' (Is. 19.4). The Arabic D-form also means 'lock, close'.

sl': no B, *cf.* Ar. *salā'a* 'pay (promptly)'. D once in passive 'be paid, weighed out' (Lam. 4.2).

slw: 'reject', *cf.* Ar. *salā* 'forget'. D once as 'reject' (Lam. 1.15). The Arabic D-stem is used as a causative.

smk: 'support, sustain'. D once as 'sustain, refresh' (SS 2.5).

spy: 'join s.o. (to s.th.)' D twice as 'join' (Hab 2.15), once in reflexive as 'have a share in, join o.s. to' (I Sam. 26.19).
spr: 'number, count'. D eight times as 'enumerate, count' (Ps. 22.18), but more frequently occurring as figurative 'recount, relate' (Gn. 24.66).

stm: 'stop up'. D twice as 'stop up' (Gn. 26.15).

str: 'hide s.th.' D twice as 'hide' (Is. 16.3), five times in reflexive as 'have o.s. hidden' (I Sam. 23.19). Š frequent as 'hide'. Ar. *satara* has the meaning hide in both B and D.

'zb: 'relinquish, forsake'. D twice in passive as 'be relinquished' (Is. 32.14).

'zq: no B, *cf.* Ar. *'azaqa* 'dig up'. D once as 'dig about' (Is. 5.2).

'ṣb: 'grieve, displease'. D twice as 'grieve, annoy' (Ps. 56.6), twice reflexive as 'grieve for, be grieved' (Gn. 6.6). Š also occurs as 'grieve' (Ps. 78.30). All three stems may well be denominative in function and origin, or D and Š may have been originally associated with a stative 'be angry' (*cf.* Ar. *ġaḍaba*).

'ṣm: 'close (one's eyes)' (Is. 33.15). D once as 'make (the eyes of s.o.) closed' (Is. 29.10).

'ql: no B, but *cf.* Ar. *'aqala* 'confine'. D once in passive as 'be confined' or 'be bent' (Hab. 1.4).

'qr: 'root up, pluck out (a plant)', *cf.* Ar. *'aqara* 'wound'. D five times in the specialized meaning 'hamstring' (Jos. 11.9). In this case B may be the secondary development, since D appears to be an original factitive connected with Ar. *'aqura* 'be barren'.

'qš: no B, *cf.* MHb 'twist'; Syr. *'aqiš* 'twisted'. D four times as 'pervert, defraud' (Mic. 3.9). Š once as estimative-factitive 'regard as crooked' (Job 9.20), suggesting that D may also be an original factitive 'make crooked', the two stems taking on complementary meanings, figurative in D, literal in Š.

'šq: 'oppress, wrong'. D once as passive 'be wronged' (Is. 23.12).

pgš: 'meet, encounter'. D once as 'encounter' (Job 5.14).

pzr: 'scatter' (once: Jer. 50.17). D eight times as 'scatter, spread' (Joel 4.2). Ar. *fazara* also has identical meanings in B and D.

plg: no B, *cf.* N-stem 'be divided'; Ar. *falaja/fallaja*, both 'divide, split'. D once as 'divide' (Ps. 55.10); once as 'form' (Job 38.25).

plḥ: 'cleave'. D three times as 'cleave, open' (Pr. 7.23), once figuratively as 'deliver (offspring)' (Job 39.3).

pll: no B, *cf.* Old Assyrian *palālum* 'judge, arbitrate'. D once as 'judge' (Gn. 48.11).

pls: no B, *cf.* Syr. *plš*, Akk. *palāšu* 'bore through'. D three times as 'level, break through' (Is. 26.7), *cf.* Ar. *fallasa* 'rend'.

pṣḥ: 'break out (in song)'. D once as 'shatter'. (Mic. 3.3).

pṣl: no B, *cf.* Ar. *faṣala*, Syr. *pṣl* 'divide'. D twice as 'peel off, split' (Gn. 30.37). Ar. *faṣṣala* likewise means 'divide'.

pqd: 'look to, number'. D twice as 'make numbered, muster' (Is. 13.4), once as 'summon' (Is. 38.10).

prd: 'separate, spread (the wings)'. D once as 'separate (intr.)' (Hos. 4.14), once in passive as 'be separated' (Est. 3.8), four times reflexive as 'separate o.s. (from others)' (Ps. 92.10). Š likewise means 'separate, divide' (trans.). Thus BH B, Š and D reflexive parallel respectively Arabic *farada/'afrada/tafarrada* 'spread out/separate/be alone'. The active D-stem seems to have acquired reflexive-passive value here.
prṣ: 'destroy'. D once in passive as 'be destroyed' (Neh. 2.13).

prq: 'tear away, remove'. D three times as 'tear off, rend' (I K. 19.11), twice reflexive as 'tear o.s. away from' (Ex. 32.3), once as 'be torn away' (Ez. 19.12). Ar. *faraqa* likewise has similar meanings in B and D.

prś: 'spread out'. D nine times as 'spread out, scatter' (Is. 25.11).

prš: 'explain', *cf.* Ar. *faraša* 'spread out'. D once in passive as 'be explained' (Nu. 15.34), once as 'be divided, separated' (Neh. 8.8).

pśq: 'open wide (the lips)', *cf.* Syr. 'cleave'. D once as 'separate (the legs)' (Ez. 16.25).

pšṭ: 'strip (off)'. D three times as 'make s.o. stripped (of garments)' (Is. 31.8), once reflexive as 'make o.s. stripped' (I Sam. 18.4).

ptḫ: no B, *cf.* Akk. *patāḫu* 'bore'; Ar. *fataḫa* 'engrave'. D eight times as 'engrave' (I K. 7.36).

ptḥ: 'open'. D eighteen times as 'loosen, free' (Gn. 24.32), once in reflexive as 'be loosened' (Is. 52.2).
ṣmd: no B, *cf.* Akk. *ṣamādu* 'bind together'; Ar. *ḍamada* 'bandage'. D once in pple. of passive 'be bound' (II Sam. 20.8).

ṣmt: 'press upon, imprison'. D once as 'press upon' (Ps. 88.17). Another possibility is that D means 'silence' as does the Š-form, *cf.* Ar. *samata* 'be silent'. Two roots may have fallen together here.

ṣpy: 'arrange in order', *cf.* Ar. *ṣaffa* 'put right'. D frequent as 'overlay, plate' (Ex. 25.11), a specialization of the root meaning, *cf.* Arabic *ṣaffafa* 'array'.

ṣrʿ: 'afflict (with skin disease)', in pass. pple. only; but *cf.* Ar. *ṣaraʿa* 'fell, strike down'. D ten times in pass. pple. with the same meaning (Ex. 4.6). The two stems alternate freely, sometimes within the same passage, probably for variety. Clearly, a general verbal concept 'afflict' has been narrowed in usage to refer to a specific disease, probably as a euphemism. Similarly, in Arabic the B-stem passive is used to refer to epilepsy.

ṣrp: 'refine'. D twice in active pple. as 'refiner' (Mal. 3.2).

ṣrr: 'wrap', *cf.* Ar. *ṣarra* 'lace, bind up'. D once in pass. pple. as 'bound up, wrapped around (a torn wine skin)' (Jos. 9.4).

qbl: no B, *cf.* Ar. *qabala* 'accept, receive'. D ten times as 'accept' (Est. 4.4). The Arabic D-form has the specialized meaning 'kiss'. This makes it likely that the more general meaning was conveyed in the D-stem in Common Semitic, and reverted to B in Arabic as a result of D's specialization. The stem is probably an original factitive-denominative as 'have s.th. before o.s., in one's presence', associated with the preposition *qbl*.

qbṣ: 'collect, assemble'. D frequent as 'gather together' (Mic. 1.7). In Arabic *qabaḍa* 'collect' both stems likewise have the same meaning.

qbr: 'bury'. D seven times as 'bury' (Nu. 33.4).

ql': 'sling'. D twice as 'sling' (I Sam. 17.49).

qmṭ: 'seize'. D once in passive as 'be seized' (Job. 22.16).

qpd: no B, *cf.* Syr. B-reflexive 'be drawn together'; Ar. *gafada* 'wind up'. D once as 'roll up, draw together (the strands of life)' (Is. 38.12).

qṣy: no B, *cf.* Ar. *qaḍā* 'complete, terminate'. D three times as 'cut off' (II K. 10.32).

qṣ': no B, *cf.* Aram. *qṣ'*, Ar. *qaẓa'a* 'cut off'. D twice in pass. pple. as 'be cut off', in the specific meaning 'made into a corner, corner' (Ex. 26.23). The Š pass. pple. also occurs with this meaning (Ez. 46.22).

qṣṣ: 'cut off'. D nine times as 'cut off, cut up' (Ex. 39.3). Arabic *qaṣṣa* likewise means 'cut off' in both stems.

qr': 'call'. D seven times in passive as 'be called' (Is. 48.8).

qrṣ: 'pinch', *cf.* Ar. *qaraṣa/qarraṣa* 'pinch/pinch, shape', the original reference apparently having been the shaping of clay with the fingers. This meaning seems to have been specialized in the D-stem. D once in passive as 'be shaped' (Job 33.6).

qšr: 'tie, bind'. D twice as 'tie' (Job 38.21).

r'y: 'see'. D once in passive as 'be seen' (Job 33.21). Š occurs as 'cause to see, cause to know' (Gn. 12.1).

rdp: 'persecute, pursue'. D eight times as 'hunt, persecute' (Hos. 2.9). Arabic *radafa* 'follow' has no D-stem, but employs Š in a comparable manner, *i.e.* with the same meaning as B.

rḥṣ: 'wash'. D twice in passive as 'be washed' (Pr. 30.12).

rtš: no B, *cf.* Aram. *rtš* 'cast away, reject'. D seven times as 'cast (down)' (Is. 31.18), in the sense of destroying (usually children).

rmy: 'throw, shoot'. D eight times as 'cast away, forsake' (Lam. 1.19) and 'send off, deceive' (Gn. 29.25), a figurative use in the sense of throwing a person off from his purpose.

rp': 'heal'. D seven times as 'heal, make healthy' (Ez. 34.4), three times reflexive as 'have o.s. healed' (II K. 8.29).

rṣṣ: 'crush, oppress'. D three times as 'crush' (Ps. 74.14), Š also occurring once in this meaning (Jd. 9.53). In addition the *pôlel* occurs once as 'oppress' (Jd. 10.8), once in reflexive as 'oppress one another' (Gn. 25.22). Ar. *raṣṣa* 'press together' also means the same in B and D.

rqḥ: 'mix, blend'. D once in passive as 'be blended' (II C. 16.14).

rqm: 'weave' (pple. only). D once in passive as 'be woven' (Ps. 139.15).

rqʿ: 'beat out'. D four times as 'beat out' (Ex. 39.3).

rtq: no B, *cf.* Ar. *rataqa* 'close up, repair'; Aram. *ritqâ* 'enclosure'. D once in passive as 'be bound (in fetters)' (Nah. 3.10).

śbr: 'examine, look for', *cf.* Ar. *sabara* 'examine'. D five times as 'look for' (Is. 38.18).

śn': 'hate'. D fifteen times in active pple. as 'one who makes hated, enemy' (Nu. 10.35). Cf. *'hb* 'love' (above).

śrg: no B, *cf.* Syr. *srg* 'intertwine'. D once in passive as 'be intertwined' (Job 40.17), once in reflexive as 'be fastened together' (Lam. 1.14). Arabic *saraja* 'braid' also has the same meaning in B and D.

śrp: 'burn'. D once in passive as 'be burned' (Lv. 10.16).

šbṣ: no B, *cf.* Syr. *šbṣ* 'mix'; MHb 'decorate with patterns'. D once as 'weave' (Ex. 28.39), once in passive as 'mixed (into gold), set (in gold)' (Ex. 28.20).

šbr: 'break'. D equally common as 'break' (Ex. 23.24). Š once as 'cause to break (through), bring to birth' (Is. 66.9), once as passive 'caused to break, wounded' (Jer. 8.21). There is no contextual evidence for the opinion that where D is used, breakage into smaller pieces is indicated.

šgl: 'violate, ravish'. D once in passive as 'be violated' (Jer. 3.2).

šḥr: 'look for' (once: Pr. 11.27). D twelve times as 'look for' (Job 7.21). The B-stem is probably a back-formation, especially since it occurs only in the active participle.

šḥt: no B, *cf.* Ar. *saḥata* 'destroy'. D frequent as 'destroy, corrupt' (Gn. 6.17), the meaning also of the much more common Š (Gn. 18.28). The absence of B may indicate that D and Š are denominative in origin.

šṭp: 'rinse, wash'. D once in passive as 'be bathed, rinsed' (Lv. 6.21).

škḥ: 'forget'. D once as 'make s.o. forgotten' (Lam. 2.6), once reflexive as 'be forgotten' (Ecc. 8.10). This is an instance in which the difference between 'do s.th.' and 'have s.th. done' is significant for the meaning of the sentence, because it is not the subject (Jahweh) who does the forgetting, but some unidentified party. Š, as 'cause to forget', identifies the forgetful party (Jer. 23.27). This exemplifies the true difference between D and Š. The former is concerned with a quality of its object ('forgotten'), the latter with an action of its object ('forgets'). This is the difference between factitive and causative, a distinction which of course was blurred in usage.

šlḥ: 'send'. D very common, demonstrating no qualitative or quantitative difference from B in context (Ex. 22.4, Job 18.8). Š also occurs several times with the same meaning.

šnn: no B, *cf.* BH šny, Ugaritic *ṯnn* 'do again, repeat'. D once as 'repeat' (Dt. 6.7).

šsp: no B, *cf.* MHb. 'separate'; BH *šs'* 'cleave'. D once as 'separate' (I Sam. 15.33).

špy: no B, *cf.* Ar. *safā* '(the wind) sweeps away (the dust)'; BH N-stem 'be swept away (by wind)'. D once in passive as 'be bared' (Job 33.21).

špk: 'pour out'. D twice in passive as 'be poured out' (Nu. 35.33), once as 'be caused to slip' (Ps. 73.2), a construction which assumes a root meaning 'slide, flow' complementary to 'pour out' as an intransitive.

šqy: no B, *cf.* Ar. *saqā* 'irrigate, water'. D once in passive as 'be watered' (Job 21.24). Š is common as 'water, give drink', as a denominative which in Hebrew had displaced the B-form of the cognate languages.

tkn: 'determine, fix'. D five times as 'measure out, adjust' (Ps. 75.4).

tly: 'hang s.th. upon'. D twice in this meaning (Ez. 27.10).

tpr: 'sew together'. D once as 'sew' (Ez. 13.18).

tpś: 'seize, handle'. D once as 'grasp' (Pr. 30.28).

The most striking fact emerging from our survey of the roots included in Group I-C is the degree to which the use of the B and D stems seems to be complementary, even as their meanings are not easily differentiated. In many cases where D is employed Biblical Hebrew will have no B-form, and one must have recourse either to an N-form (assumed to have a passival-reflexive relationship to B) or to forms from later Hebrew and cognate languages in order to reconstruct a B-stem meaning. The fact that these Middle Hebrew, Aramaic and Arabic forms are not completely trustworthy as indication of a common Semitic B-form of the root in question, that they may represent back-formations from an original common Semitic D-stem (as we suggested a number of times in Chapter IV), is not particularly relevant. What is important, is that in such cases there was no consciousness of a 'special function' of the D-stem which could not as well be expressed in B. In other cases, roots which occur regularly in D appear in B only as active participles or as infinitives. Such B-forms may be the remnants of a full series truncated by an inexplicable idiomatic preference for the D-stem of the particular root; or again, they may be back-formations which evolved in order to provide simpler infinitival and participial forms than the prefixed forms of the D-stem. Finally, there is a significant number of roots in which D-forms appreciably outnumber those of B.

Conversely, there are many roots in this group which occur more or less commonly in the B-stem, while a D-form which has the same meaning may occur only once, twice or three times. Such cases are most frequent when a B- and D-form occur in the same sentence or paragraph, suggesting that the D-form was created by the writer for variety of expression, perhaps ex nihilo, and also that the two stems were in many contexts interchangeable. In sixty or so of these cases the D-form occurs only in the passive; both the passive and the reflexive of D seem often to configurate with the B-stem of the same root, just as the B reflexive (N) of a root often seems to configurate with D. By every indication these roots, which express what one might describe as simple transitive concepts such as 'smash', 'cover', 'wash', and which constitute nearly half of all roots considered in this chapter, are freely used in both or either of the two stems. Complementary in use, B and D here would best be taken as alternate (though not mutually exclusive) stems which in this case are also interchangeable. How may such a situation exist, in light of the dictum that a differing linguistic form implies a differing linguistic function? This question may not be ignored, in light of the large number of roots involved (a few cases might be explained away as false analogical extensions). As we have pointed out previously, this dilemma has led directly to the theory of implied intensiveness or repetition of action in the D-stem. Yet other and more systematic hypotheses have been offered by semitists, of which we may mention only two here.

The large number of D-stems passive which seem to configurate with the B-stems active has been explained as resulting from Hebrew phonetic laws. Reconstruction of this process would begin with the loss of a fully developed stative in West Semitic, so that only the 'neuter verbs', those corresponding to the Akkadian 'durative' statives, were retained from common Semitic, making it necessary for the 'passive' stative to find an alternative medium of expression in the west. According to this view, this came about through two steps. First came the development in the west of an originally stative form *qaṭal* as a means of expressing past, completed acts, incorporating most of the concepts expressed in the Akkadian 'perfect stative'. The second stage was the independent development in the west of an internal passive utilizing and distinguished by the vowel sequence *-u-a-*, which became assimilated to both B- and D-forms, these becoming *quṭal* and *quṭṭal* respectively. It was the former of these which assumed the function of the Akkadian 'passive stative', for all the transitive verbs upon which the latter form had depended were now part of the *qaṭal* system. By this time, of course, the universal sense of the stative/permansive found in Akkadian was lost.

Finally, as Proto-Canaanite evolved into literary Hebrew, the latter language began to develop its own phonetic rules, including one which forbade a short vowel to stand in an open unaccented syllable. As a result of this the passive form of the new B-stem, *quṭal*, could not stand unaltered. As Barth states it, this change could have come about either by lengthening the pretonic /u/ or by sharpening the following consonant. While both solutions are found, the latter is more common, insofar as it is more consonant with the prevailing phonetic laws of Hebrew.[9] The outcome then was a passive B-form *quṭ(ṭ)al* which was indistinguishable from the D passive *quṭṭal*, and which in practice alternated with the N-form in expressing the passive aspect of B (N-stem and D-stem passive are virtually mutually exclusive in distribution among the roots). *Puʿʿal* participles such as *mᵉqôraʾî* (Is. 48.12) are explained by Barth as

[9] J. Barth, "Das Passive Qal und seine Participien", in *Jubelschrift zum siebzigsten Geburtstag des Israel Hildesheimer* (Berlin, 1890), 147.

false creations by analogy with the true passive participle of the D-stem. König sums up this aspect of the process thus: "seiner Bedeutung nach vertritt Quṭṭal das Passivum zu Qiṭṭel und nur, wo dieses scheinbar, d.h. für unser unvollkommended Sprachgefühl und nach dem wenigen uns übriggebliebenen Sprachmaterial, in seiner Bedeutung mit dem Qaṭal übereinstimmt, vertritt es das Passivum auch zu diesem."[10]

This is an ingenious and attractive scheme, but one which could solve the problems raised by this group of roots only if all of them fell into this category of forms. As it is, however, these isolated D passive forms constitute only a fraction of the total group. König's note of caution appended to his preceding statement seems to us to be well taken: "... aus dem blossen Fehlen eines entsprechenden Qiṭṭel in der übriggebliebenen Literatur lässt sich nicht das Fehlen desselben in der lebenden Sprache erschliessen."[10] When we have a large group of D-stems with (apparently) the same meaning as the corresponding B-stems, most of them occurring only a few times, there is nothing improbable about the fact that a number of them will appear as passives. To be sure, a Proto-Canaanite *quṭal* would have been untenable according to Hebrew phonetic practices; but one could as well say, that for this reason it disappeared and was replaced either by the N-form or, where a D-stem of the root existed with a comparable meaning, by the passive of that stem. This would also explain the fact that N-forms and D passive forms usually do not occur within the structure of an individual root. The fact that B- and D-stems active (on the one hand) and N- and D-stems passive (on the other), configurate in all possible combinations within this group of roots, inclines us to dismiss any explanation which accounts for only one of these combinations but leaves unanswered the broader question of the stems' interchangeability and does not even touch upon the more basic question concerning the origin of that D-form upon which the *-u-a-* pattern was imposed.

These larger problems are approached in the hypothesis, put forward at various times by many semitists, that many seeming D-forms (including many of those in this group) are actually remnants of a common Semitic present-future tense or cursive aspect corresponding to Akkadian *iqáttal.* In the Amarna letters, according to Dhorme[11], this present-future has the two forms *yuqaṭṭil* and *yuqâṭil,* the former of which became Hebrew *y^{e}qaṭṭēl,* homonymous with the D-stem. Earlier, Götze had considered the possibility of a present tense in Ugaritic, and concluded, "It can be said, at this early stage, that neither *qatila* nor *yaqtulu* (and its moods) could have served for such a purpose. Precisely for this reason the exiatence of the theme yaqat(t)al(u) has been surmised."[12] Greenberg suggested that the Hamitic form called the 'habitual' is cognate with the forms just mentioned[13], while the Ethiopic *y^{e}nagger* (Stem II Imperfect) has obvious affinities with the Canaanite form. The supposition, in relating these data to the question of the D-stem, is that this cursive form was

[10] König. *Historisches-Kritisches Lehrgebäude,* 192-193.
[11] Dhorme, "La Langue de Canaan", 432-433.
[12] A. Götze, "The Tenses of Ugaritic", in *JAOS* 58 (1938), 296.
[13] J. Greenberg, "The Afro-Asiatic (Hamito-Semitic) Present", in *JAOS* 72 (1952), 5.

given up because of its similarity to the form of the D-stem, whereupon its function was taken over by the original preterite *yaqtul*, but that some forms instead of disappearing were assimilated to the D-stem and remained to confuse the issue of its origin.

If this is so, then we must assume that this was the single most important factor in the constitution of the D-stem as employed in literary Hebrew. But one may question the validity of the whole approach, except insofar as it concerns the roots of Group II-B (the so-called 'cursives'). In the first place, it is quite unlikely that the present-future would have disappeared from Canaanite-Hebrew because of homonymy with the D-stem, and have left its vital function in the language unfilled until *yaqtul* bridged the gap. It is far more likely that, as West Semitic *qaṭala*-forms evolved as the active counterpart to stative *qaṭila* and *qaṭula* it began to infringe upon the function of the original preterite *yaqṭul* (Akk. *iprus*). This theme was originally not temporal but aspectual, embodying the concept of action performed once, as opposed to the cursive aspect *yaqaṭṭal* (Akk. *iqáttal*). This originally timeless aspect of *yaqtul* made it possible for this form to begin to assume the present and future functions of original *yaqattal*; its simpler form would have given impetus to this process of displacement, by which *yaqattal* dropped from use.

Secondly, the assumption of homonymy is itself of questionable value. While homonymy might have existed in Hebrew as a result of the reduction of a cursive *yaqatta/il* and D-stem *yuqattil*, this would not have been the case in Arabic, and probably not in Aramaic; yet both of these languages present us with problems parallel to those of Hebrew. Furthermore, if homonymy had been a major problem it is more likely that the much less frequently used D-stem, rather than the ubiquitous present-future of the simple stem, would have been forced to take another form. Such a form was in fact at hand in the alternative *yuqāṭil* of the Amarna latters, which was of course used later for precisely this purpose in some weak roots of Hebrew which could not conveniently be expressed in the geminated form.

Finally, since there is no trace of a cursive meaning in the D-forms of our Group I-C, one would have to assume that nearly fifty percent of all roots employing the D-stem did so by reason of a false analogical extension – a questionable assumption, and one which would of necessity limit severely the expressive function of the stem, making it impossible to attain any general picture of the stem as a unique linguistic feature.

In general, one may say that most such explanations as those we have just cited deal not with the origins and meanings of D itself, but with aspects of the stem which seem inconsistent with the meanings assigned to it, whether intensive, causative or factitive. The greatest single virtue of Götze's article is that he concentrates not upon explanation of apparent inconsisṭencies but upon the search for some element of consistency within the stem. As part of our own similar search, we would analyze the D-forms of Group I-C as being identifiable with Götze's third category of D-stems corresponding to the Akkadian "passive stative", of which he writes that "it denotes a state of affairs which result from another person's action; but the agent remains unspecified. This type always goes with transitive verbs; one may call it a passive participle in predicative use. Any transitive verb may have such a form at its side."[14] He later adds, "The difference between D and B is very slight. With B the emphasis is laid on the action performed, with D however on the effect of the action." This corresponds to our previous distinction of B and D as 'subjective' and 'objective' respectively: in B emphasis is upon what (A) does, in D upon the effect which the action has on (B), (A) being merely the auxiliary. In other words, the D-stem is factitive and transformative because it involves the transferral of (B) from one state into another (of which he is the subject). Moreover, (A) need not be the agent in this process. For instance, *škḥ* in B means 'forget' and occurs once in D as 'make s.o. forgotten' (Lam. 2.6). In this case Jahweh is the subject (frequently the case in the D-stem), yet the writer can not mean that Jahweh did the forgetting. Again, *g'l* in B means 'loathe', in D 'make s.th. loathesome (to others as well as oneself), pollute' (Dan. 1.8). Finally, *'zr* in B usually refers to 'gird oneself', in D 'make s.o. girded' with the emphasis of (A)'s action and (B)'s state, respectively.

In most cases, of course, the distinction between 'do.s.th.' and 'have s.th. done' is not clearcut; (A) is in fact often the agent in both B- and D-stems of a root. Where the difference in meaning between B and D is scarcely noticeable, the choice between them may be determined by lexical classification within a language, or a question of stylistic effectiveness on the part of an individual writer. These cases in which the D-form of a root may be used both when (A) performs an action and when (A) has an action performed can be referred to as 'double D-stems'; they are particularly common in roots which have both simple and reflexive D-stems. Such cases might be cited as *kšy*, B and D 'cover', D reflexive 'make o.s. covered, dress'; *prd*, B and D 'separate', D reflexive 'make o.s. separated, be apart'; *rp'*, B and D 'heal', D reflexive 'have o.s. healed'. In such cases the reflexive may be described as 'auto-transformative' in significance, rather than as the reflexive of the simple stem, and it often takes on specialized or idiomatic semantic functions. In many cases, of course, when B and D are used alike, this reflexive will have the same meaning as the N-stem; in cases where the basic D-stem or the N-stem of a root is missing it may well seem to configurate with the B-stem, as does the passive D-form when the active D-forms have not been preserved.

In order to associate those D-stems with Götze's "passive stative" one will have to say that for the most part an originally factitive D-stem meaning became to all intents and purposes the equivalent of the corresponding B-stem, via the processes of lexicalisation already mentioned. This would help to account for the fact that wherever B or D is quite common the other is likely to occur only a few times, and then quite possibly for stylistic variety. The adoption of a verbal concept into the lexicon in either B or D seems quite arbitrary to the reader (except for such instances as the

[14] Götze, "The So-Called Intensive", 6.

preference for D in verbs of destruction or division), and generally does not reflect the original distinction between the stems. Since this is so, one or the other tended to drop from common use without any consequent net loss in lexicon.

Probably this took place because of what Götze called "the West Semitic loss of the stative" which "cut the D form loose from the ground on which it was grown," for "this must necessarily have obscured its original function."[15] What happened in Hebrew, for instance, was that other forms assumed the function filled by the "passive stative" in Akkadian, such as the passive participle or the passive D-form. Most frequently this function seems to have been taken over by the N-stem. To us, this can account for the fact that so many D-forms seem to act as factitives of an N-stem where no B form occurs in the literature; it seems likely that in such cases no B-stem was in regular use, its normal function having been taken by D. In other words, a possible pair B-N (active-mediopassive) is replaced by a pair D-N. In fact, however, no such 'substitution' has taken place in most cases; instead D-N may be regarded as an alternative type of evolution, an alternative lexical means to the same linguistic end.

By whatever means the function of the Akkadian "passive stative" may have been accomplished in Hebrew, one recognizes that each of these means stood for the same thing: an implicit stative alongside the active form of the root in question. In other words, we must posit as existing in theory for each root that which exists in actually surviving forms for only a few, such as *mālē'* which means both 'fill' and 'be filled' (though for many more roots in Arabic than in Hebrew). It is this implicit stative which is the foundation of the D-stem. If such a stative is assumed, whether or not it actually existed either in West Semitic or common Semitic, the D-stem may be seen to preserve the factitive-transformative significance which we saw in Groups I-A and I-B in this latest group of roots as well. Although the transformative and non-transformative functions are in practice scattered haphazardly among the three basic stems, their passives and reflexives, we may at least say that factitive-transformative is the primary categorization of the D-stem, comprehending approximately 75% of all the roots which occur in D, and an even higher percentage of the D-forms which occur in Biblical Hebrew. We will now turn our attention to the forms of the minority.

Part II. *D-Stems Non-transformative*

A. *Associated with Nominal Forms*

'hl: 'pitch a tent' (Gn. 13.12). D once with this meaning (Is. 13.20). Both stems are denominative, associated with *'ōhel* 'tent'. In such a case it is impossible to say, without evidence from cognate languages, which form, if either, had priority, or whether each evolved independently.

'wy: no B. D fourteen times as 'desire' (Dt. 12.20), very often with *nefeš* 'soul, self' as subject; also fourteen times in reflexive 'desire for o.s.' (II Sam. 23.15). Clearly both forms amount to the same thing. The original meaning may be 'have a desire for', associated with *'awwah* 'desire'.

[15] Götze, "The So-Called Intensive", 8.

'šr: no B. D eight times as 'bless', usually translated as 'call blessed' (Gn. 30.13). The latter translation rests on the assumption that D is a factitive from *'ašrē* 'blessed'. However, since the adjective itself is a derived form, D may as well be a denominative 'give a blessing', even though there is no specific noun in Hebrew with which it is associated. Compare, however, Ar. *yasr* 'ease, pleasantness'; to 'bless' may well be to 'give ease'.

b'r: no B, nor associated noun in BH, but *cf.* Akk. *ba'ûru* 'proof' and D form *bu''ūru* 'prove'. D three times as 'explain' (Dt. 1.5), which would seem to be the same denominative.

bkr: no B, *cf.* Ar. *bakara/bakkara* 'be early/do early'. D three times: once as 'do early', *i.e.* 'make early' something determined by the context (Ez. 47.12), and twice as 'regard s.o. as the first-borne', associated with *b^ekor* 'the first-borne' in a denominative-estimative use (Dt. 21.16). Š also occurs once as 'bear the first child' (Jer. 4.31). The D and Š denominatives thus may serve specialized functions.

brk: 'bless' (in pass. pple. only). D common as 'bless' (Gn. 1.22). It seems to be a denominative associated with *bere<u>k</u>* 'knee', and to refer to the act of a father who legitimized his son by setting him upon his lap (see Job 3.12, cf. Gn. 30.3). He who is 'blessed' is thus legitimized by Jahweh, or adopted by him. The B participle is probably a back-formation, possibly employed in place of the D passive participle because of its simpler form. B and D denominatives also exist with the meanings 'kneel' and 'cause to kneel' respectively (Ps. 95.6; Gn. 24.11).

grm: no B. D twice as 'gnaw bones' (Nu. 24.8), associated with *gerem* 'bone' (*cf.* *'zm*, below).

gšm: no B. D once in passive as 'be rained upon', *i.e.* 'be sent rain' (Ez. 22.24). Š occurs once with the same meaning 'send rain, bring a shower' (Jer. 14.22), both stems associated with *gešem* 'rain, shower'.

dbr: 'speak' (pple. and inf. only). D extremely common, and would seem to be the original form, a denominative meaning either 'make words' or 'treat a matter'. In this case B would be secondary, developed for variety or for simplicity of expression.

hll: 'shine', *cf.* Ar. *halla* 'show (new moon)'. D common as 'praise' (Gn. 12.15), which might at first be thought of as a factitive-causative 'make shine, make brilliant', *cf.* Ar. *hallala* 'acclaim'; this may be the case. However D might perhaps better be derived from some noun or expression such *hal^elû* (which may itself have an original connection with 'shine'), in which case D would be denominative.

zmn: no B. D three times in passive as 'made the appointed time (a season)' (Ezra 10.14), associated with *z^eman* 'fixed date'.

znb: no B. D twice as 'smite at the rear', *i.e.* 'treat as the tail end' (Dt. 25.18), associated with *zanab* 'tail, end'.

ḥbl: no B. D three times as 'be in travail, undergo birth pangs' (SS 8.5), associated with *ḥēbel* 'birth pangs'.

ḥṭ': 'sin', *cf.* Š 'cause to sin'. D eleven times as 'purify from sin' (Nu. 19.19), once as 'bear a loss' (Gn. 31.39), nine times reflexive as 'purify o.s.' (Nu. 8.21), once reflexive as 'bear the loss (of one another)' (Job 41.17). D is not directly associated with the other verbal stems, but with the noun *ḥēṭ'* 'sin, loss, offense', thus means literally 'regard s.th. as sin', *i.e.* 'purify by repentance' or 'regard 'regard s.th. as (one's own) loss'.

ḥmš: 'be in five parts (an army)'. D twice as 'take a fifth part' (Gn. 41.34), *i.e.* 'make s.th. five'. Both stems are denominative, standing in an absolute-causative relationship to one another, yet probably independent.

ḥpš: no B. D once in passive as 'made free' (Lv. 19.20). Since neither BH nor any cognate language has a stative 'be free' from this root, while an original norminal stem *ḥofš-* can be reconstructed from the BH derivatives, D may be originally 'give s.o. freedom', in the passive 'be given freedom'.

ḥrf: 'reproach'. D more frequent in this meaning (Jd. 8.15), and is perhaps the original verbal stem, associated with *ḥerpah* 'disgrace, reproach', thus 'offer reproach' or 'think s.th./s.o. a disgrace'.

ṭll: no B. D once as 'cover (the top of a gate), protect' (Neh. 3.15). It is likely that this form arises from a dialect variant of *ṣēl* (Ar. *ẓill*) 'shade, shelter, protection'. Thus D would be 'give protection', *cf.* Ar. *ẓallala* 'shelter s.o.'. The only noun associated with BH *ṭll, i.e. ṭal* 'dew' is also related in meaning.

ybm: no B. D three times as 'act as brother-in-law (to s.o.)', *i.e.* 'consummate a brother's marriage' (Gn. 38.8), from *yabam* 'brother-in-law'.

khn: no B. D frequent as 'act as priest' (Ex. 40.13) from *kohēn* 'priest'.

kḥš: no B. D frequent as 'tell a lie' (I K. 13.18), once reflexive as 'act deceptively', *i.e.* 'make o.s. a lie' (II Sam. 22.45), associated with *kaḥaš* 'lie'. There exists also an unrelated B stative 'be lean' (Ps. 109.34).

kzb: 'lie' (pple.). D twelve times as 'tell a lie', associated with *kazab* 'lie' (Mic. 2.11). Š occurs as 'call s.o. a liar' (Job 24.25), assuming either a B stative 'be deceitful' or a noun 'liar'. Ar. *kaḏḏaba* has the BH Š-stem meaning, which would normally be carried in BH also by D. BH apparently specialized the two stems.

kny: no B, *cf.* Ar. *kanā/kannā*, both 'call by name'. D seven times as 'call by name' (Is. 45.4). There is no BH noun, but *cf.* Ar. *kunya* 'surname', *mukannan* 'surnamed'. The BH form is probably a comparable denominative.

kšp: no B. D six times as 'practice sorcery' (Ex. 7.11), associated with a noun *kešep* 'sorceries'. Also possible is D as a specialization of the root meaning reflected in the Arabic B-form *kašafa* 'reveal, disclose'.

lbb: no B. D twice as 'make cakes' (II Sam. 13.6), associated with *l^ebībah*, generally taken to refer to a specific kind of (heart-shaped) cake. This is, however, uncertain, since the *l^ebibôth* are described as 'boiled'. The denominative nature of D is nevertheless clear.

lḥš: no B. D once as 'whisper' (Ps. 58.6), in specific reference to the whisper used to charm a snake; twice reflexive as 'whisper (to one another)' (II Sam. 12.19), associated with *laḥaš* 'whisper', used several times in reference to the spell of the snake-charmer.

lqš: no B, *cf.* Ar. *laqaša* 'be late'; Syr. D 'do s.th. later'. D once as 'do late (the vineyard)', *i.e.* 'be last to come to the harvest, glean' (Job 24.6), perhaps from *leqeš* 'latter growth' (Am. 7.1).

mḥy: no B. D once in pass. pple., apparently as 'smeared with marrow, oozing marrow' (Is. 25.6), associated with *maḥ* 'marrow'.

mlḥ: 'salt'. D once in passive as 'be salted' (Ex. 30.35), Š also occurring once with a similar meaning (Ez. 16.4). All three stems are denominatives from *melaḥ* 'salt'.

mll: 'tap (the foot)' (once, Pr. 6.13; precise meaning uncertain). D four times as 'say, utter' (Gn. 21.7). While there is no cognate noun in BH, the Aramaic forms *millā/mallēl* 'word/speak' suggest an original denominative, as does the existence of a comparable Arabic denominative of Š, *'amalla* 'dictate (a letter)'. The BH B-form may be related to Ar. *malla* 'be weary' instead of the root discussed.

n'p: 'commit adultery'. D thirteen times as 'commit adultery' (Ex. 23.37). Both stems are denominatives of a noun 'adultery' (*cf.* BH *ni'up*).

ngn: 'play' (once as pple., Ps. 68.26). D nine times as 'make music (with an instrument)'. No cognate BH noun, but *cf.* Akk. *nigūtu* 'music', and note that D does not take a direct object. The single B pple. is probably a back-formation; the participles of both stems mean 'music-maker'.

nḥm: no B. D frequent as 'comfort' (Gn. 5.29), in reflexive 'comfort o.s.' (Gn. 37.35). It seems to be a denominative construction, despite the existence of N 'be comforted'. The latter would also be denominative.

nḥš: no B. D eight times as 'seek an omen, divine' (II K. 21.6), associated with *naḥaš* 'serpent', thus literally 'use a serpent (in s.th.)'. The reference is probably to the practice of snake-sorcery (prohibited in the law), though the meaning of D has been generalized.

s'p: no B. D once as 'cut off branches' (Is. 10.33), associated with *sa'ip* 'bough', *cf.* Ar. *sa'f* 'palm branch'.

s'r: 'be tempestuous (the sea)'. D once as 'make s.o. as a storm', *i.e.* 'scatter about, hurl' (Zec. 7.14), four times in passive as 'be stormtossed, whirl away' (Is. 54.11). B and D seem to be independent denominatives associated with *sa'ar* 'storm', thus 'be a storm' and 'make a storm', respectively.

sql: 'stone'. D four times as 'stone' (II Sam. 16.6), twice as 'clear away stones' (Is. 62.10), a partitive construction. Both stems are originally denominative, though no cognate noun exists in BH (*cf.* Ar. *ṯiql* 'weight'). Since B has a dual meaning, B may have evolved from the need to distinguish the two meanings.

'bt: no B. D once in an uncertain meaning (Mic. 7.3), in reference to satisfying an evil desire of the soul. Perhaps it is a denominative associated with *'aboṯ* 'cord', *cf.* Akk. *abuttu* 'fetter'.

'ṭr: 'surround'. D three times as 'crown' (Ps. 8.6), associated with a noun *'aṭarah* 'crown'; once as 'make a wreath' (SS 3.11). Š also occurs as 'crown' (Is. 23.8). All three stems are denominative, with B meaning 'be as a wreath', but not standing in an absolute-causative relationship to D.

'ks: 'fetter'. D once as 'shake the ankle-bracelet' (Is. 3.16), associated with *'ekes* 'ankle-bracelet'. B itself is probably a denominative from some cognate term, *cf.* Ar. *'ikās* 'a hobble'.

'mr: no B. D once as 'gather cut-off ears of grain' (Ps. 129.7), associated with *'omer* 'sheaf'.

'mr: no B, nor BH noun, *cf.* Ar. *ğimār* 'risk, hazard', *ğâmara* 'take a risk'. D twice in reflexive as 'make s.o. take a risk for o.s.' (Dt. 24.7), *i.e.* (in context) 'treat s.o. as a slave'.

'ng: no B. D once in passive pple. as 'delightful', *i.e.* 'thought to be a delight' (Jer. 6.2), associated with *'oneg* 'delight' (*cf.* MHb D-stem 'take delight in'). Also once reflexive as 'regard o.s. as a delight' (Dt. 28.56), seven times as 'have one's delight in s.th.' (Ps. 37.11).

'ny: 'sing'. D twice in this meaning (Is. 27.2). The fact that Ar. *ğannā* 'sing' exists in isolation (surely not connected with *ğanā* 'be rich') suggests that D may have been the original BH verbal form, despite the preponderance of B.

'pr: no B. D once as 'fling dust at' (Ez. 32.10), associated with *'āpar* 'dust'. Ar. *'afara* has this denominative meaning in both stems.

'ṣb: no B. D once as 'make s.o. a form', i.e. 'give form to s.o.' (Job 10.8), associated with *'āṣab* 'image'. Š occurs as 'make an image' (Jer. 44.19).

'ṣm: 'be mighty'; Š 'make mighty'. D once as 'chew bones' (Jer. 50.17), associated with *'eṣem* 'bone'.

pky: no B. D once as 'gurgle forth' (Ez. 47.2), lit. 'make the sound *pak̲*', *i.e.* the sound made by liquid being poured from a bottle.

pl': no B, *cf.* MHb 'be miraculous', the meaning of the BH N-form which has, as elsewhere, assumed a stative function. D three times as 'do s.th. miraculous, perform wonderfully well (a vow)' (Lv. 22.21). Š also occurs as 'do s.th. wonderfully' (Dt. 28.59). Both are associated with *pele'* 'miracle'. D once in reflexive as 'think o.s. marvelous' or 'regard o.s. as an extraordinary thing' (Job 10.16), thus may be either denominative or factitive.

ṣwy: no B. D common as 'command, appoint' (Nu. 27.19). The only associated noun, *miṣwah* 'command' is itself a secondary or tertiary form. Arabic *wṣy*, however, which also occurs only in D and Š, has associated nouns such as *waṣāh* 'command'.

qdm: no B. D five times as 'be in front, be first' (I Sam. 20.15), frequent as 'have s.th. before one', *i.e.* 'meet, confront s.o. or s.th.' (II Sam. 22.6). Thus D may be used both as a reflexive and as a transitive form, associated with *qedem* 'in front' (as a preposition) or 'that which was before (time) or in front (the East)'. The root developed quite differently in Arabic, B meaning 'go before', D 'make precede'.

qls: no B. D twice in active, three times in reflexive, both as 'mock, disdain' (Ez. 16.31; II K. 2.23), associated with *qeles* 'derision', thus 'hold s.o. in derision'.

qn': no B. D and Š both occur as denominatives, the former principally as 'feel jealousy, excitement' (Gn. 26.14), the latter exclusively as 'cause jealousy' (Dt. 32.16), an interesting specialization.

qnn: no B. D four times as 'make a nest' (Jer. 48.28), once in passive as 'nested' (Jer. 22.23), associated with *qēn* 'nest'.

qry: no B. D five times as 'lay the beams (for s.th.)' (Ps. 104.3), associated with *qōrah* 'beam'.

rbb: 'be many'. D once in passive (Ps. 144.13), perhaps with the meaning 'made many'. However, it is more likely in context that it means '10,000 times', lit. 'made 10,000', associated with *r^{e}babah* '10,000', as the preceding word in the verse, *ma'^{a}līpōt̲* is an Š denominative from *'elop* '1000'.

rb': 'square' (pass. pple.) D three times in passive pple. as 'squared' (Ez. 45.2). The B participle occurs more frequently, despite the usual association of such denominatives with D, e.g. 'make s.th. four'. Perhaps this situation arose because of the primary use of the D-form in the participle, since we have noted several times the use of B-forms for the more complicated D-stem verbal nouns and adjectives.

rḥm: no B. D frequent as 'love, have compassion' (I K. 8.50), associated with *reḥem* 'womb', used as a symbol of love and tenderness.

r'y: 'have dealings with'. D once as 'act as companion to s.o.' (Jd. 14.20), twice reflexive as 'think o.s. a companion to s.o.' (Pr. 22.24), associated with *rē'* 'friend'.

śdd: no B, nor any cognate noun in BH, *cf.* Syr. *sad(d)â* 'furrow'. D three times as 'make furrows (in), harrow' (Is. 28.24). Another possibility is that the form is associated with *śadeh* 'field' (*cf.* Akk. *šiddu*), thus 'make a field', *i.e.* 'mark out a field'.

śrk: no B, nor any cognate noun in BH, *cf.* Ar. *šarika* 'share in', *šarak* 'trap, snare'. D once, perhaps as 'make a snare of (the traces)', used of a young camel in heat (Jer. 2.23).

šw': no B. D frequent as 'cry out' (Is. 58.9), lit. 'give a cry', associated with *šewa'* 'cry' (though the original noun must have been something other than this form).

šlb: no B. D twice in passive as 'made into a frame' (Ex. 26.17), associated with *šalab* 'frame'. *Cf.* Ar. *saluba/sallaba* 'be solid/strengthen'.

šlš: no B. D four times as 'make three (of one)' (Dt. 19.3) or 'do s.th. three times' (I K. 18.34); five times in passive as 'threefold' (Ecc. 4.12) or 'be three (years old)' (Gn. 15.9). All are literally 'make or do three', associated with *šālôš* 'three'.

šqr: 'be false'. D five times as 'deceive' (I Sam. 15.29), associated with *šeqer* 'deception', thus 'practice deception on'. The link between B and D is thus indirect, the former really meaning 'be a deception'. One D-form listed under the variant *śqr* is a factitive 'make deceptive' (Is. 3.16).

šqṣ: no B. D six times as 'make s.th. detestable' or 'regard s.th. as an abomination' (Lv. 11.11), associated in an estimative function with *šeqeṣ* 'abomination'.

šrš: no B. D twice as 'root out' (Ps. 52.7), in the *pô'el* twice as 'take root' (Is. 40.24). Š occurs three times in the latter meaning (Is. 27.6). All verbal forms are associated with *šōreš* 'root', and present an interesting case either of dialectal assimilation or of semantic specialization.

t'r: 'turn, incline'. D once as 'trace out (a line, a form)' (Is. 44.13), associated with *to'ar* 'form', once in passive as 'made to turn', a causative-factitive usage (Jos. 19.13).

twy: no B. D once as 'make a mark' (I Sam. 21.14), associated with *taw* 'mark'. The form and root also occur as *t'y* (Nu. 34.7), and Š occurs with the same meaning (Ex. 9.4).

tl': no B. D once in passive as 'clothed in scarlet', lit. 'made to have scarlet cloth' (Nah. 2.4), associated with *tola'* 'scarlet-dyed cloth'.

t'b: no B. D sixteen times as 'abhor, think s.th. an abomination' (Dt. 23.8), associated with *tō'ēbah* 'abomination'. Š once as denominative 'perform an abomination' (I K. 21.26). Thus D is estimative, Š causative in usage.

According to Hirschfeld, "Den. Zeitwörter imfassen ein ungeheures Gebiet in allen Sprachen und spotten jeder Regel. Sie sind das treueste Merkmal der Fruchtbarkeit lebender Sprachen, und ihre Wucherungen gehen ins unendliche."[16] Literally the term 'denominative' denotes the process during which a root loses its exclusively nominal orientation and acquires a supplementary verbal orientation. In the Semitic languages this process can and does employ any of the verbal stems as media, but as in other language groups the simplest verbal stem (B) is the principal medium of denominalization. We again recall Rundgren's reference to the B-stem as a "possessive denominative", *e.g.* 'has *qṭl*', which defines a state of the subject in relation to a specific type of action (here a 'kill' or 'killing'). This possessive denominative is a type of stative, which then is seen to be the original force of the verb.

By this definition, 'to kill' in the B-stem is 'to be the possessor of a killing' as its subject and initiator, while 'to kill' in the D-stem is 'to make someone else the possessor of a killing' as its object. This is the difference between subjective and objective, between 'kill' and 'make killed'. Thus, von Soden writes of the D-stem in Akkadian that "auch von deverbalen Substantiven können Verben in D-Stamm denominiert

[16] Hirschfeld, "Bemerkungen zum Verbum denominativum im Hebräischen", 224.

werden (z.B. *aḫāzum* "fassen": *iḫzum* "überzug, Einfassung": *uḫḫuzum* "einfassen")."[17] Ninety years ago Philippi expressed a relevant idea when he remarked that "die Sprache ... unseren Grundstamm zunächst als eine participiale Form betrachtet und behandelt hat, und demnach im Semitischen das Verbum aus einer Nominalform hervorgegangen ist... ."[18] In a later development, particularly in Aramaic and Arabic dialects, the D-stem was also used as 'make someone the possessor of a killing', as its subject but not as its initiator, *i.e.* as a 'doubly transitive' form meaning 'make someone do something', thus overlapping the type of denominative function originally denoted by Š.

Thus, the roots and forms cited under Group II-A are not, in our thinking, distinguished from those in the preceding groups merely by their denominative origin, which can readily be seen to underlie all verbal forms and which has been patent throughout our survey of the D-stem. What is distinctive about this group is first, their function within the language, and second, the strongly nominal nature of the meanings they convey, this nominal overtone not having been universally retained in the case of the other groups. Their general function may best be described (as in our heading) as 'non-transformative', *i.e.* they do not, with the exception of one subtype, involve the transformation of an external object from one state into another. We may discern five basic types of denominative within this group, with the following approximate meanings:

(1) 'make (a nest, words, a lie)', *i.e.* be the originator of something.
(2) 'act upon (a tent, a serpent, bones)', *i.e.* do something with an object which already exists.
(3) 'give (praise, a command, comfort) to someone else'.
(4) 'act as (a priest, a brother-in-law)'.
(5) 'regard or treat someone or something as (sin, the first-borne, an abomination, a fiveness)'.

It is the last category which might be described as the 'exception', since it is clearly related to the estimative-declarative function which we have discussed earlier in this chapter, and which was particularly prevalent among D-forms associated with D-stem durative stative, *e.g. qll* 'be light', D 'treat as light, of no account'. Indeed, *ḥmš* occurs in the B-stem as 'be five, in five parts', and might well have been listed under Group I-A if it were not for its clearly nominal origin. Similarly we have *sʿr*, 'be as a storm', D 'make as a storm, scatter about'; *šqr* 'be a deception, be false', D 'practice a deception, deceive'. Undoubtedly, in other cases only the accidental absence of a B-form from our texts distinguishes denominatives of this type from such a root as *kbd*, 'have weight, be heavy', D 'give weight to, honor'. Thus this

[17] W. von Soden, "Grundriss des akkadischen Grammatik", in *Analecta Orientalia* 33 (1952), sec 88g.
[18] Philippi, "Der Grundstamm des starken Verbums im Semitischen", 82.

fifth type may be viewed as transformative in function without prejudicing our interpretation of the denominatives as a group.

Vis-à-vis the roots of Group I, our first four types of denominative D-forms are characterized by the fact that in each the object of the action is internal rather than external. This is true not only semantically, but also morphologically, *i.e.* the morpheme which denotes the object of the action (*e.g.* as *qnn* denotes 'nest') is also an element in the morphological structure of the verb itself. This last feature may be compared with the function of the infix /t/ in the morphological structure of the reflexive D-stem (and in the reflexives of other stems in cognate languages), which we described as 'auto-transformative'. These denominatives are analogous, and might also be referred to as auto-transformative, since they most often involve the subject's preoccupation with the object or process expressed in the noun and thus have reference to his own state; or as inner-transformative, since they often involve the performance of some action or process upon the associated noun. In addition to the inner object, many of these D-stems may also take an indirect object, *i.e.* indicate a recipient of the action taken or the object produced, *e.g.* 'tell a lie; give comfort; act as Levir' to someone else. The second person involved is the beneficiary and not the direct object of the subject's activity, as would be the case with D-stems of *šlm* or *qṭl*, where the object of and recipient of the action are identical.

These four types of 'pure' denominative D-stems are those referred to in Götze's dictum that "verbs of this type remain outside the verbal system in the stricter sense of the word."[19] As we indicated earlier, this judgment seems to us to be overly rigid, since denominative usage in all stems overlaps that of the 'regular' verb at many points. The principal difference between the 'regular' verb and those under discussion is morphological and syntactic, since in these denominatives an object, process or product intervenes between the subject and the recipient of his activity – which does not occur in the action-type verb of any stem. This is what is meant by the 'strongly nominal' nature of these D-forms, which puts them at odds with the subject-object relationship normally found in the D-stem. Yet we find this element in common with other D-stems: that often these denominatives either involve the removal of the subject from one state into another or denote some object in the process of formation – which is the denominative counterpart of a state in process of being achieved. As indicated under various roots, this aspect is particularly clear where B or Š denominatives also exist. These D-forms are different from, not other than, the main body of the stem, of which Götze himself says that the denominative function constitutes their primary force.

B. *Associated with Intransitive B-stems*

'rb: 'lie in wait (for s.o.), ambush'. D twice as 'waylay, lay an ambush for s.o.' (Jd. 9.25). Š once with the same meaning (I Sam. 15.5).

[19] Götze, "The So-Called Intensive", 3.

bṭ': 'speak rashly' (once: Pr. 12.18). D twice with this meaning (Lv. 5.4).

dlg: 'leap' (once: Zep. 1.9). D four times as 'leap' (SS 2.8). The Arabic root *drj* 'depart' likewise has the same meaning in both stems.

hlk: 'walk, go'. D frequent in the active as 'walk' (Ps. 8.14), and in the reflexive as 'walk about, disperse' (Gn. 13.17; Jd. 21.24). Š is also frequent as 'cause to go, lead' (Dt. 8.2). The use of both B and D forms for 'go, walk' could be explained in at least these two ways: (1) the result of an effort to vary the language for a common verb, or (2) the result of denominative usage in the D-stem. In the latter case the sequence would be 'walk/take a walk/take a walk for oneself' as in English, all having substantially the same meaning. Another, probably better explanation of the D reflexive is, that it is at least partially related in meaning to the Š-form, *i.e.* it may be related to a causative type of D-stem which does not appear as such. This is suggested by the fact that the reflexive is often employed in such phrases as 'walk with God, behave o.s., wander', all of which might be literally construed as 'cause o.s. to walk, lead o.s.'.

zmr: no B, *cf.* Akk. *zamāru* 'sing, play (an instrument)'; Ar. *zamara*/*zammara*, both 'blow, play (an instrument)'. D frequent as 'sing, praise, play (an instrument)' (Ps. 147.1). The last meaning occurs with a preposition, thus means literally 'sing (by means of or with) an instrument'.

znq: no B, *cf.* MHb 'leap forth'; Syr. 'throw'. The root idea seems to be that of forward motion, which came in Syriac at least to have transitive significance, but in Hebrew remained intransitive both in B and in D. D once, seemingly as 'leap forward' (Dt. 33.22). It is also possible that the root is connected with Ar. *zanaqa* 'constrict' (*cf.* BH *ziqqîn* 'fetters'), in the sense of 'make a constricted move'.

ḥky: 'wait for' (once in pple.: Is. 30.18). D twelve times as 'wait for' (Is. 8.17). Since MHb and Aramaic likewise employ this root in D, it seems that B here is the aberrant form, especially as it is participial.

ḥmd: 'desire, delight in'. D once as 'desire' (SS 2.3). Both stems may be denominative, as 'attribute loveliness to', associated with *ḥemed.*

yḥl: no B, *cf.* Ar. *waḥila* 'be stuck, in a deadlock'; MHb *yiḥûl* 'expectation'. D frequent as 'wait for' (Ps. 118.49). Š also occurs with this meaning (I Sam. 10.8). The fact that both D and Š occur, with no B, suggests that the original form is denominative, *i.e.* 'have an expectation (of s.th.), have hope for (s.th.)'.

yrš: 'take possession of'. D once in this meaning (Dt. 28.42). Š occurs frequently, usually with this meaning (Nu. 14.24), twice as 'cause to possess' (Job 13.26). For the cognate Arabic root *wariṯa* 'inherit', the D-form serves a causative function, as with BH *nḥl* 'take possession'.

khy: 'grow dim, weak'. D twice as 'be faint' (Lv. 13.6), once as 'be weak' (Ez. 21.12). This is an unusual case of a stative meaning in both B and D. D occurs once more regularly, as 'weaken, discourage' (I Sam. 3.13).

ktr: no B, *cf.* Aram. *ktr* 'surround'; BH *keter* 'headdress'. D twice as 'lie in wait for, ambush' (Ps. 22.13), once as 'wait for, bear with' (Job 36.2). Š occurs twice as 'surround' in the literal sense (Hab. 1.4), as opposed to D's figurative use.

m'n; no B, *cf.* Eth. *mnn* 'refuse'. D frequent as 'refuse' (II K. 5.16), usually with a verbal noun as object, thus as 'refuse to'. MHb has specialized D as 'refuse (in marriage)'. If the B-form of this root was ever in use, it may have been supplanted by the partially homonymous *m'ṣ* 'reject, refuse', D being left principally in its infinitival combination.

mhr: no B, *cf.* N 'be carried headlong, be hasty'; Ar. *mahara* 'be skillful, adroit', *i.e.* 'be quick (in doing s.th.)'. D common as 'hasten, hurry' (Jos. 4.10). The difference between B and D forms associated with this root in the various languages may be the difference between stative and active aspects, *i.e.* 'be quick' and 'act quickly'. Or, the D-forms may be denominative, as 'be in a hurry'.

mʿṭ: 'become few (in number), diminish'. D once in this meaning (Ecc. 12.3), again a use of D for a stative concept. Š occurs as 'make few' (Ex. 16.17), a meaning one might have expected for D as well.

nhg: no B, *cf.* Syr. 'sigh'; Ar. *nahija* 'pant'. D once as 'sigh, moan' (Nah. 2.8). The Arabic D-form means 'make breathless, cause to pant'.

nḥr: no B, *cf.* Ar. *naḫara* 'snort'. D once as 'snort, be angry with' (SS 1.6).

nṭl: 'hold (up, over, out)'. D once as 'hold up' (Is. 63.9).

ntr: 'leap, jump'. D once as 'leap' (Lv. 11.21), while Š is used as a causative (Is. 58.6).

npḥ: 'blow'. D once in passive as 'be blown (upon)' (Job 20.26).

sld: no B, *cf.* MHb 'jump'. D once as 'jump' (Job 6.10). D might also be construed as a factitive associated with a stative like Ar. *ṣalada* 'be hard (the ground)', thus 'make the ground hard (by jumping)'.

smr: 'bristle up (the hair), rise (the flesh)', *cf.* Ar. *šammara* 'make rise'. D once as 'bristle up' (Job 4.15).

ʿwl: no B, *cf.* Ar. *ʿāla* 'deviate (from the right)'. D twice as 'act unjustly, be wicked' (Is. 26.10). It might also be construed as a denominative associated with *ʿiwel* 'injustice'.

ʿqb: 'supplant', *cf.* Ar. *ʿaqaba* 'follow, succeed s.o.' D once as 'supplant' (Job 37.4). Both verbal stems have been construed as denominatives associated with *ʿaqēb* 'heel', probably because of the association of the verb with the Jacob narrative (Gn. 37.36), but in light of the existence of the Arabic cognate the Genesis passage may better be taken as a play on words.

pzz: 'leap up, emerge (from)', *cf.* Ar. *fazza* 'jump'. D once as 'leap' (II Sam. 6.16).

pḥd: 'tremble (from fear)'. D twice in this meaning (Is. 51.13). Š occurs as 'cause to tremble' (Job 4.14).

pls: no B, *cf.* Akk. *naplusu* 'look at, examine'; BH *peles* 'a balance', *i.e.* 'that which weighs, considers'. D twice as 'consider, heed' (Pr. 5.6).

psḥ: 'limp, pass over'. D once as 'limp' (I K. 18.26).

ṣmḥ: 'sprout, spring up'. D four times as 'sprout, grow out (hair)' (Jd. 16.22). The D-stem may reflect a specialization of meaning, although B does occur once in the same context (Lv. 13.37).

ṣʿq: 'cry out, call'. D once as 'cry out' (II K. 2.12). Š occurs once as 'call (together)' (I Sam. 10.17).

ṣpy: 'keep watch for, look out for'. D eight times in this meaning (Lam. 4.7). The D-form of Ar. *ṣafā* 'be intent upon' has a meaning 'settle'.

qwy: 'wait for', *cf.* Ar. *qawā* 'be tense, strong'. D more frequent in this meaning (Gn. 49.18). Arabic D-stem means 'strengthen'.

qpṣ: no B, *cf.* Ar. *qafaza* 'jump, take off'. D once as 'leap' (SS 2.8).

rḥp: 'shake, flutter'. D twice as 'flutter' (Gn. 1.2).

rnn: 'cry out (with joy)'. D frequent as 'cry out' (Is. 26.19). Š occurs both in this meaning (suggesting a denominative meaning for all three), and as a causative 'make to cry out' (Dt. 32.15).

rṣd: 'watch (for)'. D once as 'watch for' (Ps. 68.17). D of Ar. *raṣada* 'watch' is used as a causative 'make ready, cause to watch'.

rqd: 'skip, dance', D five times as 'dance' (Is. 13.21). Š occurs once as 'cause to dance' (Ps. 29.6).

š'l: 'desire, seek, ask'. D twice as 'ask, seek' (II Sam. 20.18), once as 'ask (for o.s.), beg'. The latter meaning is found in Arabic in the D reflexive form of the root. Š occurs as 'cause s.o. to ask' (Ex. 12.36).

šmr: 'keep, observe'. D once in a figurative sense as 'revere', *i.e.* 'keep (idols)' (Jon. 2.9), twice in reflexive as 'keep o.s. (from s.th.)' (II Sam. 22.24).

This group includes the second category of D-stems with which intensive-frequentative significance has traditionally been associated, namely those which express concepts of physical effort, vocal projection or expectation over a period of time, *e.g. dlg* 'leap', *nḥr* 'snort' and *qwy* 'wait', respectively, and which have similar meanings in the B and D forms. It is the last fact which again has led to the belief that D, being different in form and therefore necessarily different in function from B, must have expressed intensitivity or repetition of the action expressed in B. Thus, as Götze pointed out, "forms of the type *hillēḵ* ... were given an increasing import on the classification of the ordinary D forms."[20] This tendency was made particularly pronounced by the example of these roots, since there is some sound linguistic basis to support the hypothesis of repeated action (which is not the case for verbs of the Group I-C), even though the textual evidence is slight.

When we discussed Group I-C we mentioned those theses which concerned the existence of 'cursive' forms within the D-stem, those which Götze called "a small group of apparent D forms"[20] which remained unaccounted for after he had finished his survey of D-forms based upon the stative: forms such as Akk. *ruqqudum* 'dance' and *qubbum* 'shout', their meanings similar to those of the corresponding B-forms. Referring to these as 'cursives', he means by this term forms which denote a state of continuous action, and which therefore can not be reconciled with statives. He is particularly careful to distinguish these from 'perfect statives' such as Akk. *wasib* 'is seated' and *ṭebī* 'is sunk', which denote rest after movement and imply termination of the activity, pointing out that "cursive intransitives ... are incapable of having such statives at their side."[20] Seeking the origin of such forms he writes:

For their explanation it is well to remember that the specific connotation of Hebrew verbs like *hillck* "walk continuously, habitually" is in Akkadian ordinarily expressed by the Btn forms. That is to say, Hebrew *y^ehallēk* corresponds in meaning to Akkadian *ittallak*, the preterite whose present is *ittanallak*. ... The Akkadian forms undoubtedly developed from *ya-h-tán-lak*. ... It seems furthermore clear that the continuative force of the form is not motivated by the t-infix ...: hence it must be ascribed to the presence of an n-infix. This in

[20] Götze, "The So-Called Intensive", 6.

turn suggests that Hebrew *yᵉhallek, yᵉraqqed* may originate from *ya-ha-n-lik, ya-ra-n-qid,* and Akkadian *urraqqid* from *yu-ra-n-qid.* In other words, the question arises: may not all these forms be the remnants of an old Bn form to which Btn originally corresponded in the same way as Bt to B?

The 'different function' which Götze earlier ascribed to the *t*-infix,[21] was "to denote the action which has just been performed and still affects the situation", as opposed to the preterite which "refers to an action as a past fact." The *n*-infix, then, alone implies a continuative force for the action of the B-stem.

More recently, Speiser has called Götze's explanation of the *tán*-infix into question, maintaining that not the /n/ alone, but the whole infix is the sign of continuative (or durative) action.[22] Thus he would hold that only the D reflexive form of Hebrew shows this characteristic. He does not state what he would consider to be the force of /n/ alone, but the implication is that either he would not admit its existence apart from *-tan-*, or would give it some other significance. This difference of opinion confirms Landsberger's early note, that the presence of durative verbs of action in West Semitic could not be indicated with certainty, although he cites the nomina professionis and a few D-stems (*e.g. dbr, zmr*) as possibilities for such classification.[23]

It is here that the related hypothesis concerning the existence of an original present-future comes to our attention again, as well as Brockelmann's positing of a cursive aspect underlying the verbal stems of the western as well as the eastern languages. A third variation of this idea has been put forward by Rundgren, who, assuming that the base *-dammiq* is, *vis-à-vis damiq*, elative, intensive and iterative in connotation, sets up a tripartite opposition *damiq* 'is good'/*idammiq* 'becomes good'/*udammiq* 'makes (s.th.) good', in which the first two (unmarked) terms represent the intransitive and neutral aspects, the third (marked) term the transitive. In his view, the elative base *-dammiq* has been employed in *idammiq* not in its original morphological sense, but for "renewal of the cursive aspect", that cursive aspect having been inherent in the stative *damiq*. It is the elative-intensive-iterative mood reflected in *ruqqudum, dullupum etc.* But, according to Rundgren, this function never became a fully-developed category in Akkadian, thus forms such as *ipaqqid* and *iparras* were no longer iterative (a series of repeated acts), but were mainly an expression of the cursive aspect (an act continued for some time), replacing and strengthening the force of the older form *idmiq* (*yá-damiq*). Because the iterative-intensive function was abortive, the base *damiq* combined with *udammiq* as 'be good' and 'make good' respectively. The original use of *idammiq*, however, left its traces in the lexicon, specifically in those verbs which he, like Götze, describes as cursive intransitives, such as *uraqqid* (presumably by some process of lexical assimilation which rendered the difference in vocalization of the prefixes insignificant). It was, then, the transferral of the elative

[21] A. Götze, "The T-Form of the Old Babylonian Verb", in *JAOS* 56 (1936).
[22] Speiser, "The Durative Hithpaʿel".
[23] B. Landsberger, "Prinzipienfragen der semitischen, speziell der hebräischen Grammatik", in *Orientalistische Literaturzeitung* 29 (1926), Column 972.

base *-dammiq* from the stative verbs, to which it stood in a cursive relationship, which engendered the confusion surrounding the function of the D-stem. As evidence for his view, Rundgren cites Ethiopic, where an original *yuqattilu* became the cursive aspect of *qatala* (*réemploi de l'intensif*), while its original 'intensive' meaning was in turn renewed by the frequentative type *sabābara.*

We have outlined Rundgren's argument at length because of the fact that Group II-B contains one root which tends to confirm his hypothesis, namely *khy*. In B the root means 'be dim, faint', while in D it occurs twice as 'become faint, dim' and once as 'weaken, discourage'. This could well reflect the opposition *damiq*/*idammiq*/*udammiq*, with reduction of the last two forms to one (the stems actually occur in the perfect). The D meaning 'become faint' would then be regarded as an anachronism, a usage of the *qttl*-theme which had ceased to be a living part of the language. Moreover, such roots as *ḥmd*, *ʿqb*, *yrš*, *ʿwl*, plus all of those connected with the concept of 'waiting' or 'expectation' (*e.g. yhl*, *qwy*) have semantic relationships with the roots of Groups I-A and I-B, and in some cases are clearly stative in the cognate languages. This suggests that these D-forms may also be lexical curiosities, survivals of original *yadammiq*, while their counterparts in Group I evolved from the prevailing factitive meaning of original *yudammiq*.

Whether this, if true, implies a corresponding iterative-become-cursive meaning for the other verbs of this group, prodominantly those of motion and sound-projection, is a moot question – although the likelihood of this is increased. Together, these verbs constitute twenty of the thirty-nine in this group. All these are intransitive, but it would be stretching the term somewhat, to describe them as verbs of continuing action, particularly such concepts as 'leap', 'snort' or 'sigh'. At the same time, it must be noted that not very many comparable roots have appeared in our other groups, indicating perhaps that this group of D-stems in Hebrew does form a unit related in some way to the equivalent Akkadian group. The danger lies in classifying all of them on the basis proposed for *hlk*. If most do not conform to its pattern, then *hlk* itself may be misclassified. As we survey its occurrences in the texts, one can not say that 'walk about' or 'walk continuously' is any more appropriate a translation for D-forms than for B-forms of the root. Therefore one must conclude either that the usage of an infix *-n-* or *-tan-* was less rigid in the Western languages (at least in Hebrew), or that other factors are at work within this group of roots. One is left, then, with a choice of variations on the iterative-cursive-present-future theme, or with the possibility not yet mentioned, that these twenty D-forms are denominatives such as 'take a walk', 'make a leap', 'give a shout', comparable with roots found in Group II-A. Either explanation would comport well with the non-transformative nature of the roots; the latter would make superfluous the positing of an infix unique to these roots, which would simplify somewhat the D-stem problem.

APPENDIX A

D forms of uncertain origin

Outside of those roots covered in the previous sections of this chapter, there is a small group which has not yielded at all to analysis. They are now included for completeness.

ṭnp: no B, either in BH or in the cognate languages, which likewise employ the root exclusively in D. D once as 'soil (the feet)' (SS. 5.3).

skn: no B. D once in passive pple. with meaning unclear (Is. 40.20). Ar. *sakana* 'be peaceful' may be cognate, but a factitive meaning 'make peaceful' is not particularly apt in context.

p'r: no B. D six times as 'glorify' (Is. 60.7), seven times reflexive as 'show one's own glory' (Is. 44.25) or 'glorify oneself' (Jud. 7.2). There is probably some connection between the verbal stem and the noun *pᵉʾēr* 'headdress', but the nature of the association is unclear.

pnq: no B. D once in passive pple. as 'pampered, indulged' (Pr. 29.21), *cf.* D forms in MHb and Syriac; Ar. *tafannaqa* 'live in ease', *i.e.* 'indulge oneself'.

psg: no B. D once with meaning unclear (Ps. 48.14) and no cognates.

šrt: no B in BH or cognate languages. D common as 'serve' (Ex. 28.35), the root having no pure nominal forms. The radicals may originally be those of the divine name Ašerat, in which case the original meaning would be, *e.g.* 'act for Ašerat', later generalized to refer to any holy service.

tky: no B. D once in passive with meaning unclear (Dt. 33.3). A possible cognate is Ar. *takka* 'trample' in which case D may mean 'cause to trample', *i.e.* 'tread in another's footsteps'.

APPENDIX B

D-stems in Biblical Aramaic

As one would expect, in light of the limited number of Aramaic texts in the Old Testament, there are relatively few forms to be discussed here, and only forty-eight roots in all. In general, these fall into the same categories as the D-forms of Biblical Hebrew, and will be listed here in the same classifications. However, there are some differences in usage, which we shall note a little later, as well as some differences in provenance. These must be taken into account when we make our final remarks about the D-stem.

I. D-STEMS TRANSFORMATIVE

A. *Associated with B-stems Durative Stative*

bhl: no B, *cf.* Targum 'be disturbed, upset'. D six times as 'frighten' (Dan. 5.6), once reflexive as 'be frightened' (Dan. 5.9).

dḥl: 'be afraid, fear', *cf.* Ar. *daḥl* 'resentment'. D once as 'frighten' (Dan. 4.2).

ḥnn: 'be merciful, show mercy'. D once in reflexive as 'implore' (Dan. 6.12), *i.e.* 'make s.o. merciful to o.s.' Ar. *taḥannana* occurs as 'feel pity', *i.e.* 'show o.s. merciful'. The BA form is closer to what one would expect in Arabic Stem X, 'ask s.o. to show mercy' (does not occur).

yṣb: no B, *cf.* Ar. *waṣaba* 'be firm, persist'. D once as 'make certain' (Dan. 7.19), *cf.* BH D reflexive 'hold one's ground, take a stand'.

ndb: no B, *cf.* TA, MHb 'be willing, act willingly'. D four times as 'offer freely', *i.e.* 'show o.s. willing' (Ezra 7.13), *cf.* BH D reflexive 'volunteer'. Another possibility is that this D-form is connected with a B-form like Ar. *nadaba* 'assign, entrust', thus 'assign o.s., have o.s. entrusted'.

nṣḥ: no B, *cf.* TA 'be illustrious, shine'; Ar. *naṣaḥa* 'be sincere'. D once in reflexive as 'distinguish o.s.' (Dan. 6.4).

qrb: 'be near, approach'. D once as 'offer (a sacrifice)' (Ezra 7.17), *i.e.* 'bring s.th. near'. Š occurs twice with the same meaning (Ezra 6.10, 6.17).

rby: 'be great, grow up'. D once as 'make so.. great, honor' (Dan. 2.48).

šdr: no B, *cf.* MHb 'be strong'; Ar. *sadira* 'be reckless'. D once in reflexive as 'strive, labor (to do s.th.)' (Dan. 6.15), *i.e.* 'strengthen o.s. (for s.th.)'.

šwy: 'be like', *cf.* Ar. *sawā* 'be like'. D once as 'make like' (Dan. 5.21), once in reflexive as 'be made like' (Dan. 3.29), a meaning found in the Targum Š-stem as well.

šny: 'be different, changed'. D three times as 'change s.th.' (Dan. 3.28), four times in reflexive as 'be changed' (Dan. 3.19).

tqp: 'be strong'. D once as 'enforce, strengthen (a statute)' (Dan. 6.8).

B. *Associated with B-stems Perfect Stative*

bṭl: 'be at an end, cease'. D four times as 'stop, halt' (Ezra 4.21), *cf.* TA *bṭl*, in B 'cease (to work)', in D 'make s.o. cease (from working)'.

ṭ'm: no B, *cf.* TA 'taste, eat'; Ar. *ta'ima* 'eat'. D three times as 'make s.o. eat, give to eat' (Dan. 4.22).

qwm: 'rise, stand, endure'. D once as 'establish, set up (a statute)' (Dan. 6.8), a meaning found more frequently in Š (Dan. 6.9), in various contexts. The D-form may also be a denominative of *q^{e}yam* 'statute'.

škn: 'dwell'. D once as 'make s.th. dwell' (Ezra 6.12).

šm': 'hear'. D once in reflexive as 'obey', *i.e.* 'cause o.s. to hear' (Dan. 7.27), a meaning not found associated with this root in the cognate languages.

C. *Associated with B-stems Transitive*

bdr: no B, *cf.* TA 'scatter'; BH *bzr* 'scatter' (B and D). D once in this meaning (Dan. 4.11).

b'y: 'seek, request'. D once as 'seek' (Dan. 4.33), perhaps as a result of error in transmission of the text, since the D-form does not appear in any of the standard Aramaic lexicons, or in the cognate languages.

bqr: no B, *cf.* Ar. *baqara* 'split open'. D five times as 'investigate', *i.e.* 'make revealed, split apart' (Ezra 4.15), once reflexive as 'be investigated' (Ezra 5.17). In TA this meaning is found in B only, in BH and MHb in D only.

ḥbl: no B, *cf.* Akk. *ḫabālu* 'destroy'; Ar. *ḫabala* 'confuse, hinder'. D three times as 'destroy' (Dan. 4.20), three times reflexive as 'perish, be destroyed' (Dan. 2.44).

ḥwy: no B, *cf.* perhaps Ar. *waḥā* 'tell'. D four times as 'make known' (Dan. 2.4), a meaning found more often in Š (Dan. 2.6). D in TA means 'say, speak' as well as sharing the Š meaning 'show' (exists in Arabic also).

ḥrk: no B, *cf.* perhaps Ar. *ḥaraqa* 'burn'. D once in reflexive as 'be singed, burned' (Dan. 3.27).

yʿṭ: 'advise'. D once in reflexive (ithpa.) as 'advise one another, be agreed' (Dan. 6.8), a meaning like that of Arabic Stem III.

knš: 'assemble' (trans.). D twice in reflexive as 'be assembled, assemble (intr.)' (Dan. 3.3).

kpt: 'bind'. D three times as 'bind' (Dan. 3.20). Ar. *kafata*, 'restrain' in B, has the specialized meaning 'inlay' in D.

mny: 'number'. D four times as 'appoint' (Dan. 4.29): the same specialization of meanings found in BH.

nsk: no B, *cf.* BH *nsk*, Ar. *nasaka* 'pour out'. D once as 'pour out', used specifically of a libation or incense (Dan. 2.46).

nśʾ: 'carry (away)'. D once in reflexive as 'let o.s. be carried away (against), rise up against' (Ezra 4.19). TA has no D for this root.

str: no B, *cf.* Ar. *satara* 'hide' (B and D); BH N-stem 'be concealed, hide o.s.' D once in passive pple. as 'hidden things' (Dan. 2.22).

ʿrb: no B, *cf.* TA, Syr. 'mix'. D twice in passive pple. as 'mixed' (Dan. 2.41), once in reflexive as 'be mixed, mingle' (Dan. 2.43).

prš: no B, *cf.* Akk. *parāsu*, BH *prš* 'explain'; Ar. *faraša* 'spread out'. D once in passive pple. as 'be explained, read, interpreted (a letter)' (Ezra 4.18), or possibly a factitive 'be made clear', *cf.* TA B-form 'be clear'.

pšr: 'interpret'. D once in active pple. as 'interpreter' (Dan. 5.12). In TA, B and D are usually specialized as 'reveal' and 'set loose'.

ṣbʿ: no B, *cf.* TA, BH 'dye'; Mandaic 'baptize'. D once in passive pple. as 'be moistened, wet' (Dan. 4.22).

qbl: no B, *cf.* Ar. *qabila* 'receive'. D four times as 'receive, accept' (Dan. 6.1). The D-form was probably the original medium for this meaning as in Hebrew and Arabic, the Arabic B-stem being a back-formation as a result of the specialization of *qabbala* as 'kiss'.

qṭl: 'kill'. D twice as 'kill' (Dan. 3.22), once in reflexive as 'be killed' (Dan. 2.13), the B reflexive form occurring twice in the same verse with the latter.

qṣṣ: no B, *cf.* BH and Ar. 'cut off' (B and D). D once as 'cut off' (Dan. 4.11).

rʿʿ: 'crush' (once). D once (in the same verse) as 'crush' (Dan. 2.40).

šry: 'loosen, let loose'. D once as 'solve (a problem)' (Dan. 5.12), once as 'begin' (Ezra 5.2), twice in reflexive as 'be loosened, shake' (Dan. 5.6).

II. D-STEMS NON-TRANSFORMATIVE

A. *Associated with Nominal Forms*

hdr: no B. D three times as 'glorify' (Dan. 4.31), associated with *hᵉdar* 'majesty', thus 'attribute majesty (to s.o.)'. The BH counterpart of this form is found in B, but preserves one element of what must have been an original D-form, in the *hitpaʿʿel* 'behave arrogantly, attribute glory to o.s.' (Pr. 25.6).

mll: no B. D five times as 'speak' (Dan.7.25). Like the BH D-stem of this root, this form is probably associated with a noun like *millah* 'word', but could also be a factitive of an original B-stem corresponding to Ar. *malla* 'be weary', thus 'make s.o. weary (with speech)'.

nby: no B. D once in reflexive as 'act as a prophet, prophesy' (Ezra 5.1), associated with the nominal stem contained in such a noun as *nᵉbiyyayâ* 'prophet' (*cf.* BH *nābî'*). While the same meaning occurs also in the N-stem of BH, only the present form occurs in Targum, Syriac and other Aramaic dialects.

śkl: no B. D once in reflexive as 'consider' (Dan. 7.8), associated with some noun such as BH *śekel* 'insight'. The BH Š denominative 'have insight' or 'give insight (to s.o.)' has Aramaic parallels in both D and Š, and in the Targum B-stem 'recognize, have insight'. All Aramaic dialects however, have the D reflexive form cited here.

šbḥ: no B. D five times as 'praise' (Dan. 5.4), associated with some noun like Targumic *šᵉʾbaḥ* reward, praise'.

šmš: no B. D once as 'serve (God)' (Dan. 7.10), a meaning which seems to have been generalized from an original association with *šᵉmaš* 'sun', *i.e.* 'act in relation to the sun' or 'act upon the sun'.

B. *Associated with B-stems Intransitive*

hlk: 'walk'. D once as 'walk' (Dan. 4.26), a meaning also found twice in the Š-stem (Dan. 3.25).

sly: no B, *cf.* TA and Syr. 'bend down'. D twice as 'pray', *i.e.* 'bend down (to the earth)' (Dan. 6.11; Ezra 6.10). D seems to be a specialization of meaning, occurring also in Arabic.

While it would be unwise to make too-broad generalizations concerning the use of the D-stem in *Reichsaramäisch* from this small sampling, yet a few points of interest may be noted, the most striking of which is the degree to which B- and D-forms are kept distinct in this dialect. Thus, from the twenty-two roots of Group I-C (where, our experience with Biblical Hebrew would indicate, we might expect overlap in usage), twelve occur in D alone, and we must rely upon evidence from cognate languages that a B-stem may have existed at one time. This reminds us of what Dillmann has remarked concerning Ethiopic, that it "has mostly given up the first stem in the case of those verbal notions which it has developed in the second ... for when both stems are fully formed there is no longer any essential difference in the meaning."[24] While the absence of a B or D form in Biblical Aramaic where one

[24] Dillmann, *Ethiopic Grammar*, 144.

exists for a corresponding Hebrew root is undoubtedly in large part an outcome of the more limited Aramaic texts (and the missing form often occurs in Targumic Aramaic), yet at least one may say that in these texts the trend is against a proliferation of stems and duplication of meanings. Only four roots reveal overlap of stem usage in the present context. Twelve roots, as we have stated, occur in D alone. In addition, two (*mny*, *šry*) have specialized meanings in each stem, while one other (*bʿy*) may represent a textual error. Finally, three others (*yʿṭ*, *knš*, *nšʾ*) are found in the reflexive only, with specialized meanings quite different from those found in the corresponding B-stems.

For eight roots in various groups, the only existing D-form is either a passive participle or a reflexive form serving as a passive. The reflexive-passive form is also predominant in other roots for which a simple D-form DOES exist. In fact, in all five groups the reflexive D-stem is proportionally more common and more varied in meaning than in the Hebrew texts. This greater frequency is a result primarily of the Aramaic reclassification of the Common Semitic reflexive infix *-t-* as the principal morpheme for indicating the passive mood (in both B and D). Because of this, it occurs where one would expect the puʿʿal in Biblical Hebrew, and like the *puʿʿal* it often configurates with the B-stem. In addition, this dialect seems to have employed the D reflexive to express mutual action (*yʿṭ*) and action sought after (*ḥnn*). Moreover, for some roots the form seems to have assumed the semantic function of what would in Hebrew or Arabic be the stative aspect of the B-stem (*ḥbl*, *knš*, *ʿrb*, *šry*). Finally, in some cases it retains the Common Semitic true reflexive function, particularly in the roots of Groups I-A, I-B and II-A. This tendency toward greater lexical freedom in the use of the reflexive morpheme is accompanied in some instances by a freer use of the D-stem factitive meaning as well, this factitive aspect becoming less important from the standpoint of lexicon, if not from that of historical linguistics.

Essentially, what has transpired is that D, both simple and reflexive, is seen to stand as an alternative stem to B even more than in Biblical Hebrew. That is, its special historical relationship to B-forms (or better, stative forms), demonstrated for Akkadian in Götze's article, and for Biblical Hebrew earlier in this chapter, is partially lost or obscured in the Aramaic lexicon. While the transformative-factitive nature of the stem is always present and can be easily reconstructed, at least superficially the B and D-forms, simple and reflexive, are used independently of one another, particularly in the case of the roots in Group I-C (for which, of course, the freedom of usage was the greatest in Hebrew also). Thus most Biblical Aramaic roots express simple action in either B or D, not both; and where both exist the reason often seems to be the desire for stylistic variety (*e.g. qṭl*, *rʿʿ*). B simple and D reflexive often form an active/passive opposition, even occasionally D simple and B reflexive. D reflexive sometimes serves as a medium for the stative aspect of the root, as does the N-stem in Biblical Hebrew. Also noteworthy in this regard is the infrequent overlap of D and Š within these roots, another sign of lexical economy.

A corollary point to be noted, is that the Aramaic lexicon will sometimes associate the D-stem of a given root with a different aspect of that root's meaning than the one associated with the corresponding Biblical Hebrew D-stem. This is most obvious in the case of such semantic differences as that reflected in the two D-forms of *rby*, for which Hebrew developed the idea of making objects large in size or numerous, Aramaic that of making someone great, in the sense of important or powerful. However, it also exists more subtly in such a root as *nṣḥ*. The BH D-form of this root, 'direct, oversee', seems to be associated with the active aspect of the root reflected in MHb 'conquer, prevail over' (B) and Arabic *naṣaḥa* 'advise'. The Biblical Aramaic D reflexive form 'distinguish oneself' seems, however, to be associated with the root's stative aspect as reflected in Targumic Arabic and Syriac 'be illustrious, shine' and Arabic 'be sincere, well-disposed'. While both D-forms are factitive, the difference is that between 'make s.o. conquered' (BH) and 'make s.o. conquering' (BA). Likewise, the BH D-form of *bhl* seems to presuppose an active B-stem 'precipitate, move s.th. quickly' (on the basis of the N-stem 'be disturbed'), while the BA D-form presupposes a B-stative 'be disturbed' (which exists in Targumic Aramaic without a corresponding D-stem).

Yet, most of these differences between Old Testament Hebrew and Aramaic are lexical in nature, and do not undercut our understanding of the general function of the D-stem. In fact, this understanding is strengthened by the insignificant role which non-transformative D-forms play in this dialect, particularly by the fact that only two of the roots at most can be listed as Group II-B 'cursives'. While 75% of the D-forms of Biblical Hebrew were listed as transformative and associated with stative concepts, the proportion in Biblical Aramaic is nearly 85%. Thus there is even less ground here for positing an intensive or frequentative meaning for the stem. Biblical Aramaic, in its limited way, shares with the dialects of Targum Onkelos and the Peshiṭta the two tendencies we noted in Chapter IV, to break down the barriers between B and D stems, and to identify the individual root with one stem only of the two.

VI

THE D-STEM IN QUR'ANIC ARABIC

The purpose of this chapter is similar to that of the chapter preceding: to list and comment upon the types of D-forms which occur in the text of the Qur'an. For this purpose we shall employ the same system of classification developed for Biblical Hebrew, not only because this will facilitate comparison between the forms of the two languages, but also because this system is, if anything, more appropriate to the forms of the Qur'an than it was to those of the Old Testament.

Once again, however, we would stress the point that our classification of D-forms according to the type of B-stem or noun associated with the root does not necessarily imply that the D-form has therefore been 'derived' from the other, at least in the traditional sense of the word (which implies a conscious act). Rather, even though many of the existent D-forms MAY have been consciously derived insofar as they represent analogical extensions of the D-function to new roots, the D-stem is best thought of as an alternate way of handling the root concept. Our classification, then, is based upon the simplest existent form of the root, verbal or nominal. For instance, in several cases we note that both B and D seem to be denominative in origin, yet in most such cases the root will be found not with the denominatives of II-A but in the appropriate section of Group I, those D-forms associated with B-stems. The distinction drawn does not refute the position that the D-stem as a whole is basically denominative in its origin; Group II-A consists principally of those roots for which no B-stem happened to develop but which can be found in nouns which illuminate the meaning of the D-form involved.

Regarding the relationship of the B- and D-stems, this seems to be as appropriate a place as any to comment more fully upon the proposition of the Arab grammarians that the D-stem, where it is not clearly causative in its function, is employed to express 'multiplication' (*takṯīr*) or 'intensity' (*mubālaġa*) of action, since we are now to be concerned specifically with Arabic forms. For, even though as we survey the occurrences, say, of *qtl*, we quickly discover that the B-stem may govern a plural object equally as well as and more often than D, that a group of persons acting in concert will not necessarily do so in the D-stem, and that there is little ground therefore for Sibawaihi's assertion (cited in Chapter I) that the D-stem is the 'preferable' construction where plurality of subject or object is concerned, yet "we should not disguise features which, as far as the native speaker is concerned, bear all the evidence of being meaningful and distinctive."[1] While the interpretations of Arab grammarians may be suspect when a point of theological significance is concerned, such is not the case now, and we may assume that the distinction they make between B and D had some reality for them, since the modern axiom that difference of form implies difference of function did not prevent them from equating some occurrences of D and Š. They must have noticed the inconsistency in practice (as Sibawaihi's example shows) and accepted this either as a lapse from preferred usage or as of no importance for the definition and classification of the stem. In this we cannot follow them, yet their characterization of D as intensive and/or pluralic in some contexts must be taken into account, particularly since our examples are to be drawn exclusively from the Qur'an, which, as Nöldeke puts it, "zeigt uns einige Verstösse gegen die Regeln der classischen Sprache."[2]

In another article, Nöldeke cites as good examples of the intensive-frequentative meaning of the D-stem the following two phrases: *walam yaġlibka mitlu muġallabi* 'und nicht hat dich jemand so arg besiegt, wie einer der selbst so oft besiegt wurde', and *wa'in taqtulūnā nuqattilkum* 'tödtet ihr uns, so metzeln wir euch nieder'.[3] Do these examples support Nöldeke's characterization of the D-forms? It is clear that the author of the sentences intended some contrast by his employment of both B and D-forms of the root in each phrase. Moreover, while in similar Old Testament examples we noted that the purpose served was that of stylistic diversity, more than that seems to be involved here, *i.e.* an element of semantic contrast. But to us, the contrast cannot be so clearly drawn as Nöldeke's terminology and translations seem to draw it. Indeed, it is a contrast most difficult to express in an Indo-European translation.

If the contrast must be drawn, however, the nomenclature we would prefer is derived from Nida's suggestion that an alternative and preferable term for "intensive" would be "explicit", *i.e.* "the object is not only definite but very much so."[4] He cites as an example the nominal opposition "a man/the man/the very man", representing the indefinite, definite and explicit forms respectively. As applied to the verb the explicit form would best be expressed by the English phrases 'He really did it' or 'They really took care of him'. In these phrases the adverb 'really' no longer stands in place of the phrase 'in reality', nor is it synonymous with the adverb 'truly'; rather it is employed as an index of the speaker's own reaction to an act which has taken place or is to take place, namely a reaction of wonder or admiration – it implies that

[1] Nida, "The Identification of Morphemes", 6.

[2] T. Nöldeke, "Zur Sprache des Korans", in *Neue Beiträge zur semitischen Sprachwissenschaft* (Strasbourg, 1910) 55.

[3] T. Nöldeke, "Zur Grammatik des klassischen Arabisch, in *Denkschriften der kaiserlichen Akademie des Wissenschaften*, Phil.-Hist. Klasse, Band XLV (Vienna, 1897) 25.

[4] Nida, *Morphology*, 171.

the action has in some way impressed him deeply. Somewhat the same effect can be attained in English without an adverb by means of intonation of the voice or, in written English, underlining. The function of these circumlocutions in English (and other Indo-Germanic languages) is to give emphasis or prominence to the particular verbal or nominal concept in context. This might well be the origin also of the 'intensive' function of the D-stem in Arabic; we are reminded here of König's description of gemination as a strengthening of sound. If so, this would be a good example of what Porath calls the Semitic language group's "häufige Anwendung des Verbums auch da, wo idg. Sprachen eine andere Sprachkategorie gebrauchen,"[5] *i.e.* evolution of a verbal stem to express what Indo-Germanic languages convey through verb plus adverb, or verb plus vocalic or written stress signs.

Such a usage would, of course, be subject to further development of the type described by Wundt thus: "die Verdoppelung gibt den verstärkten Eindruck wieder, den die Empfindung der Eigenschaft auf den Redenden macht, und damit wird sie zum Ausdruck einer auch objektiv grösseren Intensität der Eigenschaften nicht bloss auf den Gegenstand selbst, sondern mehr noch auf den subjektiven Eindruck den er vorbringt."[6] There could easily have been such an evolution in the use of the Arabic D-stem, one which by its very nature would probably not be rigid or all-inclusive in its application. This hypothetical process may be compared with that undergone by the related Stem III in Arabic, which, starting from the same impulse as Stem II, then acquired a highly specialized meaning, at least in some contexts. According to Fleisch, in his full-length study of the stem, "Qātala est l'égal de qatala maʿa; maʿa 'avec' n'a pas été exprimé, mais il a été mis dans le verbe. Il y est présent et donne au verbe sa valour spéciale. ... Les Sémites d'Arabie l'ont mise dans le verbe et ont constitué une conjugaison particulière, d'après leur goût pour la multiplication des conjugaisons sur la racine."[7] The effect, according to this writer, is that one has within *qātala* the opposition: action shared/uniliteral action. In the same way *qattala* could easily be conceived as 'taking up' into the verbal stem the significance, say of *qatala qatlan* (the verbal equivalent of the repeated adjective or noun familiar in the Semitic languages), that significance once more being emphasis upon the action performed rather than upon the subject of the action. This is not to say that the morpheme R_2R_2 had emphasis as its original function. Indeed, if one imagines the morpheme as originally associated with denominative-factitive formations, one can easily imagine further, that the distinction between this function and the simple B-stem came to be lost in practice for transitive verbal concepts, and that the geminated stem came gradually to be used for emphatic or heightened or in some other way distinctive address. (Thus, in the Old Testament, the Hagiographa have the highest proportion of D-forms, while in the historical books the stem is most often used in

[5] E. Porath, "Die Passivbildung des Grundstamms im Semitischen", in *Monatsschrift* 70 (1926), 169.
[6] Wundt, *Völkerpsychologie*, 587.
[7] Fleisch, *Les Verbes à Allongement vocalique en Sémitique*, 434.

connection with divine activity.) Finally, one can imagine that on the one hand this distinction between B and D would not always be finely observed, and that on the other it could be employed loosely so as to take on overtones of 'objectively greater intensity of the attribute'.[8]

This would fulfill the stipulation of Cohen, that "La constitution de la racine sémitique permet l'expression de diverses notions par des alternances vocaliques et aussi par renforcement ou répétition d'une consonne. ... Les diverses langues peuvent créer ou au contraire éliminer des expressions de ce genre."[9] The evolution of such an emphatic usage as we have hypothesized for Arabic does not therefore necessarily imply the existence of the same usage in Hebrew or Aramaic dialects. Nor does it imply universal application to all Arabic texts. For instance, it seems to be of little importance in interpretation of the Qur'an. In the cases of the documents we have been studying, the application seldom seems to go beyond the first stage, emphasis reflecting the writer's or speaker's response to an action. Certainly in the Qur'an, for instance, there is little or no evidence for the existence of forms such as those of the Algerian dialect cited by Joly, *e.g. fawwata* 'passer en grand nombre', *mawwata* 'mourir comme les mouches', *kabbara* 'devenir grave (affaire)'.[10] Nor, as we have noted often in Chapter IV, did Saadia Gaon, who followed the Arab grammarians in his own discussion of the Hebrew D-stem, find it necessary in most cases of transitive verbal concepts, to translate Biblical Hebrew D-stems with similar forms in Arabic; most of these are translated by B or Š-forms. Only in the instances of factitive and denominative D-forms in Hebrew is one likely to find a comparable form in Arabic. We cannot and need not deny that 'objective intensity' is a facet of the Arabic D-stem, although the 'subjective intensity' of manifesting 'busyness' or 'eagerness' in performing an action still seems to be an undemonstrable proposition. But even the concept of 'objective intensity' has only limited application, and to use this subsidiary element of the Arabic D-stem as the basis for classification of the stem as a whole in the Semitic languages or in Common Semitic would be to let the tail wag the dog. Our survey of the D-forms in the Qur'an will show that 'objective intensity' is not ultimately an important factor in the D-stem.

As in the preceding chapter, each root in Table III will be followed by the meaning which it has in the B-stem, where a B-form exists in the Qur'an. We have drawn these meanings primarily from the lexicons of Lane and Wehr, and from Bell's translation of the Qur'an.[11] Where no B-form exists in the Qur'an (there are many instances of this) we have listed the meaning cited by the lexicon for occurrences elsewhere, or from Arabic lexicons. In the latter cases, the B-form meanings given for

[8] Fleisch, *Les Verbes à Allongement vocalique en Sémitique*, 48.

[9] H. Cohen, "Review of H. Fleish" *Les Verbes à Allongement vocalique en Sémitique* in *Bulletin de la Société de Linguistique* 42 (1946), 169.

[10] Joly, "Sur les Dérivations du Trilitère", 399.

[11] H. Wehr, *A Dictionary of Modern Written Arabic*, J. M. Cowan, ed. (Ithaca, 1961). E. W. Lane, *Arabic-English Lexicon*, Book I, London 1863-1893. R. Bell (tr.), *The Qur'an*, 2 vol. (Edinburgh, 1937-1939).

roots occurring in other stems in the Qur'an have sometimes been suspect as inventions or linguistic rationalizations of the Arabic lexicographers. In our listing, B-meanings not found in the Qur'an itself are followed by the symbol *. Next we list any forms, either from Qur'anic Arabic or from its cognate languages, which can help to clarify the B meaning where it is in doubt, if such forms exist. The apparent meaning of the D-form is then given, along with the number of its occurrences in both its simple and its reflexive aspect, and one textual reference given by Sura and verse, employing the enumeration system of Flügel's edition.[12] This is followed by a citation of the Š-stem meaning, with a textual reference when the form occurs in the Qur'an, and by citation of other stem forms whenever the information seems pertinent. Finally, wherever Biblical Hebrew has a cognate root of like meaning, the variation in meaning among its B, D, and Š forms is noted for comparison.

TABLE III

I. D-STEMS TRANSFORMATIVE

A. *Associated with B-stems Durative Stative*

'ḫr: no B, *cf.* BH *'aḥr* 'be after, stay behind'. D fifteen times as 'delay, leave behind, put at the end' (11.11), used once as contrast for *qaddama* 'send ahead' (82.5). Stem V three times as reflexive 'be late, put o.s. behind' or passive 'be delayed', the latter meaning found in the BH Š-stem. This D form may also be a factitive of the adjective *'aḫir* 'last'.

'lf: 'be familiar, become accustomed'*. D five times as 'join (hearts)' (3.98) or 'join (clouds)' (24.43), employed with *bayn* 'between', as though the stem were a denominative 'effect a familiarity between' – in which case B might be interpreted as 'have familiarity (with)'.

br': 'be free from, get free of'*. D three times as 'acquit, think s.o. blameless' (12.53), used in estimative sense; Stem V as reflexive 'declare o.s. free of, renounce' or 'call o.s. blameless' (28.63). Š occurs as causative 'free or cure s.o. of s.th.' (5.110). *Cf.* BH brr, for which B, D and Š forms all mean 'purify, purge', while N 'be pure' has the function of the Arabic B stative, and the D reflexive parallels Qur'anic 'think, call o.s. blameless or pure'.

bšr: 'be happy, rejoice in'*. D thirty-eight times as 'preach, bring the good news' (15.54), *cf.* BH *biśśar* 'tell good tidings'; both either factitive 'make s.o. happy' or denominative 'bring joy'. Š occurs as 'hear the good news, rejoice in s.th.', perhaps used in estimative sense 'think s.th. good news'. Stem III also occurs as 'lie with (one's wife)' (2.183), perhaps also a factitive 'make happy', or possibly a denominative associated with *bašara* 'skin'.

byn: 'be clear, apart, evident'*, *cf.* BH 'understand'. D thirty-six times as 'clarify' (2.154); Stem V eight times as passive 'be made clear, be evident' (29.37). Š also occurs once as 'make clear' (43.52).

ṯbt: 'be firm, hold firm'*. D twelve times as 'make firm, strengthen' (47.8), Š twice as 'confirm, establish' (13.39), a specialization.

ḥdṯ: 'be new'*. D three times as 'declare s.th. new, tell (news)' (93.11), used twice with preposition *bi* 'in reference to', once without it (99.4), as a figurative estimative usage. The D forms of BH *ḥdš* mean 'renew' or 'restore', *cf.* Arabic Š-form 'originate, produce'.

[12] G. Flügel (ed.), *Coranus Arabice* (Leipzig, 1837).

ḥḏr: 'be cautious, wary'. D twice as 'warn' (3.27).

ḥrr: no B, *cf.* *ḥurr* 'noble, freeborn'. D six times, as verbal noun 'liberation' (5.91) and as passive pple. 'consecrated' (3.31).

ḥry: no B, *cf.* *ḥarīy* 'appropriate, worthy'. Stem V once as 'make o.s. worthy' (72.14).

ḥrḍ: no B, but *cf.* *hariṣa* 'be intent', which might be a dialect variant of the same root. D twice as 'instigate s.o. to do s.th.' (4.86).

ḥrm: 'be sacred, taboo'*, *cf.* QA passive pple. 'excluded, excommunicated' which fills the function of a B stative form. D forty-two times as 'sanctify, forbid' (3.87). The factitive function is filled by Š in BH.

ḥss: 'be certain of s.th., perceive'*. Stem V once as 'seek information concerning (*min*) s.th.' (12.87), *i.e.* 'make o.s. certain about s.th.'

ḥṣn: 'be inaccessible, well fortified'*. D once in passive pple. as 'fortified' (59.14), *i.e.* 'made inaccessible'. Stem V once in verbal noun as 'chastity', *i.e.* 'making o.s. inaccessible'.

ḥyy: 'be alive, live'. D four times as 'keep s.o. alive', used to denote the phrase *ḥayyāka 'llāhu* 'may God preserve your life', thus coming to mean 'give a greeting' (4.88). Š occurs frequently as 'animate, revive' (5.35). Thus the two stems are specialized in meaning in Arabic, while in Biblical Hebrew both may mean either 'preserve' or 'revive', *i.e.* both 'keep life going' and 'give life'.

ḫff: 'be light, active'. D nine times as 'lighten, alleviate' (8.67). Stem X occurs three times as 'make light of s.o., regard s.o. as of little account' (30.60), an estimative use, as is often the case when D and Š factitives both occur for a single root.

ḫld: 'be immortal'. D twice in passive pple. as 'made immortal, perpetual' (76.19). Š occurs twice as 'perpetuate' (104.3).

ḫwf: 'be afraid, fear'. D four times as 'frighten' (39.37), once in the verbal noun of Stem V as 'fear' (16.49).

ḏll: 'be low, humble', *cf.* perhaps BH *dll* 'hang down, be feeble'. D twice as 'lower, humble, subdue s.o.' (36.72).

rtl: 'be regular, in order'*. D twice as 'present (the Qur'an) in order, distinctly' (73.4), used both times with verbal noun.

rkb: 'be in motion, act heedlessly' or 'mount, be upon s.th.'*. D once as 'create, compose', *i.e.* 'put one part on another' (82.8). Stem VI once in passive pple. as 'clustered (grain)', *i.e.* 'combined, put together' (6.99). *Cf.* BH *reḵeb* 'rider, upper millstone', *i.e.* 'that which is upon'.

zkw: 'be just, thrive'. D twelve times as 'purify, justify' (53.33); Stem V eight times as reflexive 'purify o.s., seek purity' (87.14).

slm: 'be whole, sound, blameless'*. D eleven times as 'make sure/sound' (2.66; 33.56). Š frequent as 'surrender, convert to Islam' (3.19), *i.e.* 'make o.s. whole' or 'make o.s. secure'. BH *šlm* also specializes D and Š, as 'complete' and 'perform' respectively, though again both are factitive.

snh: 'be very old'*. Stem V once as passive of an estimative-declarative meaning 'shown to be old', *i.e.* 'become stale' or 'rot' (2.261).

swy: 'be equal, equivalent'*. D fourteen times as 'make equal/sound, shape' (2.27; 26.98). Stem III occurs once with a similar meaning 'level' (18.95), the meaning of the cognate BH D-stem.

syr: 'be in motion, operation'. D four times as 'put into action, move' (78.20), once as 'cause s.o. to travel' (10.23).

ṣdq: 'be true, right, sincere'. D twenty-eight times as 'confirm, witness to, think s.th. true' (46.11; 92.6). Stem V eight times as 'give alms', a denominative of *ṣadaqa* 'alms'. For BH *ṣdq* the Š-stem 'call s.o. righteous' parallels the Arabic D-form.

ṣʿr: 'be awry'*, cf. Syriac *ṣʿr* 'be vile', in D 'contemn'. D once as 'look contemptuously' (31.17), *i.e.* 'regard as vile'.

ṣfw: 'be clear, pure'*. D once in passive pple. as 'purified' (47.17). Š twice as 'distinguish' (17.42), perhaps reflecting a specialized usage of the two stems, both as factitives.

ḍrʿ: 'be humble'*. D seven times in Stem V as 'beseech', *i.e.* 'humble o.s.' (6.42). BH *ṣrʿ* specializes the stem as 'bring low, strike down (with skin disease)'.

ḍyq: 'be narrow, anguished'. D once as 'make s.th. difficult for (*ʿala*) s.o.' (65.6), *cf.* BH Š-form of *ṣwq* 'oppress'.

ṭlq: 'be loosed from a bond (she-camel)'*. D twelve times as 'divorce (a woman)' (66.5).

ṭhr: 'be pure'. D eighteen times as 'purify, cleanse' (98.2). Stem V seven times as reflexive 'cleanse o.s.' (5.9). This is a more literal use than in the BH D-form 'declare s.o. clean'.

ṭwʿ: 'be obedient'*. D once as 'permit, make s.o. obedient' (5.33). Stem V three times as reflexive 'make o.s. obedient, do good willingly' (9.80). Š frequent as 'submit, obey' (4.82), probably an original factitive which assumed the function of B stative in the Qur'anic dialect.

ṭwq: 'be able'*. D once, perhaps as 'make s.o. pay s.th.' (3.176), perhaps as a denominative of *ṭawq* 'necklace, collar', thus 'be collared'. Š once as 'be able', again assuming the function of a B stative.

ʿjl: 'be in a hurry, rush'. D five times as 'make hurried, hasten' (10.12). Stem V once as reflexive 'hasten o.s.' or passive 'be hurried' (2.199). Š also occurs once as 'cause to hasten'.

ʿrḍ: 'be broad, wide'. D once as 'make s.th. broad, offer, allude' (2.235).

ʿṭl: 'be idle, lack'. D twice as 'make idle' (22.44) and 'leave untouched'. *i.e.* 'make to lack s.th.' (81.4).

ʿẓm: 'be great, glorious'. D twice as 'glorify' (22.31); Š once as 'make large' (65.5). For BH *ʿṣm* 'be strong', the Š-form likewise carries the factitive meaning 'make s.o. stronger than'.

ʿlm: 'be familiar, have knowledge'. D forty times as 'teach' (12.102); Stem V twice as reflexive 'learn, teach o.s.' (2.96).

ʿmd: 'be firm, cleave to'*. Stem V three times as 'be of set purpose, intend', *i.e.* 'make o.s. firm'. The D-form occurs outside of the Qur'an as 'stop s.th.', *cf.* BH *ʿmd* 'stand', Š 'cause to stand'.

ʿmr: 'be long-lived, thrive'*. D five times as 'make s.o. long-lived' (35.12). Both D and Š occur outside the Qur'an as 'populate (a land)', *i.e.* 'cause (a land) to thrive'.

ftr: 'be listless, abate'. D once as 'relax s.th.' (43.75).

fzʿ: 'be afraid, fear'. D once as 'frighten' (34.22).

fsḥ: 'be wide, provide room for s.th.'. Stem V once as 'spread out', *i.e.* 'make o.s. wide' (58.12), used as parallel to and synonymous with the B-form in the same verse.

fḍl: 'be superior, good'*. D seventeen times as estimative 'regard as superior, prefer' (17.72). Stem V once as 'regard o.s. as superior, get a preference for o.s.' (23.24).

fqd: 'be deprived of, lose'*. Stem V once as 'survey, seek (the lost)', perhaps originally 'regard o.s. as deprived' (27.20). Š exists outside of the Qur'an as 'make s.o. deprived'.

fqh: 'be knowledgeable, understand'. Stem V once as 'teach o.s., devote o.s. to knowledge' (9.123). D occurs outside the Qur'an as 'teach'.

fkh: 'be merry'*. Stem V once as 'make o.s. merry, slander one another'. (56.65). D occurs outside the Qur'an as 'make s.o. merry'.

fnd: 'be weak-minded, lie'*. D once as estimative 'think o.s. weak-minded' (12.94). Š occurs outside the Qur'an as 'weaken (the mind)'.

fhm: 'be informed, understand'*. D once as 'make understand, teach' (21.79).

qds: 'be holy'*. D four times as 'consecrate' (2.28), as with BH *qdš*.

qdm: 'be previous, precede'. D twenty-seven times as 'prepare, do s.th. before' (62.7). Stem V twice as reflexive 'put o.s. before, precede' (74.40), *cf.* BH D-stem 'do early, be in front'.

qrb: 'be near, approach'. D thirteen times as 'bring near, offer' (51.27), a meaning found in both D and Š forms of BH.

qfy: 'be after, follow s.o.'. D four times as 'send after, cause to follow' (57.27). Š occurs outside the Qur'an in a figurative use of the same meaning, 'prefer', *i.e.* 'cause s.o. to come after s.o.'.

qll: 'be little, few, trifling'. D once as 'make few' (8.46); Š once as 'bear s.th., treat s.th. as trifling' (7.55). In both D and Š, BH employs the root figuratively as 'curse'.

kbr: 'be great, important, large'. D five times as 'glorify' (74.3). Stem V nine times as 'glorify o.s., boast' (40.76). Š again is used in an estimative sense 'think o.s. important, praise' (12.31); Stem X as 'be proud' (46.9). BH has only the literal Š-form 'multiply'.

kṯr: 'be many, much, increase'. D once as 'multiply' (7.84); Š twice as 'increase s.th., make s.th. much' (89.11). There seems to be a specialization here, D connoting increase of number, Š increase of extent.

krm: 'be noble, precious'. D three times as 'honor, regard s.o. as noble' (17.72). Š occurs four times with the same meaning (89.14/18).

krh: 'be averse, dislike' (*kariha*) and 'be loathesome' (*karuha*)*. D once as 'make loathesome' (49.7); Š five times as 'force s.o.', *i.e.* 'make s.o. averse to' (20.75). Thus D and Š forms are associated with different aspects of the B meaning, though both are factitive.

klf: 'be intent, addicted, in love'*. D seven times as 'make s.o. intent' or 'commission s.o.' (2.286). Stem V once as reflexive in active pple. 'simulator, artificial', *i.e.* 'one who commissions himself' (38.86).

lbṯ: 'be hesitant, hesitate'*. Stem V once as 'hesitate' (33.14), perhaps originally 'make o.s. hesitant', but here assuming the meaning of B.

lwy: 'be curved, lean'*. D once as 'twist, turn' (63.5). B also occurs outside the Qur'an as 'twist s.th.', the active aspect of the stative here.

mkn: 'be strong'*. D ten times as 'establish, strengthen' (18.83); Š as both 'have power (over others)' or 'be powerful' (8.72). Both D and Š may be denominatives associated with *mukna* 'power, strength'.

mhl: 'be slow, lag'. D twice as 'make slow, give respite' (86.17); Š also occurring as 'give respite' in the same verse, probably for variety, although both forms occur outside the Qur'an.

nb': 'be high, turn away'*. D forty-five times as 'inform o.s. of s.th.' (3.43), used of a divine proclamation given either directly or indirectly through the Prophet; perhaps literally 'cause o.s. to turn away or shrink from', with the person as direct object and the subject of the proclamation introduced by the preposition *bi*. Š also occurs four times with this meaning; Stem X once as 'inquire, inform o.s.' (10.54).

nʿm: 'be soft, rejoice'*, *cf.* BH 'be pleasant'. D once as 'give ease to, soften s.o.' (89.14); Š seventeen times as 'make pleasant, bestow favor upon' (4.71). The root may well be denominative in all three stems, associated with such nouns as *niʿma* 'favor' and *nuʿūma* 'softness'.

nkr: 'be strange, ignorant'. D once as 'disguise' (27.41), *cf.* BH N-stem 'be disguised', thus perhaps associated with an active aspect of the B meaning. Stem V three times as 'deny, disown', *i.e.* 'show o.s. ignorant of s.th.' (40.81), *cf.* BH D-stem 'misconstrue'.

hjd: 'be awake, stay awake'*. Stem V once as 'stay awake, keep vigil' (17.81), perhaps originally 'keep o.s. awake', but here taking the function of B stative. D outside of Qur'an as 'awaken'.

hy': 'be of good appearance'*. D twice as 'put in good state, prepare' (18.19).

wfq: 'be proper, right'*. D three times as 'reconcile', *i.e.* 'set right' (4.65).

wfy: 'be perfect, complete'*. D nineteen times as 'complete, perfect, pay in full' (2.281). Stem V twenty-five times in a similar but specialized meaning 'take s.o. in death', *i.e.* 'make (someone's life) complete' (10.47).

wqr: 'be settled, dignified'*. D once as 'honor, call s.o. dignified' (48.9).

wly: 'be near'. D twenty-nine times as 'bring close, turn toward (trans. and intrans.)' (27.10; 30.51). Stem V occurs seventy-seven times, in two meanings. With the preposition *min* 'from' it means 'turn away'; with some direct object 'make friends with, turn toward' (2.61; 60.9). In either case the usage seems to be reflexive.

ysr: 'be easy'*. D ten times as 'make easy' (44.58). Stem V once as a passive 'be made easy', *i.e.* 'become easy' (73.20), Stem X occurring twice with the same meaning (2.192).

B. *Associated with B-stems Perfect Stative*

'ḏn: 'listen (*ilā*), learn (*bi*), permit (*fī*)'. D five times as 'make listen, proclaim' (12.70), without a direct object. Stem V twice with a similar meaning 'announce' (7.166). Š five times as 'give permission' (7.120), perhaps a specialization of meaning; Stem X ten times as 'ask permission', *i.e.* 'have o.s. permitted' (24.58).

'wb: 'return'*. D once as 'respond, echo s.th.', *i.e.* 'make s.th. return' (34.10).

bdl: 'replace s.th., change s.th.'*. D thirty-one times, sometimes as 'replace, change' (2.177), but predominantly as 'make s.th. replace s.th. else', *i.e.* 'exchange (two objects)' (14.33), suggesting an original B stative 'be in the place of'. However, Stem V occurs three times as 'exchange s.th. for s.th. else', 'cause o.s. to replace s.th. with (*bi*) s.th.' (4.2). Š also occurs as 'replace', *i.e.* 'make s.th. replaced by (*bi*) s.th.'. Thus D seems to be associated with both stative and active aspects of the root, the nature of the association being indicated by the presence or absence of the preposition *bi*, it being required by the active aspect. The D-forms are, however, primarily factitive, and refer to a perfected state.

brz: 'appear, show o.s.'. D twice in passive as 'be revealed, made to appear' (26.91).

bṣr: 'look at, understand'. D once in passive as 'be made to have perceived, understand' (70.11). Š occurs three times with the same meaning as B (32.12); Stem X once as 'seek to understand, investigate' (68.5).

blġ: 'reach, attain'. D six times as 'report, make s.th. reach s.o.' (46.22), *cf.* BH *blʿ*, D 'communicate'. Š four times as 'inform' (11.60).

tbr: 'perish'*. D five times as 'destroy' (25.41).

jrʿ: 'swallow'. D once in reflexive Stem V as 'force o.s. to have swallowed (bad water)' (14.20).

ḥṣl: 'happen'*. D once in passive as 'be made to have happened, produced' (100.10).

ḥkm: 'decide, judge'. D twice as 'make s.o. judge' (5.47). This could as well be a denominative associated with such a noun as *ḥukm*, *i.e.* 'give s.o. authority'. BH *ḥkm* occurs in B as a stative 'be wise', in D and Š as factitive 'make wise'.

ḥml: 'bear, carry'. D five times as 'impose on s.o.', *i.e.* 'cause s.o. to carry' (24.53).

ḫlf: 'succeed, substitute for, come after'. D four times as 'leave s.o. behind, make s.o. to have succeeded' (9.119), used in reference to the successors of the Prophet. Stem V once as 'stay behind', *i.e.* 'cause o.s. to come after' (9.121), the same meaning found for the Š-form of BH *ḥlp* 'pass on' (D 'change').

dbr: 'elapse, pass by, turn the back'. D five times as 'direct (affairs)', *i.e.* 'make (affairs) to have elapsed' (32.4). Stem V twice as 'reflect on, direct o.s. to s.th.' (47.26). Stem X four times as 'flee', *i.e.* 'cause o.s. to turn back' (70.17). BH shows a similar development, in D 'turn s.th. aside' and Š 'drive s.o. back'.

dmr: 'perish'*. D ten times as 'destroy' (47.11).

ḏkr: 'remember'. D seventeen times as 'remind s.o.' (51.55), thirty-seven times in Stem V reflexive as 'reflect', *i.e.* 'make o.s. remember' (28.51), the meaning of the BH Š-stem.

ḏky: 'burn, blaze'*. D once as 'immolate' (5.4), *i.e.* 'make burn'. Both stems may also mean 'slaughter, sacrifice'.

rbw: 'grow, increase'. D twice as 'make (a child) to have grown, raise (a child)' (26.17). BH *rbw* has the same distribution of meanings.

rdy: 'perish'. Stem V twice as 'bring about one's own destruction, perish' (92.11). Š three times as 'cause s.o. to perish' (41.22).

zwl: 'vanish, cease, leave'. D once as 'separate, remove' (10.29). Stem V once as reflexive 'separate o.s., turn aside' (48.25).

sbḥ: 'spread out, flow'. D forty times as 'sing (God's praises)' (40.7). While this could conceivably be an original 'make to spread abroad', it is more probable that the D-form is denominative, especially since the BH counterpart is not associated with any B-form.

ṣʿd: 'ascend'*. D occurs outside the Qur'an both as 'ascend' and 'make s.o. ascend'. Here, Stem V occurs once as 'ascend' (6.125), perhaps an original 'make o.s. ascend'. Š occurs outside the Qur'an as 'cause s.th. to go up'.

ṣly: 'burn, blaze'. D once as 'scorch s.th.' (69.31). BH *ṣly* has the transitive meaning 'roast' in B, again pointing to the flexibility of roots in Common Semitic.

fjr: 'break up, cleave, make an opening'. D eight times as 'cause (water) to bubble up, flow' (82.3), apparently associated with a specialized meaning of the B-stem. Stem V once as passive 'caused to flow' (2.69).

lẓy: 'burn, blaze'*. Stem V once as 'burn' (92.14), again replacing B stative, although D occurs outside the Qur'an as 'kindle, set ablaze'.

lqy: 'come near, encounter'. D once as 'bring into contact with' (76.11), five times in passive as 'be brought into contact with, receive' (41.35). Stem V five times as 'receive' (21.103), used as passive of D. The meaning of D active is found more commonly in the Š-form 'impose', *i.e.* 'make s.o. undergo or encounter s.th.' (4.96).

njw: 'escape'. D thirty-five times as 'help s.o. to have escaped, rescue, deliver' (21.76).

nzl: 'come down'. D seventy-eight times as 'make (revelation) to have come down (from heaven)' (17.84). Stem V four times as 'descend', *i.e.* a reflexive 'let o.s. descend' (47.4). Š also common, and is used interchangeably with D. BH *nzl* 'flow'; Š 'cause to flow', suggests that the single use of this form in the Qur'an in reference to rain rather than to revelation may embody the original sense of the word.

wṣl: 'connect, arrive, reach'. D once as 'cause to reach' (28.51).

The same general distinction between these two groups of roots which we found in Biblical Hebrew persists in the Qur'an, with some slight modification. The B-forms of I-A denote a current state of the subject at the moment he comes into view, a state which has no clearly-fixed beginning or end. This means, that not only such long-familiar concepts as 'be new' (*ḥdṯ*) or 'be holy' (*qds*), but also such concepts as 'be in motion' (*syr*) and 'be in a hurry' (*ʿjl*), not found in Biblical Hebrew or Aramaic, come under this category. The B-forms of I-B, however, while they also denote a current state, imply that this state has come about by virtue of a (recently) completed action or process. Most of these deal with concepts of motion, such as 'come down' (*nzl*) and 'reach' (*blḡ*), thus conforming to Götze's category of 'rest after movement'; but others, such as 'decide' (*ḥkm*), 'remember' (*ḏkr*) and 'understand' (*bṣr*), refer to mental processes. A few others, such as 'swallow' (*jrʿ*), 'carry' (*ḥml*) and 'cleave' (*fjr*) must be read as 'to have swallowed' (D 'make to have swallowed'), *etc.* As such, they are distinguishable from the causatives of the Š-stem type, *i.e.* 'cause s.o. to do s.th.', only insofar as they imply a completed action, while the Š-stem implies the initiation of an action. It is worth noting that such forms play a minimal role in the Qur'anic as well as in Biblical Hebrew D-stem; whereas in his discussion of the Akkadian 'perfect stative' and its corresponding D-stem Götze implies that these forms are the principal type within this category, that they may in fact stand beside any transitive verb. In Arabic and Hebrew it is his subsidiary 'rest after movement' type which seems dominant.

Particularly noteworthy in Group I-A is the high proportion of roots for which no B-form occurs: 50 out of 78, or about 65%. A survey of BH forms yields the reverse picture, of an exceptionally high occurrence of corresponding B-forms for this group. One might attribute this to chance omission if it were not for the fact that other forms of the roots seem to have assumed the stative function of B, particularly Stem V, where it is used as a passive rather than as a reflexive, such as 'become easy' (*ysr*) and 'hesitate' (*lbṯ*). Elsewhere, such D-forms exist side-by-side with B stative forms such as 'hurry' (*ʿjl*) and 'precede' (*qdm*). Furthermore, in a few cases Š-forms fill the function of B stative, such as 'obey' (*ṭwʿ*) and 'rejoice' (*bšr*); in Group I-B 'replace' (*bdl*) and 'perceive' (*bṣr*). In yet other cases a common adjective will substitute for B stative, *e.g. ḥarīm* 'sacred' for *ḥaruma* 'be sacred'. Though all these circumlocutions can be paralleled in Hebrew, they are a major factor in the Qur'an, and indicate greater flexibility in use of the stems in this dialect.

C. *Associated with B-stems Transitive*

btk: 'cut off'*. D once as 'cut off' (4.118), perhaps as a result of confusion with following root – but *cf.* BH *btq* 'slaughter'.

btl: 'cut off'*. D once as verbal noun, used as maṣdar in connection with the Stem V reflexive 'cut o.s. off', *i.e.* 'devote o.s.' (73.8), the only occurrence.

bḏr: 'sow, scatter'*. D three times as 'dissipate, waste' (17.28), the D-form being employed figuratively, as opposed to the D-form of BH *bzr* which, like B, means 'scatter'.

ṯbṭ: 'hold back, hinder'. D once as 'hinder' (9.46).

jss: 'grope, feel, spy on'. D once as 'spy on' (49.12).

jlw: 'reveal'*. D twice as 'reveal' (91.3). Stem V twice as reflexive 'reveal o.s.' (7.139). BH *gly* likewise has similar meaning in B and D.

jnb: 'avert s.th., preserve s.o. from s.th.', used with *min*. D once as 'avoid s.th.' (92.17). Stem V once as 'flout', *i.e.* 'keep o.s. from s.th.' (87.11).

ḥrf: 'turn s.th. away'*. D four times as 'corrupt, alter' (5.45), a specialized meaning. Stem V once as 'turn o.s. apart (for battle)' (8.16).

ḥrq: 'burn (tr.)'*, cf. QA Stem VIII 'be burned' (2.268). D three times as 'burn' (21.68).

ḥlq: 'shave (o.s.)'. D once as 'shave (s.o.)' (48.27). This may reflect a specialization of meaning. The BH B-form means 'be smooth'; Š 'make smooth', suggesting that the Arabic D-form may be an original factitive, and the active B-stem a back-formation.

ḫbṭ: 'beat, strike'*. D once in Stem V, but with no reflexive sense, as bring down, prostrate s.o.' (2.276).

ḫṭf: 'snatch away'*. Stem V three times as 'sweep away, extirpate', with no reflexive or passive connotation. D exists outside Qur'an as 'snatch'.

ḫlq: 'create, form'. D once as 'form' (22.5), *cf.* BH *ḥlq* 'apportion', with the same meaning in B and D.

dsw: no B, but *cf. dassa/dassasa* 'insert/put in'. D once as 'bring in' (91.10).

dlw: no B, *cf. dalla*, 'direct'; *dalw* 'bucket'; BH *dll* 'hang down', N 'be brought low'; BH *dlw/y* 'draw up (water from a well)'. D once as 'urge on (in a negative direction)' or 'cast down' (7.21), used of Satan's temptation of Adam. Stem V once as reflexive 'descend', *i.e.* 'bring o.s. down' (53.8). Š twice as 'let down' (17.19). All this suggests an original D-factitive form, with the B-form, if any existed, either the active aspect of the stative 'be low' or a back-formation from D.

ḏbḥ: 'slaughter, kill'. D three times as 'kill' (28.3). The same situation exists for BH *zbḥ* 'slaughter'.

rdd: 'send back, refuse'*. Stem V once as 'waver', *i.e.* 'repeat o.s.' or 'regard o.s. as rejected' (9.45), a reflexive use. D occurs outside the Qur'an as 'repel, repeat'.

swd: 'equip o.s.'*. Stem V once as reflexive 'equip o.s. with' (2.193). D outside the Qur'an as 'equip s.o.'

sjr: 'heat up'*. D once as passive 'be heated up, made to boil', *i.e.* 'rise, overflow' (81.6).

sḫr: 'deride, ridicule'*. D twenty-six times as 'humble s.o., make s.th. subservient' (14.37; 69.7). Both stems may be denominatives of a noun 'derision' (such as *suḫrīya*), i.e. B 'hold s.th. in derision, be derisive', and D 'make s.th. an object of derision'.

srḥ: 'release, let out to pasture'. D three times as 'release (a woman)' (33.28). BH *šrh* 'let loose' occurs only in B.

sʿr: 'kindle'*. D once as 'kindle' (81.12).

skr: 'shut, fill'*. D once as 'shut' (15.15), *cf.* BH *skr*, N-stem 'be shut up, D 'deliver up', *i.e.* 'stir up, make filled'.

sll: 'withdraw s.th.'*. Stem V once as reflexive 'withdraw o.s., escape' (24.63).

snd: 'support o.s.', *i.e.* 'lean against (*ilā*)'*. D once as 'support, prop up s.th.' (63.4). Š occurs outside the Qur'an as 'cause s.th. to lean against', *i.e.* 'cause s.th. to support itself', as opposed to D 'make s.th. supported'.

swm: 'inflict, set s.th. aside (by divine power)'. D four times in active and passive participles as 'coerce, mark, set aside' (51.34).

šqq: 'split'*. Stem V four times as passive 'be split' (2.69); Stem III seven times as 'oppose, split o.s. from s.o.' (59.4). D occurs outside the Qur'an as 'split'.

šyd: 'erect (a building)'*. D once in passive pple. as 'erect' (4.80).

ṣdʿ: 'split s.th.' D once as verbal noun 'splitting, headache' (56.19). Stem V once as passive 'be split' (30.42).

ṣrf: 'dispense with, turn s.th. away'. D ten times as 'dispense, disperse' (17.91).

ṣlb: 'crucify'. D four times as 'crucify' (7.121). Both are probably original denominatives.

ṣwr: 'shape' (meaning unclear in context; *cf.* BH *ṣwr* 'shape, fashion'). D four times as 'shape, form' (64.3).

'dd: 'count, number'. D once as 'count' (104.2). Š twenty times as factitive 'make s.th. counted out, prepare, arrange s.th.' (4.95).

'ḏr: 'excuse, absolve'*. D once in active participle as 'apologist, one who excuses himself' (9.91).

'zr: 'blame, rebuke'*, but *cf.* BH *'zr* 'support, help'. D three times as 'assist' (5.15).

'wq: 'impede, delay'*. D once as 'hinder' (33.18). BH *'wq* occurs in B as 'be impeded, totter', suggesting that the Arabic D-form may be an original factitive and the (supposed) B-form a back-formation.

ǧšw: 'cover'. D three times as 'cover' (8.11). Stem V once as reflexive used idiomatically, 'cover o.s. with (a woman)', *i.e.* 'sleep with a woman' (7.189). Š four times, both as 'cover' (36.8) and as 'cause s.o. to cover s.th.' (7.52).

ǧlq: 'close, shut'*. D once as 'close' (12.23).

ftḥ: 'open'. D four times as 'open' (78.19), *cf.* BH *ptḥ* 'open', B and D.

frṭ: 'neglect'. D five times as 'neglect' (39.57). BH *prṭ* 'improvise' occurs in B only.

frq: 'distinguish, separate'. D eleven times as 'divide, make a distinction' (6.160). Stem V nine times as reflexive 'be separate, separate o.s.' (98.3). Stem III once as 'depart', *i.e.* 'separate o.s. from s.th.' (65.2). *Cf.* BH *prq*, both B and D 'tear away, off'.

fsr: 'explain'*, *cf.* Stem X 'ask s.o. to explain', *i.e.* 'cause s.o. to explain (for one's own benefit)'. D once as verbal noun, 'interpretation' (25.35).

fṣl: 'separate, distinguish'. D twenty-one times as 'clarify, distinguish' (6.55). BH *pṣl* 'peel' occurs in B only.

fṭr: 'split'*. Stem V twice as passive 'be split' (42.3).

fwḍ: 'entrust s.th. to s.o.'*. D once as 'entrust' (40.47).

qbl: 'receive'*. D ten times as Stem V 'receive, accept' (3.21). Probably neither was the original verbal form. We might expect an original D-form 'make s.th. in front' on the order of *'ḫr* and *qdm* (q.v.), as with BH *qbl*, D-stem 'receive'. The B-form would then be seen as a back-formation, in response to the specialization of the simple D-form as 'kiss'. The emergence of Stem V could be seen as a similar process.

qtl: 'kill'. D five times as 'kill' (33.61).

qdr: 'arrange, decree'. D twenty-one times in this meaning (73.20).

qrn: 'conjoin'*. D three times in passive pple. as 'chained together' (38.37). Š occurs once in passive pple. as 'conformed, suitable to' (43.12), perhaps pointing to a specialization of function in the stems.

qsm: 'divide'. D once in active pple. as 'distribute' (51.4), the reflexive aspect being filled by Stem VI 'divide among themselves' (27.50). Stem III exists as a denominative 'take an oath' (7.20), associated with *qasam* 'oath'. Š has the same denominative meaning (5.58), but its coordinate Stem X occurs as 'seek a division' (5.4), *i.e.* 'seek to make s.th. distributed or divided'.

qṭ': 'cut'. D twelve times as 'cut' (12.31), Stem V three times as passive 'be broken off' (6.94), twice as reflexive 'break, divide (among several persons)' (21.93).

qlb: 'turn, transform s.th.' D five times in these meanings (9.48; 24.44). Stem V once as passive 'be changed' (24.37).

qyḍ: 'barter, exchange'*. D twice as 'assign, decree' (41.24). Both B and D seem to be specializations of a root meaning 'hand over'.

kfr: 'cover, hide'. D fourteen times as 'hide, forgive (sins)' (47.2), a specialization of meaning paralleled by BH *kpr*: B 'cover', D 'atone', the two D-stems being distinguished by the identity of the party who 'covers' the sin: God in the Arabic text, the sinner in the Hebrew text.

kfr: 'feed, support'. D once as 'provide for' (3.32); Š once as 'put in the charge of s.o.', *i.e.* 'cause s.o. to support' (38.22).

mḥṣ: 'clarify, refine'*. D twice as 'test, forgive' (3.148), a figurative use of the root idea of purification.

mdd: 'extend, stretch out s.th.'. D once in passive pple, as 'outstretched' (104.9). Š ten times as 'assist', *i.e.* 'extend o.s.'. Both B and D-forms of BH *mdd* mean 'measure'.

mzq: 'tear, rend'*. D four times as 'rend, disperse' (34.18).

msk: 'grab, seize'*. D once as 'take hold, seize' (7.169). Š eighteen times as 'seize, grasp', *i.e.* 'have s.th. seized (by oneself)' (67.21). BH *mšk* has the meaning 'draw' in both B and D.

mny: 'test, favor s.o.'*. D twice as 'tempt, inspire s.o. with desire' (4.118). Stem V nine times as 'long for, desire', *i.e.* 'tempt o.s. with' (22.51).

myz: 'set s.th. apart'*. D and Š occur outside the Qur'an as 'distinguish'. Stem V occurs once as passive 'be split apart, burst' (67.8).

nšr: 'spread out, unfold'. D once in passive pple. as 'outspread' (74.52). Š three times as 'resurrect' (80.22), which seems to be associated with the stative aspect of the B-stem, 'be green again (the earth)'.

nqb: 'pierce' (verbal noun). D once as 'search (a land)', *i.e.* 'bore into, make a breach in (*fī*)' (50.35). BH *nqb* 'pierce' occurs in B only.

nkṣ: 'invert, turn about'. D once as 'reverse, invert' (36.68).

hdm: 'destroy'*. D once as 'destroy' (22.41).

wdʿ: 'forsake'. D once as 'forsake' (93.3).

wsm: 'stamp, mark'*. D occurs outside the Qur'an as 'distinguish'. Stem V here as 'examine carefully', *i.e.* 'distinguish for o.s.' (15.75). Both stems are probably denominatives associated with *sima* 'mark'.

wkl: 'entrust, commission'. D twice as 'entrust' (6.89). Stem V forty-three times as a reflexive 'entrust o.s. to God', *i.e.* 'trust in, rely upon (*ʿalā*) God' (4.83; 3.118). BH *ykl* 'be able' embodies the stative aspect of the root meaning.

Several points may be noted, which provide a contrast between this group and the comparable forms in Biblical Hebrew. The first is, that there is much less specialization of meaning among B and D-forms than we noted for Hebrew. Of the 70 roots listed, only nine use the D-form in a figurative or otherwise distinctive manner. Of these, only four actually occur in both stems in the text of the Qur'an: *ʿdd* (B 'number';

D 'multiply'); *fṣl* ('separate'/'clarify'); *kfr* ('cover'/'forgive') and *nqb* ('pierce'/'overrun'). The other five depend upon the occurrence of the D-form in other texts: *bdr* ('scatter'/'waste'); *ḥrf* ('turn away'/'alter'); *qrn* ('join'/'chain together'); *qyḍ* ('barter'/'assign'); *mḥṣ* ('refine'/'test'). In addition, there is a special group of three roots, the B-form of which seems to refer to the performance of an action upon oneself, the D-form to action upon another person: *ḥlq* 'shave'; *zwd* 'equip'; *snd* 'support' (only the first and third actually occur in both stems in the Qur'an). In other words, this Arabic dialect takes less advantage of the existence of the two parallel stems for expressive purposes than does Biblical Hebrew, probably because of the greater richness of the Arabic vocabulary, which relies less upon circumlocutions and alternation of stems to achieve variety of language.

Second, the meaning 'have s.o. _____ed', which we found employed at least occasionally in Hebrew for expressive purposes, wherever the writer wished to indicate that someone was initiating an action actually to be performed by a third party, does not seem to be present in the Qur'an. If we regard this as the fundamental meaning of the D-stem, we must conclude that the Qur'anic Arabic has lost this distinction in practice, as Hebrew was in process of losing it. In any case we must regard its disappearance as yet another loss of an expressive device used effectively in the Old Testament and in Akkadian texts.

Third, we note again the high proportion of D-forms which have no B counterpart in the Qur'anic texts (38 out of 70, or 55%). Again, the proportion is higher than for Hebrew, although here the factor of chance may play a more important role. Alongside this phenomenon, however, we note that of the 70 roots only seven have the Š-stem in addition to D, and of these only three (*ğšw* 'cover'; *kfl* 'provide for'; *mdd* 'extend') use Š in a causative meaning. In Biblical Hebrew, on the other hand, we saw numerous examples of an Š-form serving as causative, while D carried the same meaning as B. Again, of course, chance occurrence of forms may be involved. But when these two phenomena are put together, the inference which we may draw is that there was at least a tendency within this dialect to employ a root in one or possibly two stems, rather than to have a fully-developed system of stems for each root – a not uncommon situation in Biblical Hebrew. In this respect, Qur'anic Arabic is more akin to Ethiopic than to Hebrew in its practice. To some extent, this tendency to crystallize a root in one or two stems must reflect the greater richness of the Arabic vocabulary. Arabic had the larger number of employable roots, and was able to utilize these to express shades of meaning, whereas Hebrew was turned inward, toward exploitation of the stem system, for the same expressive purposes. This would also help to account for the freer use of the stems in Arabic which we have already noted, including the use of Stem V both as reflexive and as passive, and also as an alternate for simple B and D-forms. It is also relevant to the Arabic proclivity for varying the use of the stem from that which was originally associated with it.

II. D-STEMS NON-TRANSFORMATIVE

A. *Associated with Nominal Forms*

'jl: 'be delayed'*. D occurs outside the Qur'an as 'delay', a factitive of the B-stem, but here three times as 'appoint' (6.128), associated with *'ajal* 'appointed time', thus 'make (a day or year) the appointed time'.

'ss: no B. D three times as 'found, lay the foundation for' (9.110), associated with *'uss* or *'asās*, both 'foundation'.

'qt: no B. D once in passive as 'be set as time for s.th.' (77.11), associated not with a noun of this root but with *waqt/wuqqit* 'time period'/'be appointed a time'. Both forms of this root are also found in *muwaqqat* and *mu'aqqat*, both 'scheduled'.

'yd: no B. D nine times as 'support, strengthen, give power' (5.109), associated with *yad* 'power, strength', with extension of the biliteral root. Modern Arabic has a B-form *'āda* 'be strong', which is probably a back-formation from the original D-form.

brj: 'fare well'*, a new root. Stem V three times as 'display o.s. (a woman)' (33.33), associated with *barāj* 'wonderful thing' or *burj* 'choice part', thus 'show o.s. a delightful object'. Š exists outside the Qur'an as 'have beautiful eyes', a similar denominative meaning, become specialized in usage.

bsm: 'smile'*. D once as Stem V 'smile' (27.19), associated with *basma* 'smile', having no apparent reflexive significance.

bw': 'incur, bear s.th.'*. D seven times as 'give lodging, give a position to s.o.' (16.43). Stem V once with the same meaning (10.87), three times as reflexive 'sojourn', *i.e.* 'take lodging for o.s.' (59.9). The stem seems to be associated with *bi'a* 'home'.

jhz: 'finish off a wounded man'*. D twice as 'equip, prepare' (12.59), associated with *jahāz* 'equipment'. The B-form is apparently a recent development, and may have been a specialization of the D meaning.

ḥrk: 'be in motion, move about'*. D once as 'excite, set in motion' (75.16). both B and D are denominatives associated with *ḥaraka* 'motion'.

ḫwl: no B. D three times as 'bestow, give s.th. as a possession' (6.94), associated with *ḫawal* 'property'. Modern Arabic has a B-form 'manage (a business)', also a denominative.

ḫyl: 'believe'*. D once in passive as 'appear', *i.e.* 'be made a vision' (20.69), associated with *ḫayāl* 'vision, fantasy'.

zwj: no B. D five times as 'make (two persons) a pair, mate (two persons)' (42.49), associated with *zawj* 'pair'.

zyn: 'decorate'*. D twenty-six times as 'adorn' (27.4). Both stems are denominatives associated with *zīna* 'beauty'. B is probably a back-formation in this case.

slṭ: 'be hard, sharp, eloquent'*. D twice as 'make powerful, give rule' (59.6), associated with *sulṭa* 'power, rule'. The B meaning may have evolved from an original 'have power'.

swr: no B. Stem V once as 'scale (a wall)' (38.20). D occurs outside the Qur'an as 'enclose, wall in'. Both are denominatives associated with *sūr* 'wall'.

smy: no B. D thirty times as 'name s.o., appoint a time' (53.28; 71.4), associated with *'ism* 'name'. Š occurs in other texts with this meaning.

šbh: no B. D once as 'give s.th. a likeness' (4.156), associated with *šibh* 'resemblance', used here in the passive as 'be given the likeness of', *i.e.* 'appear' (*cf.* *ḫyl*, above).

ṣbḥ: no B. D once as 'come in the morning, do early' (54.38), associated with *ṣubḥ* 'dawn'. In general, D and Š are specialized as 'do s.th. in the morning' and 'be s.th. in the morning', respectively, the latter generalized as 'become s.th. new, fresh'. The B stative *ṣabuḥa* 'be radiant' is also a denominative of this root, but developed independently.

ṣlw: no B. D thirteen times as 'pray' (3.33), associated with *ṣalwa* 'prayer', or perhaps *ṣalā* 'middle of the back, rump'; *cf.* Aram *ṣly* 'bend'.

ṭyr: 'fly'*. D and Š occur outside the Qur'an as 'make s.th. fly'. Stem V here three times as 'see an evil omen' (36.17), associated with *ṭayr* 'birds'. Both meanings are denominative: B 'be as a bird', Stem V 'act upon birds (for divination)', *cf.* BH *nḥš* (q.v.).

ẓll: 'become, persist'. D twice as 'give shade, make s.th. as a shade' (7.160), associated with *ẓill* 'shade, shadow'. B is perhaps originally 'be a shadow, hang over (events)'.

'ḏb: 'be sweet, pleasant'*. D forty-eight times as 'punish, give pain' (5.115), associated with *'aḏāb* 'pain, punishment'.

ğyr: no B. D five times as 'exchange, alter' (4.118), associated with *ğayr* 'something other, change', thus 'make s.th. something else, changed'.

fy': 'return, shift from west to east (a shadow)'. Stem V once in the same meaning (16.50), perhaps with a reflexive overtone of shadows extending themselves. Both stems are associated with *fai'* '(afternoon) shadow', as is the D-form, which occurs outside the Qur'an as 'give shade'.

kḏb: 'lie'. D one hundred ninety-three times as 'think or call s.th. a lie', *i.e.* 'deny s.th.' (34.44), an estimative use (unusual for denominatives). Š exists outside the Qur'an as 'cause s.o. to lie'. All stems are associated with *kiḏb* 'lie'.

klb: 'be mad'*. D once as 'treat s.o. as a dog', *i.e.* 'train (birds) as dogs' (5.6). Both stems are denominatives of *kalb* 'dog', thus B 'be as a dog', D 'make s.th. as a dog'.

klm: 'wound'*. D twenty-one times as 'speak to' (13.30), associated with *kalima* 'word, speech'. Stem V four times with the same meaning (78.35). The original association may have involved *kalm* 'slash, cut', now reflected in B, especially since we noted that BH *mll* (q.v.) was also connected with the idea of 'cutting' (into time, words *etc.*).

kwr: 'hasten'*. D three times as 'roll up, make round' (81.1), associated with *kura*/*kūra* 'ball/sphere'. Thus B 'be as a ball, roll along, hurry'; D 'make s.th. as a ball'.

mt': 'carry away'*. D nineteen times as 'give s.o. enjoyment (Allah)' (43.28), in passive 'be given enjoyment, be content'. Stem V ten times as 'be content', *i.e.* 'make o.s. content' (51.43). There seems to be no connection with the later B-stem.

nfs: 'be precious'*. Stem V once as 'breathe' (81.18), associated with *nafs* 'life, breath', perhaps originally 'give o.s. life'. B was probably also a denominative 'be as life and breath'.

wjh: 'be distinguished'*. D twice as 'present (one's) face, direct o.s., direct s.o.' (6.99; 16.78). Stem V once as 'turn (one's own) face, direct o.s.' (28.21). All are associated with *wajh* 'face'.

wṣy: 'connect'*. D eleven times as 'enjoin, impress, entrust' (42.11), associated with *waṣīy* 'administrator' and *waṣāh* 'direction', thus 'give s.o. the direction of s.th.'.

B. *Associated with B-stems Intransitive*

bṭ': 'be slow, walk slowly'*. D once as 'linger, fall behind' (4.74), used as transformative only with prepositions, as 'delay' (*'alā*), *i.e.* 'be slow with reference to s.o.'

byt: 'spend the night' (once: 25.65). D once as 'plot at night' (27.50), three times as 'plot' (4.83), the meaning having been generalized. Perhaps the difference between B and D is the difference between the subject's state at night and his action at night, respectively. Š occurs outside the Qur'an as 'spend the night'. Both are probably original denominatives associated with *bayt* 'house', perhaps as 'have a house' (B) and 'employ a house (for purposes of secrecy)' (D).

rbṣ: 'wait for (*li*) s.th.'*. D seventeen times as 'wait, wait upon' (57.13).

rqb: 'observe, watch'*. D twice as 'anticipate, make o.s. watchful' (28.17).

ṭwf: 'go around'. Stem V twice as 'go around' (22.30); D occurs outside the Qur'an with this meaning. An alternative view would see here a denominative from *ṭawf* 'circuit', thus 'make a circuit'.

'qb: 'follow, ensue'. D once as 'follow' (13.12).

fkr: 'consider, reflect'*. D once as 'consider' (74.18). Stem V sixteen times as 'contemplate' (7.175). Again, this may be a denominative from *fikr* 'thought, idea'.

lhy: 'be oblivious of (*'an*) s.o.'*. D once as a Stem V reflexive 'neglect, be distracted from (*'an*)', *i.e.* 'show o.s. distraught' (80.10); *cf.* BH *lhy*, hithpalpal 'behave like a madman'.

'wk : 'lean'*.D once as Stem V 'lean' (20.19). Š occurs outside the Qur'an as 'cause to lean'.

This group is numerically less significant here than it was in Biblical Hebrew, constituting only 17% of all roots occurring in the D-stem, most of these appearing only a few times (*kḏb*) being the notable exception). Moreover, at least for II-A, the usage of the forms is somewhat different from that in Hebrew, in that most of the forms which occur are not translated as 'make something' or 'act upon something', such as Hebrew 'pitch a tent' or 'throw stones', a type which we called 'pure denominatives', *i.e.* action and object comprehended within the one form. Possible examples of this type in the Qur'an are *ṣwr* 'scale a wall' or *ṭyr* 'divine with birds'. Rather, most are of a type translated 'give someone something' or 'make someone something'. In other words, these denominatives tend to be quasi-transformative in nature, as was true of a minority of examples in Hebrew.

In connection with this, we may note also the distinction between B and D-forms of Group II-A where both exist, either in the Qur'an or in other texts. B generally has the meaning 'be something' or 'have something'; D 'give someone something' or 'make someone something'; Š, where it occurs, 'cause someone to be something' or 'cause someone to have something'. We have previously seen the same distinction for some Hebrew roots; it is a situation like that which we earlier inferred from Rundgren's description of B as 'have *qtl*', D as 'make *qtl* for someone' (becoming 'cause someone to have *qtl*'), and Š as original 'cause someone to have *qtl*'. This gives us another reason for regarding the D-stem as denominative in origin, as did

Götze. This would suggest that we might apply more thoroughly the notion that many D-forms are denominalized from verbally-derived substantives.

The roots found in Group II-B add nothing new to our consideration of this group in the Hebrew texts. We may only remark that in this group, small as it is, a relatively high percentage of the forms seem capable of being construed also as denominatives.

While the most significant aspect of the Qur'anic D-stem lies in its flexibility of usage as compared with that of the Old Testament, there are several other general points which may be mentioned before we go on to our summary of the D-stem material in the final chapter.

The first concerns the relationship between the D-stem and Stem III. Perhaps the most significant point here is the negative fact, that forms of the two stems occur for the same root only five times in the entire Qur'an. Stem III itself occurs only three times. The first time it stands in a factitive relationship to the root *swy* 'be equal', with the meaning 'level' as opposed to the D meaning 'make equal, shape'; this may be regarded as a specialization of meanings. The second time it means 'come forth (to battle)', associated with a B-form 'appear, show o.s.' and a D-form 'make appear, reveal'. Thus here it carries on the D meaning, either directly or as a quasi-reflexive 'make o.s. appear'. The third time the form is a denominative of *qasam* 'oath', not directly associated with B or D, both of which mean 'divide, distribute'. All three of the cases are reminiscent of similar instances within the D-stem both in Hebrew and in Arabic. In addition, Stem VI occurs twice, once as a passive participle of *rkb* 'be in motion', here with the reciprocal overtone traditionally associated with the stem, having the meaning 'clustered', which seems to be a factitive 'put in motion'. In the second occurrence of VI, again *qsm*, it acts as the reflexive of the D meaning 'distribute', rather than of Stem III 'take an oath'. No clearer indication of the link between Stems II and III could exist. The situation is like that of Ethiopic, where Stems II and III were complementary in their distribution. In short, the Qur'anic evidence, as well as that of Ethiopic, seems to bear out Fleisch's statement (referring back to Zimmern) that *pā'al* "ne répresente primitivement qu'une forme secondaire du pi''el, avec un signification d'intensif, qui par la suite fut nuancée d'une façon particulière."[13] To this one may add only, that for the dialect and time represented by Qur'anic materials, the 'particular nuance' does not yet seem to have evolved, except perhaps in *rkb*.

Probably more important is the connection between the D and Š-forms in the Qur'an. Both stems occur for forty roots, or about 18% of all those found in the D-stem. Again this is a smaller percentage than that discovered for the comparable group in Hebrew, and bears out the Arabic tendency toward use of the root in a minimal number of stems. Furthermore, of these forty only eight can truly be said to have the same meaning in both stems: *ẖld*, *'jl*, *kbr*, *krm*, *mhl*, *nb'* (I-A); *lqy*, *nzl*

[13] Fleisch, *Les Verbes à Allongement vocalique en Sémitique*, 19.

(I-B); *dlw* (I-C). In other words, in seven instances the Š-form has a factitive meaning like that of D; in the last case, *dlw*, the origin of both stems is unclear, perhaps factitive. Thus we see that where overlap of the two stems occurs the D-stem at no time assumes the causative function of Š. This confirms Porges's statement that "Doch unterscheidet sich wenigstens ursprünglich der Intensitätsstamm mit annähernd causativischer Bedeutung vom eigentlichen Causativum erstens dadurch, dass ersterem die Kraft eines ächtens Causativum, aus einfachen Transitivis doppelt transitive Verba zu machen, völlig abgeht", although "der Gebrauch der Piel-Form anstatt das Causativum ward in den einzelnen Sprachen mit der Zeit immer häufiger, und so ist z.B. in der arabischen Vulgärsprache jetzt von vielen Verbis Conj. II im Gebrauch da, wo die Schriftsprache Conj. IV hat."[14]

In most of the forty instances where the Š-stem occurs in association with a D-form, the form does not have the causative meaning one would expect in Š. We have noted that in several instances it replaces the B stative form, which is not itself in use. In many more, found in I-A and I-B, it has a factitive value, related to that of D but specialized in meaning, as in *br'* (D 'acquit'/Š 'cure'); *ḫff* ('lighten'/'disregard'); *ṣfw* ('purify'/'distinguish'). We have noted under some of these roots that Š usually has the estimative-declarative value, where such a value exists for the root, or a figurative value, where literal and figurative usages can be distinguished. This is interesting because it is, generally, the reverse of the situation in Biblical Hebrew. Of course, it is possible that one of the usages seems figurative to us because one of the original meanings of the root has dropped out of use. Under *krh* we noted that D 'make loathesome' and Š 'make averse' were associated with different meanings of the root, here embodied in the dual forms *kariha* and *karuha*. One might well assume that distinctions of this type were just as real for other roots, though the physical evidence is no longer at hand.

Whatever the case, one may at least say that in these examples we observe Arabic doing what Biblical Hebrew did very much, namely avoid ambiguity of meaning in one stem through the transfer of one of the meanings to another stem. In Arabic as in Hebrew, this sometimes led to the re-employment of stem forms for purposes not inherent in them. The use of an originally causative Š as a factitive exemplifies this, as does the use of an original reflexive form as a passive in Arabic and Aramaic. This re-employment of forms is one of the factors which lead us into confusion as we seek to trace an original function for any one stem.

On the basis of the D and Š forms which we have just described, it is difficult to understand how Sibawaihi classified them together. Either he was influenced by the process within the vulgar language just described by Porges, or he made his classification on the basis of a relatively few forms which give the impression of being true causatives, such as *syr*, *bṭ'*, and *ḥrk* (I-A) or *jr'*, *ḥml*, and *dkr* (I-B), but which are not doubly transitive, being based on stative aspects of their respective roots. But in order

[14] Porges, *Über die Verbalstammbildung*, 45.

to classify the D-stem on the basis of such forms one must assume that all other D-forms represent a dilution of the stem's original force – which is untenable in light of the respective numbers of roots involved. The Arab grammarian's position here arises out of his purpose, which was to classify according to the most distinctive use of each stem, without much concern for classification of the original distinctions among the various stems. As a result, in Flügel's words, "durch den Gang, den die grammatischen Studien von ihrem Ursprung an nahmen, war allem folgerichtigen Systematisieren der Weg abgeschnitten."[15]

[15] G. Flügel, "Die grammatischen Schulen der Araber", in *Abhandlungen für die Kunde des Morgenlandes*, II Band, No. 4, Leipzig 1862, 74.

VII

THE D-STEM: ORIGIN AND FUNCTION

Our research into the origin and functions of the D-stem has not provided any definitive solution to our initial problem, but rather indications of the area within which a solution may be found. Thus what we shall now attempt is, not to draw a 'conclusion' but to outline those reasonably clear phenomena which we have noted in the course of our study. As the framework for these we shall employ the scheme first utilized in our introductory remarks, concerning the three 'assumptions' about the D-stem and their possible alternatives, namely:

(1) The D-stem had a single point of origin and a basic function.

(2) The D-stem is 'derived' from the B-stem, and must therefore have a meaning distinct from that of the B-stem.

(3) That meaning connotes 'intensity' or 'plurality' of the root concept embodied in the B-stem.

The evidence is least conclusive with regard to the first of these three assumptions, but it seems in general to be valid. Concerning origins, we may say that the principle of reduplication or partial reduplication has been active from the earliest known to the latest stages of the Semitic languages, as in the Indo-European and other language groups. This principle may be witnessed in the extension of original biliteral roots in order to make them conform to the prevailing triliteral pattern of the Semitic verb. The gemination of the D-stem seems to be a similar extension of the triliteral root in order to conform to a quadriliteral pattern originally associated with denominative (or nominal) verbs. These denominatives in turn seem to have come into existence as a result of an impulse external to the verbal system proper, whereby the prefixal and suffixal morphemes of the verbal system were combined with the nominal stems to create new verbal forms. Whether this extension of the triliteral root represents a direct gemination of the middle radical or whether it represents an indirect secondary gemination by way of assimilation of an original *alif* is not clear. In light of the connection of *qaṭṭala* with *qâṭala* and *'aqṭala*, both of which are also widely used for denominative purposes, the latter explanation seems to have the greater credibility, and is closely related to the most frequent extension of biliteral roots by use of the so-called 'weak' consonants. This strengthening of the first syllable also links the

D-forms with other deverbal forms such as *qâṭil* and *qaṭṭâl*.

Nevertheless, most D-forms do not seem to have been directly derived from nouns. The vast majority of D-forms seem to have arisen from verbally derived substantives such as 'killing', and from stative verbs, which we have referred to, with Rundgren, as 'possessive denominatives'. Thus behind the D-stem we sense such forms as 'he has strength' (*i.e.* 'he is strong'), 'he has possession' (*i.e.* 'he possesses') and 'he has a killing' (*i.e.* 'he kills'); these forms are usually transmitted through the B-stem. D itself may then be construed as meaning 'he has made strong (someone or something)', 'he has given possession' and 'he has made a killing' (which would not be clearly distinguishable in meaning from B in most instances) or 'he has a killing made' (which would at times give the impression of being causative in the manner of Š). Since such meanings as 'he is strong', 'he possesses' and 'he is killed' are all found in the Akkadian stative as 'durative', 'perfect' and 'passive' statives respectively, and since this stative is most conveniently thought of as a verbal adjective, D is therefore most easily thought of as a factitive stem. We thus regard D as being denominative in origin and predominantly factitive in its function. This accounts for the existence of a smaller group of denominatives, not connected with any B-forms (Group II-A), which are seen to be inconsistent not with the origin but with the predominant function of D. The relatively small group of 'cursive' D-forms (Group II-B), the existence of which has often been attributed to the presence of an n-infix assimilated to the middle radical and resulting in an orthographic similarity to and confusion with D, may indeed have such an explanation. These forms on the other hand may also be denominative in origin, as we have suggested.

This interpretation of the D-stem makes superfluous any suggestion that the D-stem is in any way 'derived' from B. It has seemed to us more convenient to describe B and D as alternate stems, one of which is triliteral, the other quadriliteral in construction; the former a possessive denominative essentially non-transformative, the latter its factitive or transformative counterpart. We have also described this distinction as 'subjective-objective', *i.e.* the difference between 'bury a corpse' and 'make a corpse buried', when both B and D are transitive. B connotes a greater emphasis on the doer of the act, D a greater emphasis on the object of the action. Thus D could be used to connote the impersonality of an action, as when the stem is employed to indicate the acts of Jahweh in the Old Testament. B and D manifest no significant 'marked-unmarked' opposition in meaning, because there is no consistent opposition in meaning between them. They are two different types of verbal stem, the distinctions between which were often diluted or broken down in vulgar usage through the confusion of similar, though originally different, functions of the two. At times also, popular usage seems to have led to the association of a particular root concept with one stem or the other, as in the cases of verbs of division and destruction associated with D. In many individual cases such associations seem, at least superficially, to have been completely arbitrary and accidental. This process seems especially marked in the later Aramaic and Arabic forms which we have reviewed. Finally, we have at several points noted that D may be used in place of B for purposes of variety within a phrase or group of phrases, or to emphasize a verbal concept, or to elevate the mood of a phrase. These uses account for the frequent employment of D-forms in the prophetic and poetic or literary writings of the Old Testament.

Since we have construed D as being distinct in origin from B, thus not in any sense 'derived' from it; and since we have taken the distinction between the two stems, in the cases where both are transitive, to be 'possessive/factitive' or 'subjective/objective', there is no longer any necessity for us to refer to the D-stem as 'intensive' either in its origin or in its function. We regard this designation as a linguistic rationalization, based upon a pseudopsychological or romantic confusion of a strengthened form with a strengthened meaning (despite the fact that reduplication of the nominal or verbal root is sometimes used both in Indo-European and in Semitic languages to denote elativity), by means of which the superficially similar meanings of some B/D pairs might be accounted for. In particular, any interpretation of the D-stem as 'energic' or as referring to a subjective heightening of experience, seems to us to be not only an over-romanticizing of the stem's function by comparison with an interpretation of D as factitive-denominative, but also a misconstruction of the reference which the Arab grammarians made to the D-stem, as denoting *takṯīr* or 'increase'.

The examples cited by Sibawaihi and Ibn Jaiš suggest that instead of 'intensification' of action they referred to the 'extension' of an action, either in time or in physical extent. If either of these two exists, it is to be regarded as a function and not origin of the form. The element of temporal extension may be reflected in the imperfective or iterative value which the D-stem often seems to have assumed, the most noteworthy example of this occurring in Ethiopic, where the *yqttl* theme provides the imperfect aspect of the preterite *qtl* theme, though traces of similar present-future usage can be found in Arabic and perhaps in other Western languages as well. There is also some evidence to suggest that the D-stem in Arabic sometimes denotes a physical extension of an activity, although this might be construed as a development out of the concept of temporal extension, *e.g.* the extension in *qawwamat* and *mawwatat* does not refer primarily to the number of persons who performed the act but to the amount of time they consumed in performing it. If this situation exists in Arabic and/or Ethiopic, however, we are justified in taking this as a function which accrued to the D-stem and not as an indication of the stem's origin. In Chapter VI we referred to this function as the 'explicit', *i.e.* that which draws the reader's or auditor's attention to the verbal concept *per se*. Such a usage is similar to the frequent Hebrew use of D in referring to the acts of Jahweh, and to other usages of D for emphasis. None of these uses are inconsistent with the origin of D as a denominative-factitive stem; we have been compelled to pay much attention to them only because Semitists have so often employed them as the starting-point and standard for their interpretations of the D-stem's origin and general function.

Basically, then, we accept the first but reject the second and third of the three 'assumptions' listed at the beginning of our study, the last two of which might roughly be described as the 'traditional' interpretation of the D-stem. While we can easily understand how they came to be held, they seem to us to be inconsistent with good linguistic science and, more important, inadequate as explanations of the D function as it has been revealed through our study of the actual occurrences of the stem in West Semitic texts. We assert that the D-stem is unique and distinctive both in origin and in function, and that the several functions which it assumed in one or more Western languages are mutually consistent from the standpoint of the stem's denominative-factitive orientation.

BIBLIOGRAPHY

LEXICONS, CONCORDANCES AND CRITICAL EDITIONS

Barnes, G. E., (ed.), *Pentateuchus Syriacus post Samuelem Lee* (1914).
Brederek, E., *Konkordanz zum Targum Onkelos* (Giessen, 1906).
Brockelmann, C., *Lexicon Syriacum* (Berlin, 1895; Halis Saxonum, 1928[2]).
Dalman, G., *Aramäisch-Neuhebräisches Wörterbuch* (Frankfurt, 1901).
Flügel, G., *Concordantiae Corani Arabicae* (Leipzig, 1842).
—, (ed.), *Coranus Arabice* (Leipzig, 1837).
Hava, J. G., *Arabic-English Dictionary for Use of Students* (Beirut, 1921, new edition).
Jastrow, M., *Dictionary of the Targumim*, the *Talmud Babli and Yerushalmi, and the Midrashic Literature*, 2 vol. (New York, 1903).
Kittel, R., *Biblica Hebraica* (Stuttgart, 1937; 1949[4]).
Köhler, L. and W. Baumgartner, *Lexicon in Veteris Testamenti Libros* (Leiden, 1948-1953); *Supplement* (Leiden, 1958).
Lane, E. W., *Arabic-English Lexicon*, book I (London, 1863-1893).
Levy, J., *Neuhebräisches und Chaldäisches Wörterbuch über die Talmudim und Midraschim* (Leipzig, 1876-1889).
Mankelkern, S., *Veteris Testamenti Concordantiae* (Leipzig, 1896).
Payne Smith, R., *Thesaurus Syriacus*, 2 vol. (Oxford, 1879-1901).
—, *Compendious Syriac Dictionary*, J. Payne Smith, ed. (Oxford, 1903).
Shah, Ahmed, *Concordance of the Qur'an* (Benares, 1906).
Sperber, A., *The Bible in Aramaic* (Leiden, 1959).
Wehr, A., *A Dictionary of Modern Written Arabic*, J. M. Cowan, ed. (Ithaca, 1961).

GENERAL AND SEMITIC LINGUISTICS

Barth, J., "Das passive Qal und seine Participien", in *Jubelschrift zum Siebzigsten Geburtstag des Israel Hildesheimer* (Berlin, 1890).
—, "Die Pôlel-Conjugation und die Pôlal-Participien", in *Semitic Studies in Memory of Dr. Alexander Kohut*, G. A. Kohut, ed. (Berlin, 1897).
Bauer, H. and P. Leander, *Historische Grammatik der hebräischen Sprache* (Halle, 1922).
—, *Historische Grammatik der aramäischen Sprache* (Halle, 1927).
al-Bayḍāwī, *Commentarius in Coranum*, H. Fleischer, ed. (Leipzig 1846-1878).
Bell, R., (tr.), *The Qur'an*, 2 vol. (Edinburgh, 1937-1939).
Bergsträsser, G., *Hebräische Grammatik*, II Teil (Leipzig, 1918).
Böhl, F., "Die Sprache der Amarnabriefe", in *Leipziger Semitische Studien* V, 2 (Leipzig, 1909).
Böhmer, J., "Spuren von Passiv-Participien des Steigerungsstamms im Hebräischen", in *Zeitschrift für Semitistik* 10 (1935).
Botterweck, G., *Die Triliterismus im Semitischen* (Bonn, 1952).

Brockelmann, C., *Geschichte der arabischen Literatur* (Leipzig, 1901).
—, *Grundriss der vergleichenden Grammatik der semitischen Sprachen* (Berlin, 1908).
—, "Die 'Tempora' des Semitischen", in *Zeitschrift für Phonetik* 5 (1951).
—, *Hebräische Syntax* (Neukirchen Kreis Moers, 1956).
Caussin de Perçeval, A. P., *Grammaire Arabe Vulgaire* (Paris, 1833).
Christian, V., "Zur inneren Passivbildung im Semitischen", in *Wiener Zeitschrift für die Kunde des Morgenlandes* 34 (1927).
—, "Das Wesen der semitischen Tempora", in *Zeitung der deutschen morgenländischen Gesellschaft* 81 (1927).
—, Bemerkungen zu Bergsträssers 'Einführung in die semitischen Sprachen'", in *Wiener Zeitschrift für die Kunde des Morgenlandes* 36 (1929).
—, *Die kausative Bedeutung des semitischen Steigerungsstammes*, in *Analecta Orientalia* 12 (1935).
—, "Untersuchungen zur Laut- und Formenlehre des Hebräischen, in *Österreichische Akademie der Wissenschaften*, Phil.-Hist. Klasse, Sitzberichte 228, Band 2 (Vienna, 1953).
Cohen, M., *Le Système Verbal Sémitique et l'Expression du Temps* (Paris, 1924).
—, *Nouvelles Études d'Éthiopien Méridional* (Paris, 1939).
—, "Review of H. Fleisch, *Les Verbes à Allongement Vocalique en Sémitique*", in *Bulletin de la Société de Linguistique* 42 (1946).
Delitzsch, F., *Studien über indogermanisch-semitische Wurzelverwandschaft* (Leipzig, 1873).
Dembitz, L. N., "The Passive of Qal", in *American Journal of Semitic Languages* 3 (1886).
Dhorme, E., "La Langue de Canaan", in *Recueil Édouard Dhorme* (Paris, 1951).
Dillmann, A., *Ethiopic Grammar* (London, 1907²).
Driver, G. R., *Problems of the Hebrew Verbal System* (New York, 1936).
Ebeling, E., *Das Verbum der el-Amarna-Briefe* (Berlin, 1909).
Eitan, I., "La Répétition de la Racine en Hébreu", in *Journal of the Palestinian Oriental Society* 1 (1920-1921).
—, "Light on the History of the Hebrew Verb", in *Jewish Quarterly Review*, New Series 12 (1921-1922).
Ewald, H., *Grammatik der hebräischen Sprache* (Leipzig 1838³).
Fleisch, H., *Les Verbes à Allongement vocalique en Sémitique* (Paris, 1944).
—, "Le Nom d'Agent Fa'al", in *Mélanges de l'Université St. Joseph* 32 (1955).
Flügel, G., "Die grammatischen Schulen der Araber", in *Abhandlungen für die Kunde des Morgenlandes*, II Band, No. 4 (Leipzig, 1862).
Friedrich, J., *Phönizisch-Punische Grammatik* (Rome, 1951).
Fürst, J., *Lehrgebäude der aramäischen Idiome* (Leipzig, 1835).
Garbini, G., "Nuovo Materiale per la Grammatica dell'Aramaico antico", in *Rivista degli Studi Orientali* 34, Fasc. I-II (Rome, 1959).
—, *Il Semitico di Nord-Ovest* (Naples, 1960).
Gelb, I., "Lingua degli Amoriti", in *Accademia Nazionale dei Lincei, Rendiconti*, Series VIII, No. 13 (1958).
Gerber, W. J., *Die hebräischen Verba denominativa* (Leipzig, 1896).
Gesenius, W., *Hebrew Grammar*, E. Kautzsch, ed.; 2nd English edtion by A. E. Cowley (Oxford, 1910).
Götze, A., "The T-Form of the Old Babylonian Verb", in *Journal of the American Oriental Society* 56 (1936).
—, "The Tenses of Ugaritic", in *Journal of the American Oriental Society* 58 (1938).
—, "The So-Called Intensive of the Semitic Languages", in *Journal of the American Oriental Society* 62 (1942).
Gordon, C., *Ugaritic Handbook* (Rome, 1947).
Gray, L., *Introduction to Semitic Comparative Linguistics* (New York, 1934).
Greenberg, J., "The Afro-Asiatic (Hamito-Semitic) Present", in *Journal of the American Oriental Society* 72 (1952).
Harris, Z., *The Development of the Canaanite Dialects* (New Haven, 1939).
—, "The Linguistic Structure of Hebrew", in *Journal of the American Oriental Society* 61 (1941).
—, "Morpheme Alternants in Linguistic Analysis", in *Language* 18 (1942).
Hartmann, M., *Die Pluriteralbildungen in den semitischen Sprachen* (Halle, 1875).

bar Hebraeus, *Buch der Strahlen*, A. Moberg, tr. and ed. (Leipzig, 1913).
Heidel, A., *The System of the Quadriliteral Verb in Akkadian* (Chicago, 1940).
Hirschfeld, H., "Bemerkungen zum Verbum denominativum im Hebräischen", in *Monatsschrift* 69 (1925).
Hjelmslev, L., "Essai d'un Théorie des Morphèmes", in *Actes du* 4. *Congrès International de Linguistes* (Copenhagen, 1936).
Hockett, C., "Problems of Morphemic Analysis", in *Language* 23 (1947).
Höfner, H., *Altsüdarabische Grammatik* (Leipzig, 1943).
Hoffmann, A., *The Principles of Syriac Grammar*, tr. Cowper (Leipzig, 1858).
Hurwitz, S. T. H., *Root-Determinatives in Semitic Speech* (New York, 1913).
Jaiš, Ibn, *Commentar zu Zamachšaris Mufassal*, nach den Handschriften zu Leipzig, Oxford, Constantinopel und Cairo, herausgegeben von Dr. G. Jahn (Leipzig, 1882).
Joly, A., "Sur les Dérivations du Trilitère et les Origines du Quadrilitère en Arabe", in *Actes du XIVe Congrès International des Orientalistes, Alger* 1905 (Paris, 1907).
Kamil, M., "Zur Bildung der vierradikaligen Verben in den lebenden semitischen Sprachen", in *Studi Orientalistici in Onore di Giorgio della Vida*, vol. I (Rome, 1956).
Kienast, B., "Verbalformen mit Reduplikation im Akkadischen", in *Orientalia* 26 (1957).
König, E., *Gedanke, Laut und Accent* (Weimar, 1874).
—, *Historisches-Kritisches Lehrgebäude der hebräischen Sprache*, vol. I (Leipzig, 1895).
Kurylowicz, J., *L'Apophonie en Sémitique* (Warsaw, 1962).
Landsberger, B., "Prinzipienfragen der semitischen, speziell der hebräischen Grammatik", in *Orientalistische Literaturzeitung* 29 (1926).
Leander, P., "Das Wesen der semitischen Tempora", in *Zeitung der deutschen morgenländischen Gesellschaft* 81 (1927).
Leslau, W., "A Parallel to the non-Gemination of the Hebrew R", in *Journal of Biblical Literature* 68 (1949).
—, *Étude Descriptive et Comparative du Gafat* (Paris, 1956).
Loretz, O., "Die hebräische Nominalform qattâl", in *Biblica* 41 (1960).
Lounsbury, F., "The Method of Descriptive Morphology", in *Anthropology* 48 (1953).
MacLean, A. S., *Grammar of the Dialects of Vernacular Syriac* (Cambridge, 1895).
Meinhof, C., *Die Sprachen der Hamiten* (Hamburg, 1912).
Meyer, R., "Spuren eines westsemitischen Präsens-Futur", in *Von Ugarit nach Qumran*, J. Hempel and L. Rost, eds. (Berlin, 1958).
Morag, S., "The Pa'el and Hithpa'el Verbal Stems", in *Tarbiz* XXVI (1957).
Moran, W. L., "The Hebrew Language in Its Northwest Semitic Background", in *The Bible and the Ancient Near East*, G. Wright, ed. (Garden City, 1961).
Nida, E., *Morphology: the Descriptive Analysis of Words* (Ann Arbor, 1946).
—, "The Identification of Morphemes", in *Language* 24 (1948).
Nöldeke, T., *Mandäische Grammatik* (Halle, 1875).
—, "Zur Grammatik des klassischen Arabisch", in *Denkschriften der kaiserlichen Akademie der Wissenschaften*, Phil.-Hist. Klasse, Band XLV (Vienna, 1897).
—, *Die semitischen Sprachen* (Leipzig, 1897).
—, "Zur Sprache des Korans", in *Neue Beiträge zur semitischen Sprachwissenschaft* (Strassburg, 1910).
Nyberg, H. S., "Zur Entwicklung der mehr als dreikonsonantischen Stämme in den semitischen Sprachen", in *Westöstliche Abhandlungen R. Tschudi*, ed. Meier (Wiesbaden, 1954).
O'Leary, de L., *Comparative Grammar of the Semitic Languages* (London, 1923).
Oppenheim, L., "Die mittels T-Infixes gebildeten Aktionsarten des Altbabylonischen", in *Wiener Zeitschrift für die Kunde des Morgenlandes* 42 (1935).
Philippi, F. W. M. "Der Grundstamm des starken Verbums im Semitischen", in *Morgenländische Forschungen, Festschrift Fleischer* (Leipzig, 1875).
Pittman, R., "Nuclear Structures in Linguistics", in *Language* 24 (1948).
Poebel, A., *Studies in Akkadian Grammar* (Chicago, 1939).
Porath, E., "Die Passivbildung des Grundstamms im Semitischen", in *Monatsschrift* 70 (1926).
Porges, N., *Über die Verbalstammbildung in den semitischen Sprachen* (Vienna, 1875).

Pott, A. F., *Doppelung (Reduplikation, Gemination) als eines der wichstigsten Bildungsmittel der Sprache* (1862).
Praetorius, F., *Äthiopische Grammatik* (Leipzig, 1886).
Rabin, C., *Ancient West Arabian* (London, 1951).
Reckendorff, H., *Die syntaktischen Verhältnisse des Arabischen* (Leiden, 1895).
Rosenthal, F., "Review of H. Fleisch, *Les Verbes à Allongement vocalique en Sémitique*", in *Orientalia* 16 (1947).
—, *A Grammar of Biblical Aramaic*, Porta Linguarum Orientalium, New Series V (Wiesbaden, 1961).
Rundgren, F., *Intensiv- und Aspektkorrelation* (Uppsala, 1959).
—, "Das altsyrische Verbalsystem", in *Sprakvetenskaplige Sällskapets i Uppsala, Förhandlingar* (Jan. 1958-Dec. 1960).
—, "Der aspektuelle Charakter des altsemitischen Injunctivs", in *Orientalia Suecana* 9 (1960).
—, *Das althebräische Verbum: Abriss der Aspektlehre* (Uppsala, 1961).
—, "Das Verbalpräfix yu- im Semitischen und die Entstehung der der factitiv-kausativischen Bedeutung des D-Stammes", in *Orientalia Suecana* 13 (1964).
de Sacy, S., *Sur la Vers on Arabe des Livres de Moïse* (Paris, 1808).
—, *Grammaire Arabe*, 2 vol. (Paris, 1831).
Sibawaihi, *La Livre de Sibawaihi*, H. Derenbourg, ed., 2 vol. (Paris, 1881-1889).
—, *Sibawaihis Buch*, G. Jahn, tr. and ed. (Berlin, 1895-1900).
Skoss, S. L., *Saadia ha-Gaon, the Earliest Hebrew Grammarian* (Philadelphia, 1955).
von Soden, W., "Grundriss der akkadischen Grammatik", in *Analecta Orientalia* 33 (1952).
Speiser, E., "The Durative Hithpaʿel", in *Journal of the American Oriental Society* 75 (1955).
Spitaler, A., "Zur Frage der Geminatendissimilation im Semitischen", in *Indogermanische Forschungen* 61 (1952-1954).
Spüler, B., "Der semitische Sprachtypus", in *Handbuch der Orientalistik*, B. Spüler, ed. (Leiden, 1954).
Toy, C. H., "On Hebrew Verb-Etymology", in *Transactions of the American Philological Association* 7 (1876).
Ullendorff, E., *The Semitic Languages of Ethiopia* (London, 1955).
Ungnad, A., "Uber Analogiebildungen im hebräischen Verbum", in *Beiträge für Assyriologie* 5 (Leipzig, 1906).
Wolfenson, L. B., "The Piʿel in Hebrew", in *Journal of the American Oriental Society* 27 (1906).
Wright, W., *A Grammar of the Arabic Language*, 2 vol. (Cambridge, 1859, 1955[3]).
Wundt, W., *Völkerpsychologie*, I Band: *Die Sprache*, Erster Teil (Leipzig, 1900).
Zimmern, H., *Vergleichende Grammatik der semitischen Sprachen* (Berlin, 1898).

INDEX

Printed in the USA
CPSIA information can be obtained
at www.ICGtesting.com
LVHW070849100124
768548LV00013B/608